Miracle in Chavez Ravine

ALSO BY WILLIAM F. MCNEIL
AND FROM MCFARLAND

*All-Stars for All Time: A Sabermetric Ranking
of the Major League Best, 1876–2007* (2008)

*Black Baseball Out of Season: Pay for Play
Outside of the Negro Leagues* (2007)

*Backstop: A History of the Catcher and a
Sabermetric Ranking of 50 All-Time Greats* (2006)

The Evolution of Pitching in Major League Baseball (2006)

*Visitors to Ancient America: The Evidence for European and
Asian Presence in America Prior to Columbus* (2005)

*Gabby Hartnett: The Life and Times
of the Cubs' Greatest Catcher* (2004)

*The Single-Season Home Run Kings: Ruth,
Maris, McGwire, Sosa, and Bonds,* 2d ed. (2003)

*The California Winter League: America's First
Integrated Professional Baseball League* (2002; paperback 2008)

*Cool Papas and Double Duties: The All-Time
Greats of the Negro Leagues* (2001; paperback 2005)

*Baseball's Other All-Stars: The Greatest Players from the
Negro Leagues, the Japanese Leagues, the Mexican League,
and the Pre–1960 Winter Leagues in Cuba,
Puerto Rico and the Dominican Republic* (2000)

*The King of Swat: An Analysis of Baseball's Home Run Hitters
from the Major, Minor, Negro and Japanese Leagues* (1997)

Miracle in Chavez Ravine

The Los Angeles Dodgers in 1988

William F. McNeil

McFarland & Company, Inc., Publishers

Jefferson, North Carolina, and London

LIBRARY OF CONGRESS CATALOGUING-IN-PUBLICATION DATA

McNeil, William.
   Miracle in Chavez Ravine : the Los Angeles Dodgers in 1988 /
William F. McNeil.
      p.   cm.
   Includes bibliographical references and index.

   ISBN 978-0-7864-3501-2
   softcover : 50# alkaline paper

   1. Los Angeles Dodgers (Baseball team)   2. World Series
(Baseball) (1988)   I. Title.
GV875.L6M39   2008
796.357'640979494 — dc22 [B]   2008015800

British Library cataloguing data are available

Cover photograph: Kirk Gibson raises his arm in celebration after hitting a game-winning two-run home run to beat the Oakland A's 5-4 in the first game of the World Series, Dodger Stadium, Oct. 15, 1988 (AP Photo/Rusty Kennedy)

Manufactured in the United States of America

McFarland & Company, Inc., Publishers
  Box 611, Jefferson, North Carolina 28640
  www.mcfarlandpub.com

To the memory of
Jamie Lee Kruger,
My "Peanut,"
January 17, 1981–November 16, 2006.
*Beautiful, talented, vivacious, optimistic, loving,
and genuine. Her smile could light up a room.*

And to her son,
Anthony James Kruger.
*He inherited his mother's good looks,
sense of humor, and charm.*

ACKNOWLEDGMENTS

I would like to thank the following people and organizations for their unselfish assistance in the production of this book.

Pete Palmer, editor of the *Baseball Encyclopedia*, for permission to use player statistics from the book.

Mark Langill, team historian, and the Los Angeles Dodgers for permission to quote from their publication, *Dodger Blue*, and for permission to use photographs of Dodgers players from their archives.

The Montreal Expos for permission to use the photograph of Gary Carter.

Tot Holmes for permission to quote from his publication, *Dodgers Dugout*.

Jay Sanford for permission to use his photographs of Nolan Ryan, Ozzie Smith, Keith Hernandez, and Dennis Eckersley.

TABLE OF CONTENTS

INTRODUCTION

The Dodgers have been a storied franchise since their birth in Brooklyn in the mid–19th century. Their ancestors were the Brooklyn Excelsiors and the Brooklyn Atlantics, who were two of the top amateur baseball teams in the country in the 1850s and 1860s. The Excelsiors, in fact, employed the game's first professional player, pitcher Jimmy Creighton, who they paid under the table in violation of the amateur rules. The Atlantics went undefeated in 1864 and 1865 and won three successive national championships from '84 through '86. Another Brooklyn pitcher, William Arthur "Candy" Cummings, was credited with inventing the curveball while pitching for the Excelsiors. The first organized professional baseball league, the National Association of Professional Base Ball Players (NA), began play in 1871 with nine teams. The Brooklyn Atlantics joined the league in 1872 and were part of the league until its dissolution in 1875.

The first true major league, the National League, replaced the National Association in 1876 and has continued in operation since that time. Another major league, the American Association, began operations in 1883 to compete with the National League. The Brooklyn franchise that would become the Dodgers joined the AA in 1884, and they have been a winning franchise over the past 100-plus years except for the period between 1921 and 1939 when, as the Daffy Dodgers, they provided baseball fans with hours of entertainment but little success. In the 1880s they were usually referred to as the Brooklyns, the Church City Nine, or the Grays. Brooklyn won its first professional baseball pennant in 1889, and the team was called the Bridegrooms at that time because six members of the team were married during the season. The following year, the Brooklyn team joined the National League and won its first National League pennant in its first year. The National League expanded from eight teams to twelve teams in 1892 to absorb the players from the American Association after it went out of existence. The Brooklyn franchise inherited a new nickname around 1896 when a heavy concentration of electric trolley car tracks in front of Eastern Park, Brooklyn's home park, caused fans, on their way to the game, to dodge the trolleys as they crossed the street. Manhattanites, and other visitors, began calling the Brooklyn fans "Trolley Dodgers," and the nickname stuck. Within a few years, it was shortened to just Dodgers.

During their first three decades in the National League, the Brooklyn Dodgers were a force to be reckoned with, winning pennants in 1890, 1899, 1900, 1914, and 1920. After a twenty-year hiatus in which they often finished sixth in an eight-team league, Brooklyn returned to prominence in the early 1940s. They won their first pennant in twenty-one years in 1941, beginning a dynasty that ruled the league for the next seventeen years. They won seven pennants during that period and, in 1955, after years of frustration, they celebrated a world championship. It was the era of the famous Boys of Summer, with Jackie Robinson, Pee Wee Reese, Roy Campanella, Duke Snider, Gil Hodges, Carl Furillo, Carl Erskine, Clem Labine and Don Newcombe.

Two years after winning the world championship, Brooklyn owner Walter O'Malley uprooted the team and set it down in sunny Southern California. The new Los Angeles Dodgers finished in seventh place in 1958, their inaugural season in L.A., but the next year they shocked the baseball world by winning not only the National League pennant, but the world championship as well. With a new home in Chavez Ravine, and a pitching staff headed by Sandy Koufax and including Don Drysdale, Johnny Podres, Claude Osteen, and Ron Perranoski, the Dodgers won National League pennants in 1963, 1965, and 1966, and captured world championships in two of those years. The 1963 championship was particularly satisfying because they swept the hated New York Yankees, four straight, holding the proud Bronx Bombers to just four runs.

After the 1966 season, the Dodgers fell on hard times until 1974 when a new dynasty was born. It included The Infield, four men who played together on the same infield for eight and a half years—Steve Garvey, Davey Lopes, Bill Russell, and Ron Cey. Los Angeles won National League pennants in 1974, 1977, and 1978, but fell short in the world championship competition each time. Then, in 1981, with The Infield still intact, and with a pitching staff that included 20-year-old phenom Fernando Valenzuela, Burt Hooton, and Jerry Reuss, Tommy Lasorda's Dodgers scaled the heights, coming from behind to take the measure of the New York Yankees in six games. Los Angeles fans envisioned the beginning of a new dynasty but, just when things looked bright for L.A., their plan came apart at the seams, and over the next six years, they struggled to remain competitive, some years succeeding and other years failing. The situation came to a head after the team suffered through two successive sub-par years, finishing fifth in 1986 and fourth in 1987, with identical 73–89 records. During the spring of 1987, the Dodgers went through a change in general managers, with Fred Claire replacing the departing Al Campanis.

The rest of the story follows.

1

VIEW FROM THE TOP

As the sun rose on the morning of October 23, 1981, the outlook for Tommy Lasorda's Los Angeles Dodgers was bleak. They trailed the New York Yankees in the World Series two games to none, so, in a season of comebacks, they would need one more if they were to realize their dream of a world championship. Looking back, the past six months seemed like a dream, and it all began on opening day. The Dodgers' starter that day, Jerry Reuss, was unable to pitch because of a strained left calf, and Burt Hooton was sidelined with an ingrown toenail, so manager Tommy Lasorda was forced to call upon a 20-year-old Mexican southpaw named Fernando Valenzuela to throw out the first pitch in Dodger Stadium. The poised youngster, with just 18 innings of major league baseball under his belt, responded with a brilliant 2–0 victory. According to inside sources, Fernando was so relaxed before the game he fell asleep on the trainer's table.

Valenzuela's rise through the Los Angeles Dodgers' minor league system had been meteoric. Dodgers scouts discovered him pitching for Guanajuantro in the Mexican League in 1978, a baby-faced 17-year-old left-handed pitcher with a devastating screwball and poise far beyond his years. His record with Guanajuantro was a lukewarm 5–6, but he led the league in strikeouts and had an outstanding 2.23 ERA. The next season, Fernando pitched for Yucatan in the Mexican League, compiling a 10–12 record, with a 2.49 ERA. Al Campanis purchased Fernando's contract before the end of the season and sent him to Lodi in the Class A California League, where he appeared in 3 games, with a 1–2 record and a brilliant 1.13 ERA. The precocious lefty spent most of the 1980 season with San Antonio in the Texas League, running up a 13–9 won-loss record, with 141 strikeouts in 181 innings, and a commendable 3.10 earned-run average. When the home club geared up to challenge the first place Houston Astros for the National League Western Division pennant in September, they were in desperate need of a left-handed arm out of the bullpen, so they sent for Valenzuela. Over the last three weeks of the season, the pudgy, 5', 11", 202-pound southpaw appeared in 10 games for Los Angeles, winning two games without a loss, and saving one, while posting a perfect 0.00 ERA.

Fernando Valenzuela, under the watchful eye of Sandy Koufax (right), had a break-out season in 1981 (author's collection).

The Dodgers won ten of their first twelve games in 1981, and Fernando won four of them including three shutouts. It was the beginning of a phenomenon that would be known as Fernandomania, a frenetic time that encompassed the first eight weeks of the season, with Fernando running up a perfect 8–0 record, with four shutouts and an almost invisible earned-run average of 0.50. Dodgers fans didn't think Fernando would ever lose a game. "They began to wink knowingly at each other whenever it was Fernando's turn to pitch. An 'OK' gesture with their thumb and forefinger coupled with a sly 'Fernando goes tonight' whisper, was a sure guarantee of a Dodger victory."[1] All was well in Dodgerland.

On May 1, the Dodgers visited the Montreal Expos, and the two teams battled for 13 innings before the Expos prevailed by a score of 9–8. The 4 hour, 18 minute game tied the record for the longest game in L.A. history. Two days later, Fernando saw his scoreless innings streak snapped at 36 in the eighth inning at Montreal, but he still came away a 6–1 winner when the Dodgers pushed across five runs in the 10th inning on run-scoring singles by Reggie Smith and Ken Landreaux, a sacrifice fly by Dusty Baker, and a two-run single by Steve Garvey. Fernando took Montreal to task again on May 14, whipping them 3–2 on Pedro Guerrero's leadoff home run in the bottom of the ninth inning, upping his record to a perfect 8–0 for the season, tying him with Dave "Boo" Ferris of the Boston Red Sox for the fastest start by a rookie in major league history. Fernando limited the Expos to three hits, with seven strikeouts and a single base on balls. Steve Garvey drove in two runs for the Dodgers.

Montreal

Name	Pos	AB	R	H
White	LF	4	0	0
Scott	2B	4	0	1
Dawson	CF	4	1	1
Carter	C	4	0	0
Cromartie	1B	3	0	0
Wallach	RF	3	0	0
Parrish	3B	3	0	0
Speier	SS	2	1	1
Phillips	SS	0	0	0
Gullickson	P	2	0	0
Smith	PH	1	0	0
Raines	PR	0	0	0
Ratzer	P	0	0	0
Totals		30	2	3

Los Angeles

Name	Pos	AB	R	H
Lopes	2B	4	1	1
Landreaux	CF	4	0	0
Baker	LF	4	1	1
Garvey	1B	4	0	1
Cey	3B	4	0	0
Guerrero	RF	3	1	1
Scioscia	C	3	0	1
Russell	SS	3	0	1
Thomas	SS	0	0	0
Valenzuela	P	3	0	2
		32	3	8

```
Montreal       0 0 1   0 0 0   0 0 1 — 1 — 3 — 2
Los Angeles    0 0 0   0 0 2   0 0 1 — 3 — 8 — 0
```

Doubles— Scioscia, Russell
Home Runs— Speier, Dawson, Guerrero

Name	IP	H	R	ER	BB	SO
Montreal						
Gullickson	7	7	2	2	0	6
Ratzer (L 1–1)	1+	1	1	1	0	1
Los Angeles						
Valenzuela (W 8–0)	9	3	2	2	1	7[2]

The dream finally ended on May 18 when the young lefty was jolted for a first inning home run by Mike Schmidt and suffered through a three-run Philly fourth as Marty Bystrom blanked L.A. 4–0. It was Fernando's first loss as a major leaguer after ten straight victories, including his two wins in 1980. The Dodgers got their revenge two days later against Steve Carlton, as Pedro Guerrero pounded out four base hits and Rick Monday hit a tenth inning home run to nip the Phillies 3–2. Ron Cey had a celebration of his own on the 23rd of the month when he slugged his 200th career home run in Cincinnati to pace the Dodgers to a 9–6 ten inning victory.

The youngster known as "El Toro" was practically unbeatable through May and the Dodgers, spurred on by his spectacular start, raced to a 29–11 record by May 23, giving them a comfortable 6½ game lead over the Cincinnati Reds. Fernando boasted an 8–2 record at that point with a miniscule 1.24 earned-run average. Burt Hooton was close behind with a perfect 6–0 mark and a 2.11 ERA, and Jerry Reuss checked in at 4–1 and a 1.50 ERA. The staff ERA was 2.35.

The first half of the season came to a sudden halt on June 12 when the players marched out on strike, leaving the Dodgers and their 36–21 record with a slim ½ game lead over the fast-charging Cincinnati Reds. In the last game before the strike began, Fernando Valenzuela, who had received a death threat the previous night, went down to defeat before the St. Louis Cardinals by a 2–1 count. The Dodgers' 20-year-old screwball artist held the Redbirds to three hits in eight innings, struck out nine batters and walked three. The only St. Louis runs crossed the plate in the first inning on a two-run, inside-the-park homer by George Hendricks.

The strike centered around a contentious issue, free-agent compensation, a proposal by team owners that would allow them to be paid back with another player if they lost a quality free agent to another club. The players refused to accept the proposal because they believed it would limit their movement between teams and lower their salaries.

The strike dragged on for two months, and when it was finally settled in early August, baseball commissioner Bowie Kuhn declared the Philadelphia Phillies and the Los Angeles Dodgers to be the winners of the first half of the season, with a second half yet to be played. The Dodgers went back on the attack as soon as the second half began, and Fernando Valenzuela immediately tied the National League mark by rookies when he threw his seventh shutout, blanking the St. Louis Cardinals 5–0. It was his 12th victory of the season. But L.A.'s offensive thrust was scuttled by several unfortunate incidents, the most important of which was an injury to third baseman Ron Cey. The Penguin was a key ingredient in the Dodgers offense as well as being a defensive specialist. On September 9, Tom Griffin of the San Francisco Giants let loose a fastball that was headed right at Cey's skull. In an effort to divert the missile, Cey threw his arm up in front of his head and the ball struck him full force, breaking his forearm and sending him to the sidelines for the better part of a month. The Dodgers lost the game 6–3 in 11 innings. Eight days later, Fernando kept the Dodgers within two games of first place by blanking the Atlanta Braves 2–0. It was his eighth shutout of the season, equaling the major league rookie record set by Ewell Russell of the Chicago White Sox in 1913. As the *North Adams Transcript* noted, the talented southpaw, "13–4 with a 2.37 ERA, leads the National League in victories, complete games (11), shutouts, and strikeouts (162). He walked two and struck out six against the Braves. The husky pitcher, now hitting .259, also drove in his seventh run of the year with an infield single in the sixth inning."[3]

Disaster struck the West Coast nine the next night. The Dodgers held a 4–2 lead over the Cincinnati Reds in the top of the ninth inning at Dodger Stadium, but they couldn't close the door. Johnny Bench, sent up as a pinch hitter with two men on base and two out, sent a screamer over the left field fence sending shock waves through Dodgerland. The team never recovered from that loss. They dropped 11 of 16 games, and eight of their last ten.

Embarrassment was added to frustration on September 26 when Nolan Ryan tossed the fifth no-hitter of his illustrious career, blanking Lasorda's cohorts 5–0 in the Astrodome, as 32,115 excited fans screamed with delight. Dodger right-hander Ted Power was touched up for two runs in the bottom of the third to give Ryan a lead he never relinquished. The 34-year-old fireballer was in complete command, fanning 11 and walking 3. Only two balls came close to being base hits. "Steve Garvey led off the seventh with a slow grounder up the middle. Second baseman Phil Garner dashed to his right and backhanded the ball. He whirled and rifled a throw to first to nip Garvey. After Pedro Guerrero made an out, Mike Scioscia blasted a line drive into deep right center. Right fielder Terry Puhl, an excellent defensive player, was off and running at the crack of the bat. He sprinted to the warning track and snared the potential double."[4]

On October 4, Dave Goltz lost his seventh straight decision going back to August 19, a Los Angeles club record, as the Dodgers closed out the season with a 5–3 loss to Houston, and limped home in fourth place in the second half of the season, their 27–26 record leaving them a full six games behind the Houston Astros. Strangely, the Cincinnati Reds compiled the best record in the National League West for the season, going 66–42, four games better than Los Angeles, but they failed to win either half, and had to watch the post-season competition on television.

One of the reasons the Dodgers were able to stay loose and relaxed during the pressure of the pennant race was because they were blessed with two of baseball's premier jokesters, Jay Johnstone and Jerry Reuss, and things never got too serious with those two around. Hotfoots were always a danger for unsuspecting rookies, and if a player left his clothing unattended, he was likely to find it cut to shreds when he returned to the locker room after the game ended. Occasionally Steve Garvey joined the duo as he did one evening in Dodger Stadium when the three men dressed in maintenance uniforms and helped the ground crew drag the infield after the fifth inning, much to the delight of the home fans. Johnstone's favorite target was Ron Cey, the Dodgers' 5', 7" third baseman, and he tormented the stocky infielder on a regular basis. One night, as reported by Johnstone, he sneaked Hollywood actor Billy Barty, the diminutive 3', 9" midget, into the Dodgers' locker room, and dressed him in Cey's uniform. Then he took Barty out on the field and positioned him at third base, as 50,000 fans roared with laughter.[5] Another time, the L.A. funnyman built a miniature, three-foot locker out of wood, hammered nails inside the locker to hang clothing on, hung Cey's uniform on one of the nails, taped the third baseman's name above the locker, placed a tiny stool in front of it, and positioned the entire engineering masterpiece where Cey's locker should have been. The entire team was hysterical — all except Ron Cey who went ballistic.[6]

The Big Blue Machine met Houston in a five-game playoff to determine the Western Division champion, and their woes continued in games 1 and 2.

Nolan Ryan, en route to an 11–5 season, tossed a no-hitter at the Los Angeles Dodgers on September 26 (Jay Sanford).

The Astros, behind Nolan Ryan and Joe Niekro, and playing in front of their home fans, defeated Lasorda's troops by scores of 3–1 and 1–0 in 11 innings. In game 1, Fernando Valenzuela opposed The Ryan Express, a tough assignment against a world class pitcher who owned a 1.11 ERA in the Astrodome, and who had just no-hit Lasorda's cohorts 5–0 in Los Angeles on September 26, the 5th no-hitter of his illustrious career. Ryan was almost unhittable through six innings, but so was young Fernando, so the game was still close entering the seventh inning. That's when Steve Garvey took a Ryan fastball downtown to give the Dodgers a 1–1 tie, but the Big Blue Machine was unable to keep Houston at bay. Dave Stewart, in relief of Fernando, threw a home run ball to Alan Ashby with two men out and one man on base in the bottom of the ninth, and the Astros came away 3–1 winners. The next night was more of the same. Jerry Reuss matched Niekro pitch for pitch for eight innings, with neither team able to dent the plate. But the Astros pulled it out once again, this time in the eleventh inning, winning 1–0 on a two-out, bases-loaded single by Denny Walling. Dave Stewart was the losing pitcher for the second straight game.

Returning home with their backs to the wall, L.A. needed a three-game sweep to continue their push to the world championship. Lasorda handed the ball to his knuckle-curve artist, Burt Hooton, and sent Bob Welch to the bullpen to strengthen the team's weak spot. The Dodgers responded to the challenge. Playing before the home crowd for the first time, the gutty Dodgers roared out of the starting gate like Man-O-War. They hammered Astros starter Bob Knepper for three runs in the opening stanza as 50,000 hysterical Angelinos roared their approval. Dusty Baker drove in the first run of the inning with a double, and Steve Garvey brought in the other two with a home run to left field. Burt Hooton protected that lead for seven innings, yielding a lone tally to the Astros in the third. Lefty Steve Howe and Bob Welch closed out the Astros in the eighth and ninth. The Dodgers padded their lead with three in the eighth on singles by Russell and Landreaux, and a sacrifice fly by Reggie Smith, and they were back in the hunt with a 6–1 victory. In game 4, Fernando Valenzuela returned to action, opposed by Vern Ruhle. In the Saturday twilight, before a sold out house of 55,983, the bold Mexican southpaw shut down the Astros inning after inning. L.A. finally broke through against Ruhle in the fifth inning. After retiring the first 14 Dodgers batters he faced, Ruhle got careless with Pedro Guerrero, hanging a curveball, and the Dominican slugger promptly drove it into the left field seats for a 1–0 Dodgers lead. Fernando continued to mow down the Astros through seven innings, with a fifth inning single by Caesar Cedeño the only blemish on his record. His teammates gave him a little breathing room in the bottom of the seventh, scoring an insurance run on a base hit by Steve Garvey and an opposite field single by Bill Russell to up the margin to 2–0. A two-out single by Tony Scott thwarted Fernando in his bid for a shutout but the Dodger ace quickly disposed of the tough José Cruz, retiring him on a popup to Mike Scioscia, to end the game.

Now the division playoff all came down to game 5, with Jerry Reuss, who had pitched nine shutout innings in game 2, facing Nolan Ryan, winner of game 1. As expected, the scoreboard showed nothing but goose eggs through five innings. Then, in the bottom of the sixth, the Dodgers came alive with three big runs. A walk to Dusty Baker and singles by Steve Garvey, Rick Monday, and Mike Scioscia brought the Dodgers faithful to their feet screaming. An insurance run in the seventh, on a double by Ken Landreaux and a triple by Steve Garvey, was unnecessary as Reuss closed out his shutout in style, winning 4–0.

The Dodgers' pitching excelled throughout the division playoff. Jerry Reuss went 1–0 while tossing 18 shutout innings at Bill Virdon's team. Fernando Valenzuela also went 1–0, with a miniscule 1.06 ERA in 17 innings. And Burt Hooton was 1–0 in his only start, with a 1.29 ERA in seven innings. Steve Garvey was the Dodgers' offensive catalyst, hammering Astros pitching for 7 base hits in 19 at-bats, a .368 average, with a triple, two home runs and four RBIs. The rest of the lineup hit sporadically, but one of them always came through at a critical time to pave the way to ultimate victory. The Penguin missed the entire division series, still nursing his broken left forearm, but he was available for duty on October 13 when L.A. faced the Montreal Expos in the best-of-five National League Championship Series.

The Expos had defeated the Philadelphia Phillies three games to two to win the Eastern Division Playoff Series, and they were at full strength in the NLCS. This time, the Dodgers had the home field advantage to start the play-offs, a three-game winning streak under their belt, and a feeling of confidence born of success. In game 1, under a bright sun, with Ron Cey back in action after 33 days on the injured list, Burt Hooton got the Dodgers off on the right track pitching 7⅓ innings of shutout ball, yielding six hits while fanning 2 and walking 3. He won the game 5–1. Cey got the Dodgers on the board first when he ripped a double into the right field corner to score Steve Garvey, and he was eventually squeezed home by Bill Russell. In the bottom of the eighth, L.A. added three more when Cey singled and Pedro Guerrero and Mike Scioscia followed with home runs.

Montreal	0 0 0	0 0 0	0 0 1 — 1 — 9 — 0	
Los Angeles	0 2 0	0 0 0	0 3 x — 5 — 8 — 0	

Montreal manager Jim Fanning sent Ray Burris to the mound in game 2, and the journeyman right-hander was at the top of his game, stifling the Dodgers on three base hits and winning by the score of 3–0. Fernando Valenzuela pitched adequately for Lasorda's team, but he was nicked for two runs in the second inning and another in the sixth, and that was more than enough for the big 6', 5", 200-pound fireballer who went 9–7 during the season, and 0–1 in the division playoff.

Montreal	0 2 0	0 0 1	0 0 0 — 3 — 10 — 1
Los Angeles	0 0 0	0 0 0	0 0 0 — 0 — 5 — 1

The Montreal momentum continued in game 3 before the home fans as the Expos' ace, Steve Rogers, put the Dodgers on the brink of extinction once again, by out-pitching Jerry Reuss for a 4–1 victory. The Dodgers big blond right-hander held a 1–0 lead after 5½ innings before the Expos exploded for four big runs in the bottom of the sixth. Reuss retired the first two batters to face him in the sixth, but the all-important third out didn't come until it was too late. A bloop single by Andre Dawson started the avalanche. A walk to Gary Carter, and a seeing-eye single by Larry Parrish tied the score. Light-hitting Jerry White, who hit just three home runs in 119 at-bats during the season, then jerked a Reuss fastball over the left field fence, and suddenly the Expos were home free — within one game of the World Series.

Los Angeles	0 0 0	1 0 0	0 0 0 — 1 — 7 — 0
Montreal	0 0 0	0 0 4	0 0 x — 4 — 7 — 1

Once again, with their backs to the wall, Lasorda's crew took a deep breath and flexed their muscles. They refused to accept their fate. Burt Hooton squared off against Bill Gullickson, a seven game winner in the regular season, in game 4. Hooton, who had compiled an 11–6 record over the summer months, and who had thrown 7⅓ shutout innings against the Expos in game two, was just as magnificent in this game, limiting Montreal to one unearned run in 7⅓ innings. A two-out double by Dusty Baker gave the Dodgers a 1–0 lead in the third. Montreal tied it an inning later on a single by Gary Carter. Hooton became the winning pitcher when Steve Garvey put a Gullickson fastball into orbit with Dusty Baker on base in the top of the eighth, sparking a 7–1 win. The final score was misleading because the game was deadlocked at 1-all after seven innings, before Garvey's heroics put two runs on the board for the West Coasters, giving them a 3–1 lead. L.A. added four more runs in the ninth to ice the decision. Dusty Baker drove home two runs with a single, and Ron Cey and Reggie Smith each plated one. Steve Howe blanked Montreal in the bottom of the ninth to wrap up the victory and set the stage for the big finale.

Los Angeles	0 0 1	0 0 0	0 2 4 — 7 — 12 — 1
Montreal	0 0 0	1 0 0	0 0 0 — 1 — 5 — 1

Game 5 at Le Strade Olympique was rained out on Sunday, and when it finally got underway the next day, the weather was still cold and damp, and a chill hung in the air as Ray Burris took the mound for the Expos, attempting to repeat his game-two magic. He was opposed by Fernando Valenzuela, who had taken the loss against Burris in Los Angeles. The contest was another tight pitcher's duel with both pitchers in top form. Montreal drew first blood in the opening stanza, scoring on a double play. L.A. tied the score in the fifth when Fernando's ground ball plated Rick Monday, who had singled. It was nail-biting time in Montreal as the game remained tied through the next three innings. As the ninth inning got underway, a packed house of nervous Canadians sat on the edge of their seats. Montreal manager Jim Fanning brought his ace, Steve Rogers, into the game to hold the Big Blue Machine in check, but Rogers was found wanting. Steve Garvey, the first batter, popped up. The Penguin, Ron Cey, then drove a Rogers fastball to deep left, but Tim Raines ran it down for out number two. Rick Monday strode to the plate determined to keep the Dodgers' hopes alive. Rogers, working carefully, fell behind in the count 3–1. The next pitch was a hanging sinker and Monday unloaded, sending a screamer to straightaway center field, as 36,491 Expos fans sat in stunned silence. Dawson followed the flight of the ball all the way to the fence, and then watched helplessly as the ball cleared the right center field fence and settled into the stands for a dramatic home run as NBC-TV announcer Dick Enberg informed his listeners, "And Monday will touch 'em all." Fernando tried to close out the Expos in the bottom of the ninth, but the pressure of the day finally caught up with him. After retiring the first two batters, the crafty southpaw lost his touch and walked Gary Carter. When he also walked Larry Parrish, Lasorda brought in Bob Welch to wrap it up. That he did, retiring Jerry White on an easy grounder to Davey Lopes, and the Dodgers were National League champions, and were on to their way to the World Series to face their long-time nemesis, the New York Yankees, once again.

Rick Monday, the smooth-swinging left-handed batter, who had hit eleven home runs in 130 at-bats during the regular season, became an instant Dodgers hero, and a baseball legend, with his dramatic pennant-winning home run in the Canadian cold.

	Los Angeles					Montreal			
Name	*Pos*	*AB*	*R*	*H*	*Name*	*Pos*	*AB*	*R*	*H*
Lopes	2B	4	0	1	Raines	LF	4	1	1
Russell	SS	4	0	2	Scott	2B	3	0	0
Baker	LF	4	0	0	Dawson	CF	4	0	0
Garvey	1B	4	0	0	Carter	C	3	0	1
Cey	3B	3	0	0	Manuel	PR	0	0	0
Monday	RF	4	2	2	Parrish	3B	3	0	1
Landreaux	CF	0	0	0	White	RF	3	0	0
Guerrero	RF	4	0	1	Cromartie	1B	3	0	0
Scioscia	C	3	0	0	Speier	SS	3	0	0
Valenzuela	P	3	0	0	Burris	P	2	0	0
Welch	P	0	0	0	Wallach	PH	1	0	0
					Rogers	P	0	0	0
Totals		33	2	6			29	1	3

Los Angeles	0 0 0	0 1 0	0 0 1 — 2 — 6 — 0
Montreal	1 0 0	0 0 0	0 0 0 — 1 — 3 — 1

Doubles— Raines, Parrish
Triple — Russell
Home Run — Monday

	IP	H	R	ER	BB	SO
Los Angeles						
Valenzuela (W 1–1)	8⅔	3	1	1	3	6
Welch (S 1)	⅓	0	0	0	0	0
Montreal						
Burris	8	5	1	1	1	1
Rogers (L 1–1)	1	1	1	1	0	1[7]

There was no rest for the weary, however, as the team had to pack hurriedly and fly to New York City. The World Series opened in Yankee Stadium the following day. Bob Lemon's edition of the Bronx Bombers won the first half of the American League Eastern Division, and met the Milwaukee Brewers, winners of the second half, in the division playoffs. The Yankees disposed of Buck Rodgers' Brewers in five games, winning the decisive battle 7–3 behind home runs by Reggie Jackson, Oscar Gamble, and Rick Cerone. The New Yorkers met little resistance in the ALCS, sweeping the Western Division champion Oakland Athletics three straight while outscoring them 20 to 4.

With that success behind them the Bombers were primed to capture another in their long line of world championships, against a tough Los Angeles Dodgers team that had earned a reputation for scratching and clawing for every advantage. On paper, the two teams seemed evenly matched. The Yankees had scored 421 runs to 450 runs for the Dodgers, and their pitching staff had surrendered 343 runs to 356 runs for L.A. The Yankees were not the Bronx Bombers of old, but they still had some punch in their lineup with sluggers like Reggie Jackson (15 home runs, 54 RBIs, .237 batting average), Dave Winfield (13, 68, .294), and Lou Pinella (5, 18, .277), and slick fielding Graig Nettles. Their pitching staff was anchored by Ron "Gator" Guidry (11–5, 2.76 ERA), Tommy John (9–8, 2.64), young Dave Righetti (8–4, 2.06), and Goose Gossage (3–2, 20 saves, 0.77 ERA)

The Series opened in Yankee Stadium on October 20, with Ron Guidry selected to open the Series for the Yankees, opposed by the Dodgers' crafty lefty, Jerry Reuss. After Guidry retired the Dodgers in order in the top of the first, the Yankees stormed out in front in their half of the inning. A single by Jerry Mumphrey and a two-out double by Lou Pinella set the table for big Bob Watson, who promptly drilled a three-run homer into the right center field bleachers. The Bronx Bombers added single runs in the third and fourth innings, knocking Reuss out of the box in the process. L.A. finally got on the scoreboard with a run in the fifth on a Steve Yeager home run. Guidry protected the 5–1 lead into the seventh inning, when he tired and was replaced by Ron Davis. After issuing walks to Derrel Thomas and Davey Lopes, Davis was yanked in favor of Goose Gossage, the Yankees' closer. Pinch-hitter Jay Johnstone greeted the Goose with a line single to right, plating Thomas and sending Lopes scurrying around to third. After a sacrifice fly cut the Yankees' lead to 5–3, Steve Garvey smashed a line drive that seemed headed for the left field corner and a tie game. But it was not to be on this night. The incomparable Graig Nettles, he of the magic glove, reacted instantaneously to the crack of the bat and, with one leaping backhand motion, he speared the liner ending the rally. That was it as far as the Dodgers were concerned. Gossage slammed the door in their faces in the ninth, and New York got the quick jump 5–3.

| Los Angeles | 0 0 0 | 0 1 0 | 0 2 0 — 3 — 5 — 0 |
| New York | 3 0 1 | 1 0 0 | 0 0 x — 5 — 6 — 0 |

The Yankees made it two in a row the next day when crafty southpaw Tommy John gained the verdict over a gallant Burt Hooton by the score of 3–0. John tossed seven shutout innings for the victory while Hooton yielded just one unearned run in six innings. The game was scoreless for four innings, but New York dented the plate in the fifth inning on a two-out double by Larry Milbourne. They added two more in the top of the eighth off Steve Howe on RBIs by Watson and Willie Randolph.

| Los Angeles | 0 0 0 | 0 0 0 | 0 0 0 — 0 — 4 — 2 |
| New York | 0 0 0 | 0 1 0 | 0 2 x — 3 — 6 — 1 |

Now it was back to L.A., and once again the Dodgers found themselves in a big hole, trailing two games to none. Tommy Lasorda's team was discouraged, but not beaten, remembering how they had rallied from a two game deficit to defeat the Houston Astros in the Western Division playoff, and how they rallied from a two-games to one deficit to stop the Montreal Expos in the National League Championship Series. This Series was just more of the same. Lasorda sent his ace, Fernando Valenzuela, to the mound to face New York's rookie left-hander, Dave Righetti in game three. Fernando struggled with his control throughout but hung tough, and his manager, Tommy Lasorda, stuck with him. After the Dodgers had touched up Righetti for a three-spot in the bottom of the first on a three-run homer by Ron Cey, the Bronx Bombers chipped away at Fernando, scoring two runs in the second and two more in the third for a 4–3 lead. Catcher Rick Cerone, who had doubled and scored in the second inning, took Valenzuela deep in the third, sending a shot over the left center field fence with Lou Pinella on base. L.A. countered with a brace of runs in the fifth, and Fernando made it stand up for a 5–4 win. The biggest play of the day, and perhaps of the Series, was made in the Yankees' eighth. After New York put the first two men on base on singles by Aurelio

Rodríguez and Larry Milbourne, Bobby Murcer was sent up to sacrifice the runners along. He popped a bunt toward third base for what looked like a successful sacrifice. But Ron Cey had other ideas. The fiery Dodgers third baseman raced toward the plate with his characteristic waddle and threw himself at the ball as it dropped earthward. The ball settled in Cey's glove as he landed on his stomach on the foul line. Getting to his feet, he quickly rifled the ball across the diamond to Garvey to double Milbourne off first. It was a game-saving play. In the ninth, Fernando disposed of Mumphrey and Winfield easily, and then fanned the tough Lou Pinella to lock up the victory. It wasn't an easy win for the rookie, as he walked seven men along the way and was nicked for nine base hits, but he prevailed in a gutty performance, and his lead gave the Dodgers the momentum they needed to derail the Yankees express.

| New York | 0 2 2 | 0 0 0 | 0 0 0 — 4 — 9 — 0 |
| Los Angeles | 3 0 0 | 0 2 0 | 0 0 x — 5 — 11 — 1 |

Game 4 was the turning point of the Series. It was another memorable game as Lasorda's team, drawing on their experience in the Division Series and the NLCS, fought back from 4–0 and 6–3 deficits to win a slugfest 8–7. The big blows of the game were Jay Johnstone's game-tying two-run homer in the sixth inning and Bill Russell's tie-breaking single in the same inning. Dodgers starter Bob Welch failed to retire a single batter on this bright, sunny California afternoon. With the temperature a balmy 72 degrees, Bob Lemon's Bombers nicked Welch for three base hits and a walk, good for a 2–0 lead. They added single runs in the second and third innings, before the Big Blue Machine could break through. L.A. scored two runs in the bottom of the third, and another run two innings later, cutting the New York lead to 4–3. But, once again, Lasorda's bullpen failed. Tom Niedenfuer, in his second inning of relief, was touched up for two runs and the Yankees were back on top by a 6–3 count. "Again the Dodgers failed to fold. In their typical style, they scratched and clawed their way back. In the bottom of the sixth, Mike Scioscia drew a one-out walk, Jay Johnstone, pinch-hitting for pitcher Tom Niedenfuer, made what may have been the key hit of the entire Series, hitting a long home run to right center field. Suddenly, Tommy Lasorda's boys were back in the game once more. They still trailed 6–5, but in their minds, they had the lead. They tied the game moments later when Reggie Jackson dropped Davey Lopes' fly ball down the right field line for a two-base error, and Bill Russell, atoning for an earlier miscue, brought home the tying run with a line-drive single to left. The momentum had shifted. The atmosphere was electric. The Dodgers were on the move and they couldn't be stopped."[8] They scored what proved to be the winning runs in the bottom of the seventh off George Frazier, tagging him with his second loss of the Series. A single by Dusty Baker, a double by Rick Monday, and a walk to Pedro Guerrero loaded the bases, and Steve Yeager came through with a sacrifice fly to plate the eventual winning run. A second run scored moments later on an infield single by Lopes. The Yankees pushed over a run in the eighth making the final score 8–7.

| New York | 2 1 1 | 0 0 2 | 0 1 0 — 7 — 13 — 1 |
| Los Angeles | 0 0 2 | 0 1 3 | 2 0 x — 8 — 14 — 2 |

The Dodgers had everything going for them in game 5. They had the momentum and the confidence, and they had the home crowd behind them. The game matched Game 1 adversaries Jerry Reuss and Ron Guidry. New York struck first with a run in the top of the second inning on a double by Jackson, an error by Davey Lopes, one of three he made in the game, and a single by Lou Pinella. Louisiana Lightning made the run stand up until the seventh when Pedro Guerrero and Steve Yeager touched him for back-to-back home runs, and that was all L.A.'s big blond southpaw needed. He completed the game, limiting New York to five base hits, while striking out six and walking three. Dave Winfield singled in the fifth inning. It would be his only hit of the Series, as the $21 million free agent finished with a .045 batting average in 22 trips to the plate. "A potential tragedy occurred in the bottom of the eighth. Goose Gossage, the man with the 94 mile-per-hour fastball, threw an inside pitch to Ron Cey. The Penguin was unable to get out of the way of the speeding pellet, and took the full impact of the shot on the left temple. After several nervous minutes, the game Dodger third baseman was able to leave the field under his own power, suffering nothing more than a concussion."[9]

| New York | 0 1 0 | 0 0 0 | 0 0 0 — 1 — 5 — 0 |
| Los Angeles | 0 0 0 | 0 0 0 | 2 0 x — 2 — 4 — 3 |

The Series returned to the Bronx for game 6, but Lasorda's cohorts couldn't be stopped, nor could the Penguin. After suffering a beaning three days before, Ron Cey left his hospital bed and returned to the Dodgers lineup for the finale. Burt Hooton and Steve Howe combined to hold the Yankees in check while the big Dodgers bats exploded for a 9–2 Series-clinching victory. The turning point in the game came in the fourth inning when New York manager Bob Lemon made a strategic blunder, pinch hitting for his starting pitcher, Tommy John, with the game tied at 1–1. John, who had a 0.69 ERA in 13 innings in the Series, was noticeably upset and, when the pinch-hitter failed to produce, the Dodgers jumped on relief pitcher George Frazier for three runs in his one inning of work, pinning him with his third loss of the Series, and coasting to a 9–2 win. In the big Dodger fifth, Ron Cey, back in action, drove in the tie-breaking run with a single, and Pedro Guerrero netted two more with a booming triple. Guerrero added a two-run single in the sixth and a solo home run in the eighth, completing the scoring. Cey, Yeager, and Guerrero were voted co–MVPs of the Series.

Manager Tommy Lasorda and Ron Cey (at right) lead the charge from the dugout after the final out in Game 6 of the World Series (courtesy of Los Angeles Dodgers).

Los Angeles

Name	Pos	AB	R	H
Lopes	2B	4	2	1
Russell	SS	4	0	2
Garvey	1B	4	1	1
Cey	3B	3	1	2
Thomas	3B	2	1	0
Baker	LF	5	2	2
Guerrero	CF-RF	5	1	3
Monday	RF	3	0	1
Landreaux	CF	1	0	0
Yeager	C	5	0	1
Hooton	P	2	1	0
Howe	P	2	0	0
Totals		40	9	13

New York

Name	Pos	AB	R	H
Randolph	2B	3	1	2
Mumphrey	CF	5	0	1
Winfield	LF	4	0	0
Jackson	RF	5	0	0
Watson	1B	5	0	0
Nettles	3B	3	0	2
Rodríguez	3B	1	1	1
Cerone	C	3	0	0
Milbourne	SS	2	0	0
John	P	1	0	0
Murcer	PH	1	0	0
Frazier	P	0	0	0
Davis	P	0	0	0
Reuschel	P	0	0	0
Gamble	PH	0	0	0
Pinella	PH	1	0	1
May	P	0	0	0
Brown	PH	1	0	0
LaRoche	P	0	0	0
Totals		35	2	7

L.A. Dodgers co–MVPs (left to right) Pedro Guerrero, Steve Yeager, and Ron Cey (courtesy of Los Angeles Dodgers).

Los Angeles	0 0 0	1 3 4	0 1 0 — 9 — 13 — 1
New York	0 0 1	0 0 1	0 0 0 — 2 — 7 — 2

Doubles— Nettles, Randolph
Triple — Guerrero
Home Runs— Randolph, Guerrero

	IP	H	R	ER	BB	SO
Los Angeles						
Hooton (W 1–0)	$5\frac{1}{3}$	5	2	2	5	2
Howe	$3\frac{2}{3}$	2	0	0	1	3
New York						
John	4	6	1	1	0	2
Frazier (L 0–3)	1	4	3	3	0	1
Davis	$\frac{1}{3}$	1	3	2	2	1
Reuschel	$\frac{2}{3}$	1	1	0	2	0
May	2	1	1	1	1	2
LaRoche	1	0	0	0	0	2[10]

Euphoria settled over Dodgerland as the world champions looked forward to perhaps another dynasty, but it wasn't to be. Age was catching up with several of the Dodgers players. Burt Hooton was nearing 32 years of age. Jerry Reuss was 32. And the famous Dodgers infield of Garvey, Lopes, Russell, and Cey, all of whom were at least 33 years old, had been together for a major-league-record 8½ years, culminating in the Series triumph. Steve Garvey was a third baseman when he arrived in Los Angeles in 1970, but when Ron Cey joined the team three years later, he was installed at the hot corner and Garvey was moved over to first base. Bill Russell became a Dodger in 1969, as an outfielder, but took over as the regular shortstop in 1972. Davey Lopes completed the quartet in 1973 when he moved up from Albuquerque where he had just sparked Tommy Lasorda's Dukes to the Pacific Coast League pennant with a .317 batting average and a league-leading 48 stolen bases. The Dukes were loaded that year with Cey (.329, 23 homers, a league-leading 123 RBIs), Von Joshua with a league-leading .337 batting average, and Tom Paciorek who hit .307 and led the league in runs scored (125), base hits (186), doubles (33), and home runs (27).

The Infield never played as a unit again after their 1981 World Series triumph. Davey Lopes was the first to go. He was traded to the Oakland Athletics on February 8, 1982, and Steve Garvey left as a free agent on November 10 of the same year, subsequently signing with the San Diego Padres. And Ron Cey went to the Chicago Cubs in 1983. Only Bill Russell ended his career in Los Angeles, retiring as a player in 1986, and then staying in the organization as a coach and a minor league manager until 1996 when he replaced Tommy Lasorda as the manager of the Dodgers.

The 1981 Los Angeles Dodgers earned the nickname "Team Comeback" after storming back from an 0–2 deficit to defeat the Houston Astros in the Western Division playoff, overcoming a 1–2 deficit to sink the Montreal Expos in the National League Championship Series, and rallying from an 0–2 deficit to send the proud Bronx Bombers packing in the World Series. Actually, the team had begun the legend a year earlier when they erased a three-game deficit in the last three games of the 1980 National League pennant race, to tie the Houston Astros for first place. And they would continue the saga in 1982 against the Atlanta Braves.

Sadly, for Dodgers fans everywhere, the team lost one of its greatest players on October 25 when "Pistol Pete" Reiser died in Los Angeles of a respiratory ailment. The handsome center fielder might have been the greatest player ever to play the game if fate had treated him more kindly. As his former manager, Leo Durocher, once said, "He had everything but luck." Reiser captured the National League batting championship in 1941 at the age of 22, when he hit .343 and led the league with 117 runs scored, 39 doubles, 17 triples, and a .558 slugging average. He was leading the league in batting again the following year, stroking the ball at a .356 clip in July, when he ran into the center field wall in Sportsman's Park, St. Louis. It was just one of many times that Reiser was carried off the field on a stretcher. The numerous injuries sapped his strength until he was just a shadow of his former self, one of the game's tragic figures.

2

PEAKS AND VALLEYS—
1982 TO 1985

Davey Lopes was traded to Oakland on February 6, 1982, breaking up the long running Dodgers infield of Garvey, Lopes, Russell, and Cey, who had thrilled Dodgers fans for 8½ years. The quartet played together longer than any other infield in major league history. In fact, only three other combinations ever stayed together for more than five years: the Chicago Cubs of 1906–10, the Cubs of 1965–69, and the great Brooklyn combination of Hodges, Robinson, Reese, and Cox, who anchored the Dodgers defense from 1948 through 1952.

Fernando Valenzuela ended a three week holdout and arrived at Dodgertown to honor his contract that was automatically renewed March 1 under the second year rule. He honored the contract but he refused to sign it. As spring training got underway, Jay Johnstone, one of the team's notorious pranksters, along with Jerry Reuss, thought things were too quiet in the Dodgers enclave, so he took immediate action. First, he sneaked into manager Tommy Lasorda's town house and removed the mouthpiece speakers from both telephones. Then, about 2 A.M., after Lasorda had retired for the night, Johnstone and catcher Steve Yeager put a rope around the doorknob to Lasorda's room and tied the other end to a palm tree. When Lasorda tried to open the door in the morning, he found himself trapped in his room. He tried calling for help on the telephone but, although he could hear the girl on the switchboard, she couldn't hear him. He became frantic and started screaming out the window. Several of the players heard him, but ignored the commotion. Finally, scout Ralph Avila passed by and, hearing the forlorn cry for help, rescued the embattled skipper.

Pre-season baseball experts installed the Los Angeles Dodgers as one of the favorites to win the Western Division, along with the Cincinnati Reds and the Houston Astros. But lurking in the background were the Atlanta Braves, under the direction of new manager Joe Torre. The Braves had compiled an unimpressive 50–56 record in 1981, but had a solid core of experienced hitters in Chris Chambliss, Bob Horner, and Dale Murphy. They also had a decent pitching staff headed by 43-year-old Phil Niekro, Rick Camp, and Rick Mahler, with closer Gene Garber to shut down the opposition in the ninth.

On April 6, the Dodgers opened the 1982 season at home amid a joyous world championship celebration. They received their blue sapphire and diamond World Series rings, and they raised the championship banner to the cheers of 49,662 delirious fans. The game that followed was a thrilling pitchers duel with the San Francisco Giants, and Lasorda's cohorts scored the winning run in the bottom of the ninth when Bill Russell ripped a double down the left field line, went to third as the Dodgers loaded the bases with no outs, and scored on Dusty Baker's seeing-eye single through a drawn-in infield. Terry Forster was credited with the win in the 4–3 contest. The game marked the first time since June 23, 1973, that Garvey, Lopes, Russell, and Cey didn't hold down the infield spots as a unit, as noted above. Steve Sax, a 22-year-old dynamo, replaced Lopes at second base, and would go on to win the National League Rookie of the Year award after hitting a solid .282 with 49 stolen bases.

But, in an omen of things to come, the Atlanta Braves came out of the gate smoking. Rick Mahler tossed a two-hitter at the San Diego Padres, winning 1–0 on a double by Glenn Hubbard. Five days later, Mahler threw his second consecutive shutout, beating the Houston Astros 5–0 behind a home run by Bob Horner, racking up Atlanta's fifth straight win. On April 20, Joe Torre's crew reeled off their 12th consecutive victory, a new major league record to start the season, and the following night they defeated Cincinnati 4–3 with two runs in the bottom of the ninth, to make it thirteen in a row. The streak finally came to an end on the 22nd when the Reds took a 2–1 decision.

The team that earned the moniker Team Comeback for their three come-from-behind series victories in the 1981 post-season, as well as for their thrilling comeback from a three-game deficit in the final three games of the 1980 season when they overtook the Houston Astros, only to lose the one-game playoff for the Western Division title, would have to live up to their reputation again in 1982. By April 22, the Dodgers stood at 6–8 and were already mired in third place, 7½ games behind Joe Torre's streaking Atlanta Braves. Things didn't get any better for the Big Blue Machine as the summer progressed. They went 10–11 in April, 15–13 in May, and 16–12 in June. One bright spot in the Dodgers' summer was Steve Garvey, who played his 1000th consecutive game on June 7, with a crowd of 44,714 well-wishers giving him a standing ovation that lasted several minutes. As often happens after these types of celebrations, Garvey went zero for four in the game and the Atlanta Braves hung a 4–3 defeat on L.A. when Dale Murphy smashed a three-run homer in the ninth to snatch victory from defeat.

At the July 4 halfway point, the Los Angeles record was 41–38, seven games behind Atlanta. "Three and a half weeks later, things looked even bleaker. An 11–13 mark left them further behind, a distant 10½ games out of first. To make matters worse, the battered Los Angeles contingent had to visit Atlanta for a four-game weekend series with the league leaders."[1]

Suddenly the Big Blue Machine caught a fresh tailwind, and stormed through Atlanta like General William Tecumseh Sherman. On July 30, they downed the Braves twice in Fulton County Stadium, winning by scores of 10–9 and 8–2, shaving the Atlanta lead to a mere 8½ games. In the opener, Ron Roenicke's bases-loaded single proved to be the game-winner as the Dodgers roared back from a 6–1 deficit to win it. Bob Welch coasted to the victory in the nightcap, winning his 11th game. Tommy Lasorda's troops completed the four game sweep, by winning 3–0 behind Fernando Valenzuela's six-hitter on Saturday, and 9–4 behind two home runs by Dusty Baker and one by Pedro Guerrero, on Sunday.

One week later, Joe Torre's embattled Braves visited Tinseltown to do battle once again with the Dodgers. But this four-game series treated Atlanta no better than the first one. L.A. routed the Braves again, by scores of 3–2 in 10 innings, 5–4, 7–6 in 11 innings, and 2–0 behind Bob Welch's 13th win of the season, and suddenly, in a period of just 10 days, the huge 10½ game Atlanta lead had shrunk to 1½ games. As Tommy Lasorda noted, "It (the eight game sweep) has to be the greatest heist since the Brinks Express robbery.... I've never seen a team gain so much ground in so short a period, not even in the minor leagues."[2] On Tuesday, August 8, the Dodgers completed their dizzying dash to the top of the National League. They routed Cincinnati 11–3 while the Braves were dropping a 3–2 decision to the San Francisco Giants. The L.A. surge continued on the 11th and 12th and, on the 13th, Steve Sax swiped his 41st base of the season, in a 6–1 laugher over the San Francisco Giants. The win increased the Dodgers' lead over Atlanta to 2½ games. In the most astounding turnaround in major league history, Tommy Lasorda's streaking sluggers had reeled off 14 wins in 16 games while, at the same time, Torre's impotent Injuns were dropping 15 of 16, a flip-flop of 13 full games in the standings.

On August 17, the Dodgers and Cubs battled to a 1–1 tie over 17 innings in a game halted by darkness. The game was resumed the next day and the L.A. crew eked out a 2–1 victory when Dusty Baker's sacrifice fly plated Steve Sax with the winning run in the 21st inning. Jerry Reuss, who picked up the victory with four innings of shutout relief, also won the regularly scheduled game, hurling five innings in a 7–4 Dodgers win, running his record to 12–9. The Dodgers were four games in front of the fading Braves, but change was in the wind. On the 19th, Atlanta defeated Montreal 5–4, and the following night they beat them again, 2–1 in ten innings. Just as suddenly as they lost it, Joe Torre's charges regained their momentum. They reeled off 13 victories in 15 games and recaptured first place from the Dodgers. On September 8, the Braves broke a nine-game losing streak to the Dodgers by edging them 12–11

Steve Sax took over the second base duties from the departed Davey Lopes in 1982 (author's collection).

on Dale Murphy's game-winning single, giving them a ½ game lead over L.A. The next night they increased their lead to 1½ games with a 10–3 rout of the Blue Crew, and from there, to the end of the season, the two teams jockeyed for position.

The Dodgers made another run at Atlanta in early September and by the 17th they were back in the driver's seat, three games ahead of the Braves with just ten games to play. Two days later, an L. A. rally against the Houston Astros kept their lead intact. Things looked bleak for Lasorda's crew until Pedro Guerrero's two-run double in the bottom of the tenth inning salvaged a 5–4 victory and sent the big West Coast crowd home happy. Unfortunately, they couldn't protect the lead. They dropped the next five games while Atlanta won four, and the Braves were back on top by one game with five to play.

The entire season came down to the final game, with the Dodgers in San Francisco, and Atlanta in San Diego, protecting a one game lead. The scoreboard in Candlestick Park told the story. The Braves had lost to the Padres by a 5–1 score, so a Dodgers victory would send the two teams into a one-game playoff to decide the Western Division pennant race. But it was not to be. With the score deadlocked at two-all, the Giants' Joe Morgan cracked a three-run homer off Terry Forster, in relief of Fernando Valenzuela, giving the Giants a 5–3 win and killing the Dodgers' hopes of overtaking the Atlanta Braves. The Dodgers finished the season in second place with an 88–74 record, one game behind Atlanta.

Los Angeles					San Francisco				
Name	*Pos*	*AB*	*R*	*H*	*Name*	*Pos*	*AB*	*R*	*H*
Sax	2B	4	0	0	Venable	CF	3	0	0
Landreaux	CF	4	1	1	Wohlford	LF	1	0	0
Baker	LF	4	0	2	Morgan	2B	3	1	1
Garvey	1B	4	0	1	Clark	RF	4	0	0
Monday	RF	4	1	1	R. Smith	1B	3	0	0
Cey	3B	4	1	2	Bergman	1B	0	0	0
Scioscia	C	2	0	0	Evans	3B	3	1	1
J. Morales	PH	1	0	1	Leonard	RF	4	1	1
Bradley	PR	0	0	0	Brenly	C	2	1	1
Yeager	C	0	0	0	LeMaster	SS	0	0	0
Roenicke	PH	1	0	0	Pettini	SS	1	0	0
Russell	SS	4	0	1	Summers	PH	1	0	1
Valenzuela	P	2	0	0	Sularz	SS	0	1	0
Orta	PH	1	0	0	Laskey	P	2	0	0
Niedenfuer	P	0	0	0	Lavelle	P	0	0	0
Forster	P	0	0	0	Minton	P	1	0	0
Totals		35	3	9			28	5	5

```
Los Angeles      0 2 0    0 0 0    0 1 0 — 3 — 9 — 0
San Francisco    0 2 0    0 0 0    3 0 x — 5 — 5 — 0
```

Doubles— Leonard, Summers, Landreaux, Baker.
Home Runs— Cey, Morgan

Name	IP	H	R	ER	BB	SO
Los Angeles						
Valenzuela	6	2	2	2	5	9
Niedenfuer (L 3-4)	⅓	2	2	2	0	1
Forster	1⅔	1	1	1	0	2
San Francisco						
Laskey	6⅓	6	2	2	0	2
Lavelle	0	1	0	0	0	0
Minton (W 10-4)	2⅔	2	1	1	0	2³

On November 10, Steve Garvey, failing to reach an agreement with Dodgers owner Peter O'Malley on a new contract, became a free agent. He eventually signed a $6.6 million five-year deal with the San Diego Padres. Twelve days later, on November 22, Steve Sax became the fourth consecutive Los Angeles Dodgers player to be named the National League Rookie of the Year, following in the footsteps of Rick Sutcliffe, Steve Howe, and Fernando Valenzuela.

The Dodgers were once again one of the favorites in the Western Division as the 1983 season approached, along with the Atlanta Braves, and they were joined by the San Francisco Giants, who had finished just two games behind the Braves in 1982. Cincinnati's fortunes had taken a turn for the worse in the season just completed and, with Joe Morgan, Tony Pérez, and Pete Rose long gone, and Johnny Bench just a shadow of his former self, they were not expected to compete for the title. And Houston, which had slumped to a 77–85 record, leaving it a full 12 games behind Atlanta, did not appear to have the firepower to challenge the top two.

The Dodgers themselves were in transition in 1983. Their first move was to trade third baseman Ron Cey to the Chicago Cubs for Vance Loveless and Dan Cataline on January 19. It was not a popular move with the fans because the Penguin was one of their favorites, but a new youth movement was underway in L.A., and the old guard, who had outlived their usefulness, had to give way to the new. Greg Brock, a long-ball hitting southpaw swinger, was stationed at first base. Steve Sax was back at second. Bill Russell still held down the shortstop job, and Pedro Guerrero was brought in from the outfield to play third base. Mike Marshall, a 6', 5", 220-pound right-handed slugger, was stationed in left field.

March 4, 1983, was a dark day in Dodgers history. Closer Steve Howe admitted to being addicted to cocaine, but said he was now clean. That story proved to be false, and the talented lefty spent six weeks in drug rehab from May 17 to June 29. After his return, he ran up a brilliant 1.44 earned run average with 18 saves in 46 games, before succumbing to his habit once again. On September 23, the Dodgers fined him $54,000 and suspended him for the remainder of the season. Major League Baseball subsequently suspended him for all of 1984 as well.

As noted in *The Dodger Chronicles*, "Tommy Lasorda's team was a Jekyll and Hyde outfit. It was always a question of whether the Dodger pitchers could hold the opposition to fewer runs than the leaky L.A. infield would let in. Fortunately for L.A. fans, the pitching staff was, once again, the class of the league. They were led by Fernando Valenzuela (19–13, 2.87), Bob Welch (16–11, 3.36), Jerry Reuss (18–11, 3.11), and Alejandro Peña (0–2, 4.79). Tom "Buff" Niedenfuer, the mainstay of the bullpen, appeared in 55 games in 1982, with a 3–4 record, 9 saves, and a 2.71 earned run average. Steve Howe, in 66 games, was 7–5 with 13 saves and a miniscule 2.08 ERA."[4]

The Dodgers opened the season on April 5 in the Astrodome, and routed the Houston Astros 16–7 behind the offensive pyrotechnics of Ken Landreaux, who knocked in six runs, and Pedro Guerrero, who drove in five.

Three days later, Tommy Lasorda's cohorts got a taste of their own medicine in their home opener when the Montreal Expos ko'd Burt Hooton en route to an 8–3 victory. The Dodgers defense was a major culprit in the debacle, making three errors as well as other bad plays that weren't recorded as official errors. Mike Marshall's misplay on a fly ball by Tim Wallach in the fourth inning led to four runs and an early shower for Hooton. Andre Dawson paced Bill Virdon's team with five hits in five at-bats, including a double, a triple, and a squeeze bunt RBI single. Scott Sanderson was the winning pitcher with relief help from Bryn Smith.

No sooner had the season gotten underway than the Dodgers suffered a setback when Mike Marshall was beaned by Montreal right-hander Jeff Reardon on April 9. The big right fielder stayed in the lineup but his bat went silent over the next several weeks and he was finally benched in favor of veteran Rick Monday against right-handed pitchers.

It was Steve Garvey weekend in Dodger Stadium, and the former Los Angeles first baseman, now a member of the San Diego Padres, celebrated his 1,118th consecutive game on Saturday, April 16, breaking Billy Williams' National League record. Garvey received a standing ovation from the 50,800 fans who came to welcome him back, and he chipped in with two base hits, but they were not enough to offset the L.A. offense on this night as Steve Sax with four hits and Greg Brock with two doubles and a single paced Lasorda's crew to their sixth straight win, this one by an 8–5 score.

Ron Cey made his first return home with the Cubs on May 9, pounding out three hits, but the Big Blue Machine took the contest by a 4–3 count when Ken Landreaux, who had homered in the sixth inning, drove in the winning run with a single in the ninth.

Greg Brock got off to a sensational start as Steve Garvey's replacement, hitting nine home runs and driving in 28 runs in the first 35 games. On May 18, he slammed two home runs and drove in six runs in a 13–3 rout of the Montreal Expos.

Dodgers pitchers were in a zone between May 22 and 24, throwing three

Greg Brock and Mike Marshall gave the Dodgers a formidable one-two punch in the early 1980s (author's collection).

consecutive shutouts. Bob Welch blanked the New York Mets by a 5–0 score on Sunday, Fernando Valenzuela shut down the Philadelphia Phillies 2–0 on Monday, and Alejandro Peña took care of the Phils 3–0 the following day. Welch went on to defeat the Cincinnati Reds 1–0 in Dodger Stadium 26 days later, hitting his first major league home run off Mario Soto.

On July 31, Walter Alston was inducted into the Baseball Hall of Fame in Cooperstown, New York, in recognition of his managerial service with the Brooklyn and Los Angeles Dodgers. His 23-year career, all with the Dodgers, included 2040 victories against 1613 losses for a .558 winning percentage, seven National League pennants, and four world championships.

Steve Sax hit a psychological stone wall during the 1983 season as he was suddenly unable to make the throw from second base to first base with any consistency. By July 20 he had amassed a total of 26 errors in his team's first 108 games. His 26th came on a double-play ball and led to a 7–3 victory by the Pittsburgh Pirates. It got to the point where the fans behind first base would duck every time a ground ball was hit to second base. Sax's total of errors mounted to 30 before he got his throws under control, but he did play errorless ball over the club's final 57 games.

The Dodgers, after suffering through a 4–15 slump in July, found themselves 5½ games behind the Atlanta Braves on August 8, and the *Atlanta*

Constitution announced in large headlines, "It's Over." Los Angeles manager Tommy Lasorda didn't think so, and he held a closed-door meeting with his team two days later following a 9–2 drubbing at the hands of the Cincinnati Reds. During the meeting, Lasorda read the riot act to the team; then veterans Bill Russell and Rick Monday lectured the young players on teamwork and dedication. The meeting apparently achieved its purpose because the next night Greg Brock clubbed a three-run homer in the top of the first inning, and the Dodgers held on for a 4–3 win, starting an eight game winning streak. By August 29, the surging Dodgers had reclaimed first place.

Midway through the season, as noted by Brian Golden, "Humor became the rallying focus of the 1983 Dodger National League West titlists. Then-assistant trainer Paul Padilla, it was reckoned by some players, bore a resemblance to Mr. Potato Head, the child's toy. Eventually, Jerry Reuss bought one of the toys, and it became a sort of trophy awarded to the daily heroes of Dodger victories. The ungainly looking toy developed into a coveted possession, and helped cement clubhouse unity which ultimately helped the Dodgers run down Atlanta in the west."[5]

On September 11, rookie R.J. Reynolds squeezed Pedro Guerrero home with the winning run in the bottom of the ninth inning at Dodger Stadium, as the Dodgers nipped the Atlanta Braves 7–6 to go three-up in the National League West pennant race. The Big Blue Machine, which trailed by three runs as the ninth inning got underway, scored twice on Mike Marshall's double, before Reynolds' heroics.

The key game of the season was played on September 23. The Dodgers were visiting Atlanta for a three-game series against Joe Torre's crew, and they held a 4½ game lead over the Braves at the time, making it critical for the Braves to sweep the series. But any possibility of that happening was put to rest in the opening game when the Dodgers offense, sparked by home runs off the bats of Ken Landreaux, Pedro Guerrero, and Dusty Baker, sent Atlanta pitcher Len Barker to an early shower en route to a convincing 11–2 victory. Dodgers right-hander Jerry Reuss, the recipient of the avalanche, coasted to his 12th victory of the season. The Braves took games two and three, but it was too little, too late.

Los Angeles					**Atlanta**				
Name	*Pos*	*AB*	*R*	*H*	*Name*	*Pos*	*AB*	*R*	*H*
Sax	2B	6	3	3	Butler	LF	4	0	1
Russell	SS	4	2	1	Hubbard	2B	4	1	1
Baker	LF	3	2	1	Moore	P	0	0	0
Guerrero	3B	5	2	2	Ramírez	SS	4	0	2
Landreaux	CF	5	1	2	Murphy	CF	4	1	2
Espy	CF	0	0	0	Watson	1B	4	0	1
Marshall	RF	5	0	1	Komminsk	RF	4	0	2

Name	Pos	AB	R	H	Name	Pos	AB	R	H
Brock	1B	5	0	1	Benedict	C	4	0	0
Yeager	C	4	1	1	Royster	3B	3	0	0
Reuss	P	3	0	2	Barker	P	0	0	0
					Falcone	P	0	0	0
					Runge	PH	1	0	0
					Dedmon	P	0	0	0
					Jacoby	PH	1	0	0
					Boggs	P	0	0	0
					Brizzolara	P	0	0	0
					Johnson	2B	1	0	0
Totals		40	11	14			34	2	9

Los Angeles	1 0 3	0 2 4	0 1 0 — 11 — 14 — 0
Atlanta	0 0 0	2 0 0	0 0 0 — 2 — 9 — 3

Errors— Barker (2), Royster
Triples— Marshall
Home Runs— Landreaux, Baker, Guerrero

Name	IP	R	ER	H	BB	SO
Los Angeles						
Reuss (W12-11)	9	2	2	9	0	4
Atlanta						
Barker (L 1-3)	2⅔	4	4	4	3	4
Falcone	⅓	0	0	0	0	0
Dedman	2	2	2	2	0	2
Boggs	⅓	4	4	4	0	0
Brizzolara	2⅔	1	1	3	0	2
Moore	1	0	0	1	0	2[6]

Tommy Lasorda's Big Blue Machine went on to win the pennant by three games, their 91–71 record giving them the advantage over the Atlanta Braves. Their opponent in the National League Championship Series was the Philadelphia Phillies who, on paper, looked like the ideal opponent for the Dodgers. L.A. had handled Paul Owens' team easily during the season, winning 11 of 12 contests, and holding the big bats of Mike Schmidt, Pete Rose, Tony Pérez, Garry Maddox, Gary Matthews, and Joe Morgan, to a combined .187 batting average. Dodger pitchers had tossed 8 complete games at the Phils in 12 starts, with a 1.09 ERA. But, as history has shown, regular season records are meaningless in post-season play. It's a new season, and everyone starts with the same record.

    The NLCS opened in Los Angeles on October 4, with Philadelphia's Steve Carlton toeing the rubber against Dodgers ace Jerry Reuss. Future Hall of Fame third baseman Mike Schmidt went deep off Reuss in the top of the first inning and fellow Hall of Famer, Steve Carlton made it stand up for a 1–0

Philadelphia victory. In game 2, manager Tommy Lasorda handed the ball to his 22-year-old southpaw sensation, Fernando Valenzuela, and Fernando, as he did many times over his career, responded with a 4–1 seven-hitter. Pedro Guerrero drove in the game-winners with a two-run triple in the fifth inning, wiping out a 1–0 Philly lead that had been fashioned on a second inning home run by Gary Matthews. Returning to the City of Brotherly Love, Paul Owens and his crew watched the Dodgers self-destruct. Bob Welch, the L.A. starter, walked two men to open the second inning, then had to leave the game with a hip injury. Alejandro Peña came on, and watched two runs score on a wild pitch, a passed ball and an infield grounder. Mike Marshall's two-run home run in the top of the fourth narrowed the Philly lead to 3–2, but that was it for the Dodgers "as Gary Matthews took control of the game. The fleet footed leftfielder hit a solo home run in the bottom of the fourth off Peña, stroked a two-run single off Honeycut in the fifth, and added another run-scoring single off Zachry in the seventh, as the Phils rolled to a 7–2 triumph."[7] The next day, lefty Steve Carlton took over and clinched the best three-of-five series for the Philadelphia fans. He scattered six base hits over six innings and his Philly teammates jumped on Jerry Reuss for three runs in the first inning on Gary Matthews three-run homer, and followed that up with a brace of runs in the fifth off the Dodger starter and two more in the sixth off Rick

Steve Carlton defeated the Dodgers twice in the 1983 NLCS, sending the Phillies to the World Series (author's collection).

Honeycut. The final score was 7–2. It was the first time in five National League playoff series that the Dodgers did not advance to the World Series. It was an omen of things to come.

The Los Angeles Dodgers season ended on a sad note, but the team had a lot to celebrate for the season in general. Pedro Guerrero had a big year, rapping the ball at a .298 clip, with 28 doubles, 6 triples, 32 home runs, 103 runs batted in, and 23 stolen bases. Mike Marshall batted .284 with 17 doubles, 17 home runs, and 65 RBIs. Ken Landreaux hit .281 with 25 doubles, 17 home runs, 66 RBIs, and 30 stolen bases. Steve Sax compiled a .281 average with 94 runs scored and 56 stolen bases. Greg Brock ended the season hitting just .224, but slammed 14 doubles, 2 triples, and 20 home runs, driving in 67 teammates. The pitching was the team's strong point as shown below.

Name	G	IP	W	L	SVS	ERA
Alejandro Peña	34	177	12	9	1	2.75
Burt Hooton	33	160	9	8	0	4.22
JerryReuss	31	223	12	11	0	2.94
FernandoValenzuela	35	257	15	10	0	3.75
Bob Welch	31	204	15	12	0	2.65
Steve Howe (before being suspended)	46	67	4	7	18	1.44
Tom Niedenfuer	66	95	8	3	11	1.90

The Achilles heel on the team was the infield defense that was horrible, to put it mildly. Steve Sax was charged with 30 errors, Pedro Guerrero chalked up 29, and Bill Russell had 20. The team committed 166 errors in 155 games, last in the major leagues.

The 82nd winter baseball convention was held at the Opryland Hotel in Nashville, Tennessee, from December 5 to December 9, 1983, and Dodgers vice president of personnel, Al Campanis, was on the prowl for fresh talent. Campanis had earned the nickname of "Trader Al" over a period of fifteen years, for his propensity for dealing off bright young prospects for aging veterans who might bring a short term payback to L.A. pennant drives. Now home-grown products were few, and their minor league credentials were inflated from having played their AAA ball in the rarified atmosphere of Albuquerque, New Mexico. But that didn't stop Campanis from wheeling and dealing. He swung a four-player trade with the New York Mets, a three-for-one deal with Kansas City, and a near-trade with the Oakland Athletics. The key players for the Dodgers were reliever Carlos Díaz, who was expected to fill the void left by the potential loss of Steve Howe due to chemical dependence, and infielder Bob Bailor, a valuable utility player who had experience in both the infield and the outfield. The Dodgers lost one of their top minor league pitchers in the deal however. Sid Fernandez, who had led three minor leagues in strikeouts, and who tossed two no-hitters for Vero Beach in 1982, would go on to win 114 games in the major leagues during his career. The near-trade with Oakland, involving Dusty Baker, was vetoed by Baker whose contract gave him the right of refusal.

On December 15, baseball commissioner Bowie Kuhn suspended Dodgers closer Steve Howe for one year for drug abuse. Nine days later, on Christmas Eve, it was revealed that Howe — having been fined $54,000 by the Dodgers earlier and out much of the season — had declared bankruptcy, listing debts of $340,900.

Dusty Baker was given his outright release by Los Angeles on February 9, 1984, to allow him to make a deal for himself with another team. Several trade talks had been completed over previous months, but they were all fruitless. The release of Baker turned out to be premature from L.A.'s standpoint. Candy Maldonado, Baker's replacement, who had a solid .319 season at Albuquerque in 1983, could do no better than a .268 batting average with 5 home runs and 28 RBIs in 254 at-bats in 1984.

The National League Western Division champions were picked to repeat in '84. The pitching staff that had led the National League in ERA with a 3.10 mark in 1983, Bob Welch, Fernando Valenzuela, Reuss, Hooton, Peña, and Niedenfuer, was back and apparently healthy. The only question mark was Jerry Reuss, who had arthroscopic surgery on his elbow in January, but he appeared to be recovered as the new season got underway. The Dodgers looked forward to a productive offense now that their two potential superstars, Greg Brock and Mike Marshall, had a year of major league experience under their belt. And they anticipated an improved defense, with Bill Russell a fixture at shortstop, and Steve Sax and Pedro Guerrero entering the prime of their careers. The hope was that Guerrero would be more comfortable at third base, and that Sax would be without the heebie-jeebies in his throwing arm. And, they were particularly strong behind the plate where Mike Scioscia, a big, strapping 6', 2", 220-pound catcher, replaced Steve Yeager. The 25-year-old Scioscia would go on to a notable 13-year major league career, gaining the reputation as the best major league catcher at blocking the plate.

The season opened on April 3, 1984, and the St. Louis Cardinals were inconsiderate visitors to the West Coast as they manhandled Dodger starter, Fernando Valenzuela, en route to an 11–7 victory. Whitey Herzog's team pounded out 17 base hits including three each by Willie McGee and Darrell Porter. Both McGee and Porter hit for the circuit against the Dodgers southpaw, and Porter added an RBI triple. The Dodgers reversed course quickly however and, typical of Lasorda teams, they roared through April with a 17–8 record, giving them a one game lead in the division. Dodgers pitchers tossed six shutouts in the month, led by Rick Honeycut. The crafty right-hander, who was acquired from the Texas Rangers on August 19, 1983, was a perfect 4–0 with two shutouts, three complete games, and a 1.38 earned-run-average. Alejandro Peña was close behind, with a 4–1 record, two shutouts, two complete games, and a 1.94 ERA. The L.A. offense was triggered by Mike Marshall with 7 home runs and 22 RBIs in 25 games and Greg Brock with 6 home runs. Steve Sax was hitting .319 with 20 runs scored.

Small cracks were already beginning to show in the Dodgers facade however. Errors were piling up like blocks of stone, 26 errors in 26 games. The porous infield defense was led by Sax and Guerrero with 6 errors each. Guerrero was also mired in a batting slump at .196. Hs anemic average was almost matched by first baseman Greg Brock at .205 and shortstop Dave Anderson at .224.

The most significant event of the early 1984 season was the arrival of a talented rookie pitcher. Orel Hershiser had been with the team since opening day, but he was used primarily in mop-up situations during the first month, and not many fans were aware of him. But manager Tommy Lasorda was aware of him, and he realized he had a special athlete on his hands, a former hockey player from western New York, and a pitcher who had everything but confidence in his ability. One day in May, Lasorda called Hershiser and Dodgers pitching coach Ron Perranoski into his office where he proceeded to lay his rendition of the Sermon on the Mound on the young pitcher.

> "You remember how mad I was about how you pitched to Cruz the other day in Houston...."
>
> I [Hershiser] nodded. Did I ever. It was one of those two-out situations with two men on. José Cruz was a great contact hitter, a dangerous RBI (runs batted in) man.
>
> "...You throw low and away, ball one. Low and away, ball two. Low and away, ball three. He's takin' and you finally get a strike over, luckily, 'cause that one could'a been called low or outside, either one. He knows you can't afford to walk him, so he's sittin' on your three and one pitch, and what do you do?"
>
> I didn't want to think about it, and I sure didn't want to talk about it. The worst thing was, Tommy was getting himself upset all over again just rehashing it. He grew louder. His face reddened. He leaned closer.
>
> "You laid the ball in for him! Boom! Double and two runs! Hershiser, you're givin' these hitters too much credit! You're tellin' yourself, 'If I throw this ball over the plate, they're gonna hit it out.' That's a negative approach to pitching!"[8]

Lasorda went on to tell Hershiser that he had Hall-of-Fame caliber talent, but that he was timid about using it. "I've seen guys come and go, son, and you've got it! You gotta go out there and do it on the mound! Take charge! Make 'em hit your best stuff! Be aggressive! Be a bulldog out there. That's gonna be your new name: Bulldog."[9]

And so, the Bulldog was born. And he took Lasorda's advice to heart. With Perranoski's coaching and improved mental toughness on his part, he quickly became part of the Dodgers' starting pitching rotation. In his first appearance after Lasorda's sermon, Hershiser was called in, in relief against the San

Francisco Giants, and with his manager cheering his Bulldog on, he set Frank Robinson's club down with one run over three innings. Within days, fate took over. Jerry Reuss went down with an injury and spent five weeks on the disabled list, and Hershiser was rushed into the starting rotation to fill the gap. And he did it masterfully. Beginning on June 29, he threw 33⅔ consecutive scoreless innings, the most in the National League that year. He recorded four shutouts in July, earning him the Pitcher of the Month award. Over the final four and a half months of the season, the 6', 3", 190-pound right-hander led all Dodgers pitchers in victories, shutouts, and earned-run-average.

The tide began to turn for Lasorda's team in May, ever so slowly at first, then more rapidly as the season progressed. The Dodgers hung tough through most of June, but they couldn't forestall the inevitable. They ended the month with a 41–38 record, and were just 6½ games off the pace, but in July they went 12–16 and finished the month 12 games behind the San Diego Padres. And the leaky infield defense was a major cause of the collapse. Pedro Guerrero, after making 29 errors in 1983, accumulated almost as many through 76 games in '84. And his second base compatriot, Steve Sax, was just as bad. One day after a particularly sloppy game, according to Lasorda, he called Pedro into his office where he questioned him. He asked Pedro what he thought about just before the pitcher threw the ball. "Well, skipper," Pedro replied, "When the pitcher gets ready to pitch, I look up and say, 'Please God, don't let him hit the ball to me.' Then I look around the infield and say, 'And God, don't let him hit it to Sax either.'"[10]

Manager Tommy Lasorda took Guerrero's comments to heart and decided to return the big slugger to his favorite position in left field. He recalled Germán Rivera from Albuquerque and stationed him at third base, but the 24-year-old youngster was only marginally better than Guerrero defensively, with 14 errors in 90 games and of little help offensively, with just 2 home runs and 17 RBIs in 227 at-bats.

One bright spot for Tommy Lasorda's charges during the month was a two-hit shutout of the Cincinnati Reds by Bob Welch on July 28. The big Dodgers right-hander came away a 1–0 winner when Mike Marshall's sacrifice fly scored Dave Anderson from third base.

Cincinnati					Los Angeles				
Name	*Pos*	*AB*	*R*	*H*	*Name*	*Pos*	*AB*	*R*	*H*
Redus	CF	4	0	2	Anderson	SS	3	1	1
Oester	2B	4	0	0	Amelung	RF	3	0	0
Cedeño	1B	4	0	0	Stubbs	1B	4	0	1
Parker	RF	2	0	0	Marshall	LF	3	0	0
Walker	LF	2	0	0	Reynolds	LF	0	0	0
Power	P	0	0	0	Landreaux	CF	3	0	1
Owchinko	P	0	0	0	Scioscia	C	3	0	1
Krenchicki	3B	3	0	0	Bailor	2B	3	0	1

Name	Pos	AB	R	H		Name	Pos	AB	R	H
Foley	SS	3	0	0		Rivera	3B	3	0	2
Gulden	C	3	0	0		Welch	P	3	0	0
Hume	P	3	0	0						
Pérez	1B	1	0	0						
Totals		28	0	2				28	1	7

Cincinnati	0 0 0	0 0 0	0 0 0 — 0 — 2 — 1
Los Angeles	0 0 0	0 0 1	0 0 x — 1 — 7 — 0

Error-Oester

Doubles-Bailor, Anderson, Rivera

Name	IP	H	R	ER	BB	SO
Cincinnati						
Hume (L 3-11)	6	6	1	0	1	0
Power	1	1	0	0	0	1
Owchinko	1	0	0	0	0	1
Los Angeles						
Welch (W 7-11)	9	2	0	0	2	8[11]

One week later, Welch limited these same Reds to two hits and no runs in seven innings, winning 5–2. Mike Marshall slammed a two-run homer for the winners. Dave Anderson also drove in two runs.

The rest of the season was a rocky road for the Lasordamen. The team managed to compile a record of 60–60 by August 14, 10½ games from the top, thanks primarily to their strong pitching, but they couldn't mount a serious challenge against San Diego because of their mediocre defense and sputtering offense. One night, Fernando Valenzuela hurled ten brilliant innings against the Cincinnati Reds, holding them to one run on two hits, with 10 strikeouts, but left with a no-decision. Jerry Reuss lost the game 2–1 in 11. The next night, the Atlanta Braves, behind Rick Mahler, defeated L.A. and Rick Honeycut 2–1. Peña carried the pitching load, with a 12–6 record and a strong 2.38 ERA. Honeycut, after a blazing start, had leveled off, with a 9–7 mark and a 2.89 ERA. Rookie Orel Hershiser, who was coming of age, had compiled an 8–6 record and a 2.63 ERA. The defense was atrocious with Sax, Guerrero, Dave Anderson, and Rivera, all showing double-digit miscues. And the offense was almost non-existent. Marshall, who was on the shelf for a month after a foot operation, had 20 home runs but only 55 RBIs to show for it, in 377 at-bats. Pedro Guerrero, with 37 RBIs was the number two man on a team with a combined .243 batting average.

Lasorda did everything he could think of to right the ship, but nothing worked. He even sought divine intervention. "One weekend we were visiting Cincinnati for a series against the Reds. I walked into the Catholic Church on

Sunday morning and saw John McNamara, the Reds' manager, sitting in one of the front pews, so I joined him. After Mass was over, John walked up to the front of the church, put some money in the offering box, and lit a candle. I waited around until John left, then I walked up to the front of the church, muttered to myself, 'It won't work, John,' and blew out his candle. We won the game 13–2."[12]

If that course of action helped L.A. defeat Cincinnati, it was a one-time deal only, and the Dodgers manager said, tongue in cheek, the pressure of losing finally came to a head after his team had lost its sixth straight game. "I called my coaches together," he said, "and told them I was contemplating suicide. Joey Amalfitano said, 'Don't do it, Tom. You should talk to Suicide Anonymous. Here's their telephone number.' I took the number from Joey and dialed it, and the guy on the other end said, 'After listening to your story, I think you're doing the right thing.'"[13]

Things didn't get any better for the Los Angeles Dodgers the rest of the way, and they limped home a weak fourth in a six-team division with a 79–83 record, 13 games behind the front-running San Diego Padres. On the plus side, they finished second in ERA in the National League, their 3.17 mark trailing only the Pittsburgh Pirates (and the Pirates finished in the cellar in their division). Alejandro Peña, who missed five starts down the stretch, at 12–6, Orel Hershiser at 11–8, Rick Honeycut at 10–9, and Bob Welch at 13–13 paced the mound corps. Peña led the league with a 2.48 ERA and four shutouts. Bulldog Hershiser tied for the league lead in shutouts and finished third in ERA, sixth in complete games, and eighth in strikeouts. The offense had little to cheer about with a team batting average of .244 and 580 runs scored in 162 games, an average of 3.58 runs per game. The defense, of course, was the main culprit, allowing 86 unearned runs to cross the plate. The iron-glove brigade was led by Pedro Guerrero with 22 errors, Steve Sax with 21, Dave Anderson with 19, Rivera with 15, and Mike Scioscia with 12.

The Dodgers' weakness was exposed for the first time during the 1984 season. Their supposedly unlimited talent pool in their minor league system was found to be wanting. Highly touted prospects like Greg Brock, Candy Maldonado, Franklin Stubbs, Sid Bream, and a bevy of pitchers kept the turnstiles clicking between L.A. and Albuquerque, but none of them proved capable of holding down a full time job. So Trader Al went to the winter meetings in search of a centerfielder and a third baseman. He failed on both counts. He lost Rickey Henderson, who went to the New York Yankees, then failed in an attempt to wrest Buddy Bell away from the Texas Rangers. The Dodgers would have to make do with their 1984 squad.

Still, manager Tommy Lasorda was optimistic about 1985. "We didn't finish fourth last year because of a lack of ability. We just had an unusually high number of injuries [15 men on the disabled list]." And the Dodgers seemed to confirm their manager's confidence as they finished spring training with a gaudy

16–11 record and moved into the season, ready to reclaim their title, porous defense and all. The experts picked the Dodgers to finish no better than fourth or fifth in their division, or essentially where they finished in '84. As it turned out, 1985 brought the City of Angels another Western Division title, but it would be the last hurrah for several of their veterans. They also lost one of their top pitchers even before the season began. Alejandro Peña, who had led the National League with a 2.48 ERA in 1984, underwent surgery on his right shoulder in February and was on the disabled list until September 25.

On opening day, April 12, 1985, the San Francisco Giants defeated the Los Angeles Dodgers by the count of 4–1, touching Rick Honeycut for all four runs in the third inning. Jeff Leonard led the attack with a two-run home run. Sid Bream homered off Mike Krukow for the Dodgers' lone run. Fernando Valenzuela got off to a sizzling start, running off 41 consecutive scoreless innings to start the season, and setting a new major league record by pitching 44.1 consecutive innings at the start of the season without allowing an earned run. He finished the month with a 0.23 ERA, earning him the Player of the Month award for April, in spite of a disappointing 2–3 record caused by his team's mediocre offense and leaky defense.

Jerry Reuss, L.A.'s answer to Peter Pan, was at his mischievous best in April, when the Dodgers visited Chicago for a series against the Cubs. It so happened that the Yankees were in town at the same time for a series against the White Sox. Now trade rumors about Reuss had been circulating for weeks so Jerry decided he would take advantage of the situation. He packed his equipment bag with towels and made his way over to the players entrance at Comiskey Park. He told the guard he played for the Yankees and was admitted to the visitors clubhouse. As Jay Johnstone told it,

> Inside, Reuss didn't hesitate. He walked through the clubhouse waving to players he knew and saying, "Pleased to meet you" to those he didn't. Then he went straight to new manager Lou Pinella's office, dropped his equipment bag on the desk, reached out his hand and said, "Hi, Lou. I'm Jerry Reuss."
>
> "I know who you are," said the puzzled Pinella. "But what are you doing here?"
>
> "Didn't you hear? The deal went through."
>
> "What deal?"
>
> "I'm your new pitcher. Didn't George call you? Maybe we should close the door."
>
> "Yeah, maybe we should," said Pinella, who got up and closed the door.
>
> "I haven't pitched since Friday," said Reuss, "but I'll do whatever you want me to do."
>
> "Nobody told me anything. What's going on."
>
> Reuss, with one of his sneaky smiles, then said:
>
> "Here, open my equipment bag."
>
> Pinella did, saw the towels, and realized how firmly he'd been hooked.
>
> "He really had me," Pinella later admitted. "Hey, with this team it could have happened."[14]

After a so-so April, the L.A. brigade hit the skids in May. The team stopped hitting, the defense contributed 39 errors in 26 games, and they found themselves 5 games out of first place at month's end. Tommy Lasorda, who had reactivated the Pedro Guerrero third base experiment in spring training, finally ended it once and for all on June 1, moving his top lumberman back to left field where he was comfortable. And Pedro, with the heavy burden of third base lifted from his shoulders, responded with a vengeance. In the next 30 days, he smashed 15 home runs, breaking Ralph Kiner's National League record for the most home runs hit during the month of June, and tying Babe Ruth's major league record.

The Dodgers trailed San Diego most of the first half of the season, and were still four games behind the Padres on July 4, but they got as hot as the weather during the month. Led by Pedro Guerrero's pyrotechnics, the entire team hit as never before, averaging 5.1 runs per game. By July 12, they had pulled to within ½ game of the top after taking the measure of the Chicago Cubs by a 3–1 count. Bob Welch, with relief help from Ken Howell, held the Cubs to five base hits. L.A. broke a scoreless tie in the top of the seventh inning on singles by Russell, Cabell, Yeager, and Sax, a base on balls, and two sacrifice hits.

Los Angeles					**Chicago**				
Name	*Pos*	*AB*	*R*	*H*	*Name*	*Pos*	*AB*	*R*	*H*
Anderson	3B	3	0	0	Hatcher	CF	3	0	0
Duncan	SS	4	0	0	Sandberg	2B	4	0	2
Russell	LF	3	1	1	Moreland	RF	4	0	0
Cabell	RF	4	1	2	Durham	1B	4	0	0
Howell	P	0	0	0	Davis	C	4	0	1
Brock	1B	3	0	1	Cey	3B	1	0	0
Landreaux	CF	0	0	0	Speier	3B	1	0	0
Maldonado	CF	3	1	0	Bowa	SS	3	0	1
Yeager	C	3	0	1	Hebner	PH	1	0	0
Sax	2B	4	0	2	Fontenot	P	2	0	0
Welch	P	2	0	0	Bosley	PH	1	1	1
Matuszek	1B	1	0	0	Frazier	P	0	0	0
Totals		30	3	7			32	1	5

```
Los Angeles    0 0 0    0 0 0    3 0 0 — 3 — 7 — 0
Chicago        0 0 0    0 0 0    0 1 0 — 1 — 5 — 0
```

Doubles-Bowa, Bosley, Sandberg

Name	*IP*	*H*	*R*	*ER*	*BB*	*SO*
Los Angeles						
Welch (W 3-1)	7⅓	5	1	1	0	3
Howell (S9)	1⅔	0	0	0	1	1

Name	IP	H	R	ER	BB	SO
Chicago						
Fontenot (L 3-4)	8	7	3	3	3	4
Frazier	1	0	0	0	1	0[15]

A 20–7 surge in July, their best July in 22 years, propelled them to the top of the heap, and at month's end they held a five game lead over San Diego in the National League West. And just about everyone contributed to the fireworks. Guerrero hit a stratospheric .460, Landreaux was at .351, Marshall hit .345, Sax .327, Brock .323, and Scioscia .322. The pitchers followed suit: Valenzuela 5–0, 1.24 ERA, Welch 5–0, 1.56, and Hershiser 4–1, 2.16.

The Dodgers never let up. Snapping off an eight-game win streak in August, L.A. was 16–11 for the month and stretched their lead to seven games. In other baseball action around the major leagues, Tom Seaver, pitching for the Chicago White Sox, came to New York on August 4 and held the mighty New York Yankees in check to win the 300th game of his illustrious career, a 4–1 masterpiece. "Tom Terrific" limited Billy Martin's team to six hits while fanning seven as 54,032 fans, many of them there to see their hero enter baseball history, cheered the victory.

One hot day in Dodger Stadium, Jerry Reuss, feeling a little bored, sent the ball boy over to home plate umpire Frank Pulli with a drink between innings, but instead of something cold, he sent hot coffee. Then he sneaked a ball out of the umpire's ball bag, inscribed it, "To Frank, May God bless you. Tom Lasorda," and put it back into the bag. Unfortunately, the umpire didn't notice the inscription, and put the ball in play. Dodgers pitcher Tom Niedenfuer saw the writing, but thought the ink might give him an advantage, so he pitched it. As fate would have it, the batter fouled the pitch off, the ball went into the stands behind home plate, and was caught by a man named Frank who couldn't believe his good luck. He not only caught a ball signed by Tommy Lasorda, but it was inscribed to him.[16]

On the field, the Big Blue Machine continued to build on their lead until it reached nine full games over San Diego. Vice President and general manager Al Campanis added some late-season bench strength when he acquired Len Matuszek, Enos Cabell, and Bill "Mad Dog" Madlock. Madlock was immediately inserted into the lineup and went on a .360 tear down the stretch. The Dodgers went 18–12 in September and won the division going away with a total of 95 victories.

On Wednesday October 2, Tommy Lasorda's charges celebrated winning the Western Division pennant following a 9–3 victory over the Atlanta Braves behind Orel Hershiser's 11th straight victory. Actually the pennant was decided in the fifth inning when news of Cincinnati's 5–4 loss to the San Diego Padres eliminated the Reds from the race. L.A.'s 95–67 record gave them a comfortable 5½ game lead over the second place Redlegs.

Mike Marshall, who had a mid-season appendectomy and was on the disabled list from June 20 to July 18, still put up some impressive numbers, slugging 28 home runs, driving in 95 runs, and hitting .293 in 135 games. Guerrero had a sensational season after being returned to the outfield permanently. He batted a torrid .320 with 33 home runs and 87 RBIs in 137 games. Bill Madlock, who came over from the Pittsburgh Pirates in August, pounded the ball at a .360 clip in 34 games in L.A., and Steve Sax, who settled down defensively in mid-season, batted .311 in his last 84 games, .279 overall. Greg Brock hit .251 with 21 home runs. But it was the pitching that was the secret weapon. It was consistent from start to finish, compiling a 2.96 ERA. The big four were superlative. Fernando Valenzuela went 17–10 with a 2.45 ERA, Orel Hershiser rolled up 19 wins against just 3 losses, a league-leading .864 winning percentage, and a 2.03 ERA, Bob Welch was 14–4 with a 2.31 ERA, and Jerry Reuss was 14–10 with a 2.92 ERA. Tom Niedenfuer anchored the bullpen, pitching in 64 games with 19 saves and a 2.71 ERA. And Carlos Díaz was a pleasant surprise, pitching in 46 games covering 79 innings, with a 6–3 won-loss record and a 2.61 ERA.

The Dodgers met the Eastern Division winners, the St. Louis Cardinals, in the best of seven NLCS. The Cardinals, who had captured their division by three games over the New York Mets, were a strong, all-around team who had led the National League in batting average, runs scored, stolen bases with 314 (the most stolen bases in the National Leagues since 1912), and fielding percentage, and their 3.10 earned-run-average trailed only Los Angeles. Individually, the St. Louis rabbits included rookie Vince Coleman, who swiped 110 sacks; Willie McGee, who stole 56; Andy Van Slyke, who had 34; and Ozzie Smith and Tommy Herr, who had 31 each. In other words, everybody could run. And they could hit and field as well. Willie McGee led the National League in batting with a .353 average, in base hits with 216, and in triples with 18. He also scored 118 runs. Tommy Herr hit .302 with 97 runs scored. Jack Clark batted .281 with 22 home runs and 87 RBIs. And Vince Coleman hit .267 with 107 runs scored. On the mound, John Tudor went 21–8 with 10 shutouts and a sparkling 1.93 ERA, and Joaquín Andújar won 21 games against 12 losses.

The Dodgers won 7 of 12 games from the Cardinals during the regular season, but they were all tough games, so the National League Championship Series was considered to be a toss-up. The highlights of the series for the Dodgers, were the first two games. The Dodgers came out firing on all cylinders in the opener. Their defense was flawless, bordering on the spectacular at times. They looked like a team of gold glove stars rather than a squad that had made 166 errors in 162 games. The Cardinals were noted for their running game, but it was L.A. that ran the bases with abandon. Fired up by motivational genius Tommy Lasorda, who told his team that Whitey Herzog told his players the Dodgers were a crummy team, the Big Blue Machine throttled the Redbird offense behind their ace hurler, Fernando Valenzuela. The Dodgers broke open a scoreless game in the bottom of the fourth. Bill Madlock reached first on an error and promptly stole second. Minutes later, he scored the first run of the series on a single by Pedro Guerrero off southpaw John Tudor. L.A. added three more in the sixth. Madlock started the action again with a double that caromed off shortstop Ozzie Smith's glove and rolled into short left field. After Guerrero walked, Mike Scioscia plated Madlock with a single. Candy Maldonado caught the Cardinals defense flat footed with a bunt single. Steve Sax then followed with a double to score two more runs, and Fernando coasted 4–1.

In game 2, Orel Hershiser bested Joaquín Andújar 8–2 in Dodger Stadium. This game gave the Dodgers a comfortable two-game lead in the best of seven series. The game was decided early. After St. Louis nicked "The Big O" for a run in the top of the third inning, Lasorda's cohorts responded in the bottom of the inning with a three-run spurt, sparked by Hershiser's run-scoring single that tied the game. Later in the inning Ken Landreaux doubled in Hershiser and Bill Madlock singled in Landreaux. Greg Brock's two-run homer in the fourth iced the game for L.A.

St. Louis					Los Angeles				
Name	*Pos*	*AB*	*R*	*H*	*Name*	*Pos*	*AB*	*R*	*H*
Coleman	LF	5	0	2	Duncan	SS	4	0	1
McGee	CF	5	1	1	Anderson	SS	1	1	0
Herr	2B	3	0	1	Landreaux	CF	4	3	3
Clark	1B	3	0	1	Madlock	3B	5	0	3
Van Slyke	RF	3	0	0	Bailor	3B	0	0	0
Pendleton	3B	4	1	1	Guerrero	LF	3	0	1
Porter	C	2	0	0	Marshall	RF	4	0	1
Smith	SS	4	0	2	Scioscia	C	3	1	1
Andújar	P	2	0	0	Brock	1B	4	1	1
Horton	P	0	0	0	Sax	2B	4	1	1
Campbell	P	0	0	0	Hershiser	P	4	1	1
Braun	PH	1	0	0					
Dayley	P	0	0	0					
Lahti	P	0	0	0					
Jorgensen	PH	1	0	0					
Totals		33	2	8			36	8	13

St. Louis   0 0 1   0 0 0   0 0 1 — 2 — 8 — 1
Los Angeles   0 0 3   2 1 2   0 0 x — 8 — 13 — 1

Doubles-Herr, Landreaux (2), Duncan
Home Run-Brock

Name	*IP*	*H*	*R*	*ER*	*BB*	*SO*
St. Louis						
Andújar (L 0-1)	4⅓	8	6	6	2	6

Name	IP	H	R	ER	BB	SO
Horton	1⅓	1	2	2	2	0
Campbell	⅓	0	0	0	0	0
Dayley	1	0	0	0	0	0
Lahti	1	2	0	0	0	1
Los Angeles						
Hershiser (W 1-0)	9	8	2	2	5	4[17]

That was the extent of the Dodger's success in the postseason. They went on to lose the next four games to the Redbirds to close out their season. In game 3, speedsters Vince Coleman and Willie McGee went a combined 4 for 9 at the plate and ran wild on the basepaths, stealing two bases, drawing two wild attempted pickoff throws from Welch and Scioscia, and scoring three runs. Tommy Herr homered for the Redbirds' fourth and final run in a 4–2 Cardinals victory. Danny Cox, an 18-game winner during the regular season, was the winning pitcher while Bob Welch fell victim to the speed of Whitey Herzog's rabbits.

Los Angeles	0 0 0	1 0 0	1 0 0 — 2 — 7 — 2
St. Louis	2 2 0	0 0 0	0 0 x — 4 — 7 — 0

In game four, southpaw John Tudor tossed a five-hitter at the Lasordamen, while his Cardinals teammates pummeled Dodgers starter Jerry Reuss and two relievers for nine runs in the second inning en route to a 12–2 blowout victory. Bill Madlock hit for the circuit for L.A.

Los Angeles	0 0 0	0 0 0	1 1 0 — 2 — 5 — 2
St. Louis	0 9 0	1 1 0	0 1 x — 12 — 15 — 0

The next day belonged to Ozzie Smith, the defensive wizard of St. Louis. After Bill Madlock's homer brought the Dodgers back from a 2–0 deficit, the bullpens on both teams kept the sluggers in check until the bottom of the ninth inning when "The Wizard of Oz" took Dodgers closer Tom Niedenfuer downtown to give the local fans a thrilling 3–2 win and a three games to two lead in the NLCS. It was Ozzie Smith's first home run from the left side of the plate in 3,014 major league at-bats, including postseason play. Jeff Lahti was the winning pitcher for the Cardinals while Niedenfuer took the loss for L.A.

Los Angeles	0 0 0	2 0 0	0 0 0 — 2 — 5 — 1
St. Louis	2 0 0	0 0 0	0 0 1 — 3 — 5 — 1

The scene shifted back to Los Angeles for game six and the fans were treated to another nail-biter, but this time the hometown crowd filed out of the stadium disappointed. Dodgers starter Orel Hershiser left the game in the

Ozzie Smith, a defensive wizard, smashed a game-winning home run in game five
of the 1985 NLCS (Jay Sanford).

seventh inning with the score tied at 4-all. Once again, the outcome was turned
over to the bullpens and, once again, the St. Louis relievers came out on top.
This time, L.A. carried a 5–4 lead into the ninth inning, but once again Tom
Niedenfuer failed in the clutch. The big bat in this key game belonged to first
baseman Jack Clark, who deposited a Niedenfuer fastball into the left field seats
with two men on base to give Herzog's boys a 7–5 victory and a well-deserved
National League championship. Todd Worrell was the winning pitcher while
Niedenfuer took his second consecutive loss. Bill Madlock and Mike Marshall
homered for L.A. in a losing cause. Madlock's home run was his third home
run of the NLCS in just 24 at-bats.

| St. Louis | 0 0 1 | 0 0 0 | 3 0 3 — 7 — 12 — 1 |
| Los Angeles | 1 1 0 | 0 2 0 | 0 1 0 — 5 — 8 — 0 |

General manager Al "The Chief" Campanis, manager Tommy Lasorda,
and his staff were confident that they could retain the National League Western Division title in 1986, and that they had the team that could advance to
the World Series. But that was not the case. Injuries, old age, and unfulfilled
potential, all combined to derail the Dodgers express, and to force a re-eval-
uation of their talent.

3

HITTING ROCK BOTTOM

The Dodgers pitching staff that had led the National League in ERA in 1985 was back intact in '86 to make another run at the pennant. Every pitcher, with the exception of Rick Honeycut and Jerry Reuss, was under 30 years of age, and Honeycut was only 31. Reuss, the graybeard, would turn 37 in June. Mike Scioscia was solid behind the plate and was a dangerous presence with a bat in his hand. The outfield of Marshall, Landreaux, and Guerrero was adequate defensively and outstanding on offense, with both Guerrero and Marshall providing long-ball power. The infield of Brock, Sax, Duncan, and either Anderson or Bill Madlock, who was obtained from the Pittsburgh Pirates in August 1985, was the chink in the L.A. armor. They were shaky at best, with no proven offensive capabilities and leaky gloves.

Al Campanis, the Dodgers' V.P. of personnel, had put together a 10-year plan to keep the team staffed with the top players in the land, but a review of the players under development exposed a weakness in the L.A. talent rating system. The players who were being counted on to keep the Dodgers at the top of the National League included Hector Heredia, Félix Tejeda, Scott May, Mike Ramsey, Gilberto Reyes, Jeff Hamilton, Stu Pederson, Ed Amelung, and Reggie Williams. As it would turn out, only Reggie Williams would get any substantial playing time in 1986, and only Jeff Hamilton would contribute to a Dodgers pennant, two years later. Most of the rest of the untouchables were busts.

Campanis, probably relying on the Dodgers farm system to supply the team with the talent it needed to challenge for the pennant, made no major moves over the winter. He did acquire relief pitcher Ed Vande Berg from Seattle to give the Dodgers some left-handed punch out of the bullpen. And he did add outfielder Terry Whitfield and backup catcher Alex Treviño, but that was it.

Still, the spring forecast was rosy. According to the experts, the Dodgers were rated at 3–1 to reach the World Series. With the hot hitting Pedro Guerrero back in the outfield full time, a rejuvenated Steve Sax with his defensive demons conquered, and a healthy Bill Madlock, a four-time National League batting champion, anchoring the hot corner, Tommy Lasorda was psyching his team up for a big season. And Al Campanis was praising the talent on the team. "On paper, we would appear to be stronger and better balanced than last year. And that heightens the optimism." Lasorda seconded the vice president's comments. "I'm just excited about this season. I'm much more enthused this time than I was last year."[1]

Unfortunately for Lasorda and the Dodgers organization, the season started to unravel even before it began, on April 3 to be exact. The offensive catalyst, Pedro Guerrero, made an abortive slide into third base, rupturing a tendon in his left knee and sidelining him for the season. Without their big gun, the Lasordamen were lost. Other regulars who spent significant time on the disabled list during the season included Bill Madlock (five weeks with a pulled groin and a sprained ankle), Mike Marshall (two weeks with a lower back problem), Greg Brock (three weeks), Mike Scioscia (five weeks), Mariano Duncan (four weeks with a broken foot), Ken Landreaux (five weeks), Alejandro Peña (eight weeks), and Jerry Reuss (seven weeks with a chronic elbow problem).

On opening day, April 7, 1986, Fernando Valenzuela got Tommy Lasorda's troops off on the right foot with a 2–1 victory over the San Diego Padres. The 25-year-old Mexican pitcher, who fanned nine men during his complete game effort, was touched up for ten base hits but kept them well spaced. Dodgers left fielder Franklin Stubbs threw Carmello Martínez out at the plate in the fifth inning to keep the Dodgers in the game, and Mike Marshall hit a seventh inning home run off Eric Show for the winning margin. The only Padres run came in the ninth inning when a Dave Anderson error allowed Steve Garvey to score.

The following Sunday, L.A. broke a three-game losing streak with a 3–2 win over the hated San Francisco Giants in Dodger Stadium. Orel Hershiser limited the Giants to seven hits and Franklin Stubbs cracked his third home run in three games.

On the other side of the country, April 29 was a red-letter day for the Boston Red Sox when their ace, Roger Clemens, set a new major league standard by striking out 20 men in a nine-inning game. "The Rocket," as he is called, threw a three-hitter, with no walks, at the Seattle Mariners for his fourth consecutive victory to open the season. He was trailing 1–0 in the game until the bottom of the seventh inning when Dwight Evans hit a two-out, three-run homer to rescue the big right-hander. Clemens fanned both Spike Owen and Phil Bradley to open the ninth inning, for the record. At one point, between the fourth and sixth innings, Clemens fanned eight consecutive batters. Tom Cheney of the Washington Senators holds the strikeout record for an extra inning game, fanning 21 Baltimore Orioles batters in sixteen innings on September 12, 1962.

By May 3, the Dodgers were creeping along with a 13–13 record, hardly the type of performance their management expected. The pitching was good as usual, with Hershiser (3–2), Reuss (2–0), Valenzuela (4–1), and Welch (3–1) leading the way. But the offense and defense were horrible. The team batting average of .224 included Madlock (.237), Marshall (.245), and Duncan (.196). The defense had committed 37 errors in 26 games and had allowed 16 unearned runs. The rosy predictions of the spring were rapidly disappearing. Things continued to deteriorate over the next month, and on June 15, their record stood at 31–32. But, as Terry Johnson noted in *Dodger Blue*, one Dodger was having a banner season. Sax was sizzling. "This version of Steve Sax bears little resemblance to the one who struggled — at the plate, in the field and inside himself — the previous two years. His throws go where they're supposed to again. He's hitting the ball to all fields again and he's once again demonstrating his speed on the basepaths."[2]

From June 14 to July 5, Tommy Lasorda's charges won just 6 of 19 games and, as the season reached the halfway point, they found themselves holding down last place with a 36–45 record, 8½ games out of first. A total of 14 players had more than 100 at-bats and the trainer's room was crowded with the walking wounded. Only Duncan, Marshall and Sax had more than 217 at-bats, and only Sax would remain healthy over the final three months of the season. Duncan would accumulate only 151 more at-bats in the remaining 80 games and Marshall, who was hitting .263 with 17 homers and 46 RBIs on July 7, would bat only 52 more times with just 2 home runs and 7 RBIs. The situation was particularly distressful to Marshall, who had been injury prone since he came up to the Dodgers in 1983. In four years, he had only one season with more than 500 at-bats, and he was on the disabled list each of the last three years. The pitchers also had their share of problems. Jerry Reuss, who had thrown 213 innings in 1985, had arthroscopic surgery on his right shoulder, and was out of action from July 17 until September 3. And Alejandro Peña, who fought through shoulder problems all of 1985, missed the first half of the season, and struggled to regain his form.

On July 27, the Dodgers made a stirring comeback to defeat the Chicago Cubs 13–11, and went on to sweep a three-game series from the San Francisco Giants at home by scores of 2–1, 2–1, and 4–2. On August 1, Pedro Guerrero made his first appearance of the year as the Big Blue Machine took their fifth straight, a 9–3 rout of the Cincinnati Reds in Dodger Stadium. Guerrero, pinch-hitting for Rick Honeycut in the bottom of the seventh inning, strode to the plate amid an avalanche of cheers from the 46,000 spectators. He eventually flied out to right field — but Pedro was back, the sun was shining again, and the third-place Dodgers were only 3½ games behind the second-place San Francisco Giants and only 7½ games behind the division-leading Houston Astros. The next day, Enos Cabell clocked a grand-slam homer and L.A. routed the Reds by a 7–1 margin behind the one-hit pitching of Alejandro Peña and Tom Niedenfuer. Two days later, Mike Marshall joined his teammate in the outfield and, with Fernando Valenzuela pitching a gutsy game in search of his 15th victory, Los Angeles came from behind to defeat the Astros for their eighth straight win. Unfortunately for the Dodgers, their good luck didn't continue. Guerrero went back on the disabled list on August 11 and would stay there until September 3, and Marshall would see only limited action over the final two months of the season because of his balky back. The game of the 11th was particularly disastrous for L.A.'s pennant hopes. The Dodgers led the Houston Astros 6–3 in the bottom of the eighth inning in the Astrodome, but the bullpen blew another save, with the Astros winning 7–6. The inept L.A. bullpen was one of the major problem areas throughout the season.

On September 22, Fernando Valenzuela defeated the Houston Astros 9–2 for his 20th victory of the season. A torrid Dodgers attack that included a six run rally in the top of the fourth inning kept the Houston fans quiet. Pedro Guerrero, who was recently activated from the disabled list, showed no ill effects from his torn knee tendon as he slid hard across home plate during the uprising. He also showed that his swing was not rusty as he slugged his second home run of the season in his next at-bat.

Los Angeles					Houston				
Name	*Pos*	*AB*	*R*	*H*	*Name*	*Pos*	*AB*	*R*	*H*
Sax	2B	5	1	2	Hatcher	CF	4	0	0
Stubbs	CF	5	1	2	Doran	2B	3	0	0
Bryant	RF	4	1	2	Calhoun	P	0	0	0
Williams	RF	0	0	0	Lopes	LF	4	0	1
Guerrero	LF	4	2	2	Davis	1B	3	0	0
González	CF	1	0	0	Bass	RF	4	1	0
Brock	1B	5	0	1	Garner	3B	4	1	1
Scioscia	C	5	1	0	Ashby	C	2	0	0
Hamilton	3B	4	1	2	Thon	SS	3	0	0
Anderson	SS	3	1	1	Darwin	P	1	0	0
Valenzuela	P	3	1	1	Hernández	P	0	0	0
					Pankovits	PH	1	0	0
					Solano	P	0	0	0
					Keough	P	0	0	0
					Walker	PH	1	0	0
					López	P	0	0	0
					B. Peña	RF	0	0	0
Totals		39	9	13			30	2	2

```
Los Angeles   0 0 0   6 1 1   0 1 0 — 9 — 13 — 2
Houston       0 0 0   0 0 0   2 0 0 — 2 —  2 — 1
```

Doubles— Bryant, Sax (2), Brock
Triple — Garner
Home Runs— Bryant, Guerrero, Stubbs.

Name	IP	H	R	ER	BB	SO
Los Angeles						
Valenzuela (W 20-10)	9	2	2	1	3	5
Houston						
Darwin (L 3-2)	$3^2/3$	8	6	1	0	3
Hernández	$1^1/3$	1	1	1	0	1
Solano	1	2	1	1	1	0
Keough	1	1	0	0	0	0
López	1	1	1	1	0	0
Calhoun	1	0	0	0	0	0[3]

The Dodgers sun set along with Guerrero and Marshall, and they won only 18 games and lost 33 from August 11 through the end of the season on October 5. Hershiser went 2–5 down the stretch, Howell was 1–4, and Welch was 1–4. Only Fernando, who won 5 games against 2 losses, stood out. Steve Sax tried to hold up the team's offense, but he was alone. He batted a lusty .367 with 25 runs scored and 13 stolen bases in 36 games. Franklin Stubbs, the only power hitter with both Guerrero and Marshall on the shelf, could do no better than a .175 batting average with 2 home runs and 10 runs batted in, in 28 games.

The season ended on a sour note for the Los Angeles Dodgers, their 73–89 record leaving them 23 games behind the Houston Astros, and mired in fifth place in the Western Division. They avoided finishing in the cellar by the slim margin of ½ game, leaving the bottom spot for the Atlanta Braves. Only one player on the team hit above .280, only one player scored more than 60 runs, no one drove in more than 60 runs, and only one player hit more than 19 home runs. Franklin Stubbs hammered 23 homers, but he drove in only 58 runs. The Dodgers defense was atrocious, especially in the infield where Madlock (26 errors), Duncan (25 errors), Sax (16 errors), Anderson (11), Stubbs (7 errors), and Alex Treviño (11 errors) contributed a majority of the team's major league high 181 errors. The pitching ERA rose to 3.76 after leading the league with a 2.96 ERA the previous year. And the saves dropped from 36 to 25. The only bright spots on the team were Steve Sax, Fernando Valenzuela, and Orel Hershiser. The dynamic Sax was the only Dodger with more than 407 at-bats during the season as injuries took a heavy toll on the team. Sax ripped the ball at a .332 clip, with 210 base hits, 91 runs scored, 43 doubles, and 40 stolen bases. Fernando racked up a brilliant 21–11 record for a team that scored only 3.94 runs per game. The classy southpaw worked 269 innings with a 3.14 ERA and completed 20 of his 34 starts. The 27-year-old Hershiser, in his third full season in L.A., compiled a 14–14 record with 3.85 ERA.

In the final analysis, injuries, a porous defense, and an inept bullpen led to the Dodgers' downfall. The team's two primary closers were not up to the job. Ken Howell, who pitched in 62 games, could do no better than 12 saves against 9 blown saves, with a 6–12 won-loss record and a 3.87 earned run average, hardly the statistics a team needs out of its closer. A microcosm of his season occurred on September 25 during a doubleheader against the San Diego Padres. Howell pitched well in the opener and the Dodgers won 4–3 in ten innings. He was called on again to save the nightcap but instead allowed the tying and winning runs to score in another heartbreaking loss. Howell's counterpart, Tom "Buff" Niedenfuer was no better. He pitched in 60 games, with a 6–6 record, a 3.71 ERA, and 11 saves against 6 blown saves. According-ing to Dodgers pitching coach Ron Perranoski, Niedenfuer lost his con-fidence after giving up two cata-

Ron Perranoski watched in dismay as his vaunted pitching staff suffered through a disastrous 1986 season (author's collec-tion).

strophic home runs to Ozzie Smith and Jack Clark in the 1985 NLCS, and that lack of confidence was evident as he was touched up for 11 home runs in just 80 innings of work. Alejandro Peña was successful in his only save attempt as was Jerry Reuss, but a team with 15 blown saves in 40 opportunities, a 63 per-cent save record, cannot expect to challenge for a division title.

The Dodgers vice president in charge of personnel, Al Campanis, real-ized the weaknesses that doomed his team, and he noted the team's top pri-ority. "We've got to get a stopper. That's our No. 1 priority. I understand there were 37 games that we were ahead in the seventh, eighth, and ninth inning. And if we would have won half of them, or 20, we're in first place or there-abouts." The Dodgers, who played 10 consecutive one-run games at the start of the season to tie a major league record, played 66 of them during the sea-son and won only 28.[4]

Dan Beck, in a satirical Halloween piece in *Dodger Blue*, put the season in perspective.

• "The season begins and we have a quick series of shots of Niedenfuer throwing a pitch then turning around to watch the ball soar out of the park. Then Ken Howell is on the mound and the same thing happens. Again, and again, and...."

• "As all this happens we keep looking back at Tom Lasorda prowling around the dugout and, I don't believe it, he actually looks like he's losing weight.

• "Meanwhile, the action keeps cutting back to the field where we see the reasons for the weight Lasorda is carrying. Errors. Errors. Errors. Baserunning mistakes. Strikeouts. Terrifying relief appearances. Boy, I tell you, this is scarier than a garlic sandwich."[5]

The 1986 World Series matched the Boston Red Sox against the New York Mets in an exciting seven-game confrontation. The Series has come down through baseball lore as the Bill Buckner World Series because of the fact that the Red Sox first baseman let a ground ball from Mookie Wilson go through his legs to give the New Yorkers a stunning, come-from-behind 10-inning victory in game six. It is true that Davey Johnson's boys rallied for three runs in the bottom of the tenth inning for the win after the first two batters had been retired, but the real culprits were Calvin Schiraldi, Bob Stanley, and Roger Clemens, not Bill Buckner. Schiraldi was touched up for three consecutive base hits in the tenth inning, and reliever Bob Stanley wild pitched the tying run home before Mookie Wilson hit his seeing-eye ground ball. Clemens, who started game six, had been ko'd in just 4⅓ innings in game two, and he came up short again, but this time it was a matter of heart, not skill, that did him in. The big right-hander, who had led major league pitchers with a glittering 24–4 record during the regular season, with a league leading 2.48 earned run average, inexplicably asked manager John McNamara to take him out of the game in the eighth inning because of a blister on his pitching hand. Clemens was six outs away from locking up Boston's first world championship in 68 years and he let a blister rob him of the honor. If a similar thing had happened to the St. Louis Cardinals' Bob Gibson, for instance, his manager would have had to drag him off the mound, and then Gibson would have left claw marks in the dirt all the way to the dugout. Two days later, the New York Mets annexed their second World Series title when they raked Schiraldi for three runs in the seventh inning to break a three-all tie, and Jesse Orosco tossed two shutout innings to send the BoSox packing.

The Dodgers made an important trade with the Milwaukee Brewers as the year wound down. They obtained hard throwing right-hander Tim Leary and minor league pitcher Tim Crews, in exchange for first baseman Greg Brock. The 28-year-old Leary, at 6', 3" tall, and weighing 190 pounds, appeared in 33 games for the Brewers in '86, compiling a commendable 12–12 record for a sixth place team, and fanning 110 batters in 188 innings. Brock, who had been designated to replace hard-hitting Steve Garvey at first base for Tommy Lasorda, never lived up to expectations. The 1985 season was his best season with the Dodgers and he was still found wanting with just a .251 batting average, 21 home runs, and 66 runs batted in, in 129 games.

Tommy Lasorda and his coaches approached the 1987 season with more questions than answers. They needed a dependable closer and some defensive help in the infield. It was also critical that their walking wounded, particularly

Pedro Guerrero and Mike Marshall, be able to play a minimum of 140 to 150 games. In Lasorda's world, however, the sun always shines and the sky is always blue, so optimism once more filled the Southern California skies and the Dodgers manager, sounding like a carnival barker, expounded on the team's prospects. "We feel we have something to prove this year. We won the National League West in 1985, but we came up short last year, partly because of 16 disabling injuries. We feel we have the talent to be competitive and win our division in 1987, if we stay healthy."[6]

Lasorda felt comfortable with the talent he had at his disposal. He still had one of the top pitching staffs in the National League with Hershiser (14–14), Valenzuela (21–11), Welch (7–13 with a 3.28 ERA), Tim Leary (12–12 with Milwaukee), and Rick Honeycut (11–9), plus closers Tom Niedenfuer (6–6, 11 saves), Alejandro Peña (1–2 while fighting shoulder problems), and Matt Young (8–6 with 13 saves with Seattle). The pitching staff's 3.15 ERA was second best in the National League in 1986, trailing only the New York Mets. Mike Scioscia, behind the plate, had developed into one of the top defensive catchers in the major leagues, and was arguably the best plate-blocker the majors had seen in decades. The infield of Franklin Stubbs, Steve Sax, Mariano Duncan, and Bill Madlock presented an unknown quality. Madlock was a superior third baseman, both offensively and defensively when healthy but, at 36 years of age, the state of his health was a major concern. Steve Sax was coming off a career year, and was hoping to repeat. Madlock's backup, Dave Anderson, as well as Duncan and Stubbs, had potential, but had not yet produced as expected. The outfield of Guerrero, Shelby, and Marshall was adequate defensively and outstanding offensively, when healthy.

The 1987 season got off to a bad start for the Dodgers when they were beaten by the Houston Astros 4–3 in the Astrodome on April 6. And the evening got even worse when Dodgers general manager Al Campanis, "The Chief," appeared on the ABC late night television show *Nightline* with Ted Koppel to commemorate the memory and contributions of Jackie Robinson. It was the beginning of the end for Campanis, who shot himself in the foot during the interview. When he was asked by Koppel why there were no black managers, GMs, or owners, Campanis said, "The only thing I can say is that you have to pay your dues when you become a manager ... some of the better known black players have been able to get into other fields and make a pretty good living in that way." When asked if he thought racial prejudice still existed in baseball, he said, "No. I don't believe it's prejudice. I truly believe that they may not have some of the necessities to be, let's say, a field manager, or perhaps a general manager. So it just might be — why are black men or black people, not good swimmers. They just don't have the buoyancy."[7]

The black community immediately rose up in indignation and demanded his resignation. Hank Aaron and Jesse Jackson were in the forefront of the vigilantes. Campanis apologized publicly two days later, but it was too little, too late. The public still screamed for his scalp. On April 8, Dodgers president Peter O'Malley, succumbing to the pressure, asked for, and received, Campanis' resignation.

Campanis' dismissal was one of the saddest episodes in Dodgers history. A good man had been crucified for misinterpreted remarks. The 70-year-old general manager had been part of the Dodgers organization for 46 years, and he had played a big part in the integration of major league baseball. Don Newcombe put it in perspective when he said, "I don't believe Campanis has a prejudiced bone in his body. If Jackie were around today, I don't think he would appreciate what has happened to Al, because Al helped him and befriended him. He would tell Al, 'You've just messed up, and you've got to apologize,' and Al did apologize."[8]

Campanis had started to rebuild the Dodgers into a winner when he was unceremoniously fired. He had put a solid core of players into place before he left, including pitchers Fernando Valenzuela, Bob Welch, Orel Hershiser, Rick Honeycut, Tim Leary, Alejandro Peña, and Tom Niedenfuer, as well as position players Mike Scioscia, Steve Sax, Pedro Guerrero, and Mike Marshall.

Peter O'Malley telephoned fifty-one-year-old Fred Claire on the 8th and asked him to temporarily assume the duties of VP of player personnel following Campanis' removal. Claire, who had degrees from both Mt. San Antonio College and San José State, had been a sportswriter for 12 years, with the *Whittier News*, the *Pomona Progress Bulletin*, and the *Long Beach Press-Telegram* before joining the Dodgers in 1969 as director of publicity. He was promoted to vice president of public relations and promotions in 1975, and was appointed executive vice president of the Dodgers in 1982, being given responsibility for the day-to-day operations of the team. After assuming his new duties, he used his predecessor's roster as the base to strengthen the team. One of Claire's first moves was to sign outfielder Mickey Hatcher. Hatcher, who had been released by the Minnesota Twins after spring training, on March 31, 1987, was Claire's type of player. He was a scrapper who fought for every base hit, every base, and he was an effervescent presence on the bench and in the clubhouse who kept players on their toes at all times. Hatcher had contacted Al Campanis, but Campanis was not interested, saying the Dodgers were going with younger players. Hatcher's agent, Willie Sánchez, phoned around but there was no interest in a 32-year-old journeyman baseball player. One morning, when Hatcher was out jogging, he stopped on his neighbor's front porch to read the newspaper, and he read where third baseman Bill Madlock of the Dodgers had arthroscopic surgery on his right shoulder. By this time, Fred Claire had replaced Al Campanis as the Dodgers general manager, so he asked his agent to call Claire. He told Sánchez that he would be willing to go to the Dodgers AAA farm team at Albuquerque at his own expense to show the Dodgers what he could do. Sánchez called him back that night. "How does it feel to be a Dodger?" Hatcher recalled. "I said, 'Great. I'm on my way

Fred Claire began the rebuilding process when he signed Mickey Hatcher to a
Dodgers contract on April 10, 1987 (author's collection).

to Albuquerque [Pacific Coast].' He said, 'Wait. They want you in Los Ange-les.'"⁹ The contract was signed on April 10, and, in his first game as a Dodger, Hatcher knocked in the tying run.

Los Angeles Dodgers manager Tommy Lasorda probably broke out in a cold sweat when Claire signed the mischievous Hatcher to a contract, remem-bering the embarrassment and suffering that Hatcher had caused him in 1980 and 1984. In 1980, Hatcher and pitcher Joe Beckwith broke into Lasorda's office and left him with a visitor — a pig. When Lasorda returned to his office and found a squealing porker on the premises, he quickly made for the door, but by that time Hatcher and Beckwith had locked the door from the outside, leaving the Dodgers manager trapped in his office. As Hatcher recalled, "Tommy didn't take this too well, and when he had finally screamed long and loud enough, we opened the door — to find Tommy standing on top his desk, yelling for us to get that thing out of there — or we would never play again."¹⁰

Four years later, when Hatcher was a member of the Minnesota Twins, during a spring exhibition game between the Twins and Dodgers, Hatcher struck again. He broke into the Dodgers clubhouse, took Lasorda's pants and, as he told it, "proceeded to make them into a new style, especially for Tommy Lasorda. I cut the legs off the pants and made them into shorts, and then I cut little hearts into the rear end. I figured they'd be great designer pants, he'd walk out and everyone would have a big laugh. It didn't quite work out that way, though. Tommy was waving, all smiles before the game, until Mark Cresse leaned over to tell him what had happened to his pants. Just then, Ron Davis [Twins reliever] and I started to walk around our dugout with Tommy's pant legs on our arms. All of a sudden, he ran back into the clubhouse and we didn't see him again until about the third inning. I come up to bat and all of a sudden Lasorda starts yelling at Orel Hershiser, 'If you don't hit him, you're not gonna make the team.' I heard it, and in the middle of his windup, Her-shiser yelled, 'Watch out,' so I ducked as he threw the ball over my head. I think Hershiser eventually made the team. I heard later that Tommy sent peo-ple out looking for my car, but it was well hidden. It was a lot of fun."¹¹ After Claire signed Hatcher, Lasorda told his new outfielder that he would never play until he bought his manager a new pair of pants.

The Dodgers were coming off a disastrous 1986 season in which they won just 73 games and lost 89. They could hardly see first place from their fifth place vantage point, 23 games in arrears. But they did have some positives com-ing into the season. Fernando Valenzuela racked up a brilliant 21–11 record in spite of the Dodgers' travails, and his victory total was the highest in the National League. They were also looking forward to the return of Pedro Guer-rero, who was injured most of the '86 season. And Fred Claire was active in the main office in an effort to strengthen his squad.

On April 15, they released pitcher Jerry Reuss, a mainstay in the Dodgers pitching rotation since 1979. The handsome blond right-hander had compiled an 86–69 record over that time, with 18 wins in both 1980 and 1982. But at 38 years of age, it was time to give the reins to a younger man. Five weeks later, Claire obtained center fielder John "T-Bone" Shelby from the Baltimore Orioles in exchange for Tom Niedenfuer.

On the field, there were no noticeable changes. Mike Scott of the Houston Astros tossed a one-hitter at L.A. on April 16, although even that loss had a silver lining. Dodgers starter Alejandro Peña, who had been troubled with shoulder problems for two years, was impressive in defeat. He pitched six innings, yielding two runs on four hits, with five strikeouts and no bases on balls. Tommy Lasorda's warriors finished April with a 12–11 record, and trailed the San Francisco Giants by just 3½ games, but that would turn out to be their only winning month of the season. They were 11–15 in May and 13–14 in June. On July 7, their 37–45 record left them 8½ games behind the division-leading Cincinnati Reds. The team ERA was a decent 3.55, and the starting pitchers had thrown 16 complete games and 4 shutouts, but the bullpen was in a self–destruct mode. They had been scored upon in 35 of 60 appearances while compiling a 7–9 record with an abominable 4.28 ERA, and their 12 saves represented the fewest number of saves in the National League. The overall team performance left much to be desired. They were last in the league in team batting average, last in runs scored, ninth in home runs, tenth in errors, and tenth in unearned runs allowed.

Some of the bright spots included the old guard of Pedro Guerrero, Mike Marshall, Orel Hershiser, Bob Welch, and Fernando Valenzuela, plus journeyman Mickey Hatcher. Guerrero was hitting a crisp .316 with 16 home runs and 50 RBIs, Marshall was at .293 with 8 homers and 34 RBIs, and Hatcher was stroking the ball at a .314 clip while keeping the dugout loose and relaxed with his spirited cheerleading and innocent pranks. On the mound, Orel Hershiser led the way with a 10–7 record, a 2.90 earned run average, and six complete games, followed by Bob Welch at 8–5 with a 3.53 ERA and three complete games, and Fernando Valenzuela at 7–6 with a 3.88 ERA and six complete games.

Fred Claire spent a significant amount of his time during the summer searching the baseball markets for people he thought could help the team. On June 12, he signed free agent outfielder-first baseman Danny Heep, who had eight years of major league experience with the Houston Astros and New York Mets, while compiling a .257 batting average with 25 home runs in 1313 at-bats. One week later the Dodgers obtained 38-year-old Phil "Scrap Iron" Garner, a 14-year major league veteran who could play all the infield positions, from the Astros. And on July 10, Claire signed Tito Landrum, an outfielder with nine years service with the St. Louis Cardinals. The 32-year-old right-handed hitter brought a career .255 batting average with him but, more importantly, he also brought post–season experience with a .347 batting average in 19 games, including a tenth inning home run for the Baltimore Orioles against

Fernando Valenzuela was the only bright spot in the Dodgers' fifth place finish in 1986, as he led the National League in victories with 21 (author's collection).

the Chicago White Sox in the 1983 League Championship Series that broke up a scoreless tie and sent the Orioles on to the World Series. As it turned out, neither Garner nor Landrum survived the '87 season, but Heep stayed on to help L.A. in their 1988 pennant quest. Claire also brought pitcher Tim Crews up from Albuquerque where he had compiled a 7–2 record and 12 saves in 42 games. Crews would pitch in 20 games for L.A. the rest of the season, with a 1–1 record, and a glittering 2.48 ERA.

While the Dodgers were struggling to get back into the National League West pennant race, a big, 6', 5", 215-pound rookie was making a stir in the American League on the West Coast. Mark McGwire, a powerful right-handed slugger, connected for his 30th home run of the year on Sunday, July 5, against the Boston Red Sox. The 23-year-old Californian followed a José Canseco blast with one of his own off Bruce Hurst on Saturday, and duplicated the feat off Dennis "Oil Can" Boyd in the fourth inning of a 6–3 A's victory on Sunday. When Red Sox reliever Wes Gardner hit McGwire on the helmet with a pitch in the eighth inning, both dugouts emptied, led by A's manager Tony LaRussa and Reggie Jackson, but order was restored before the situation deteriorated. Gardner noted, "I was pitching him inside. People have been pitching him away and he's been hitting the ball out. I'm not going to try to hit anybody, but I am going to try to establish the inside by throwing inside." McGwire was also hit with a pitch in the sixth inning, after Canseco smashed his second homer of the game and 18th of the season. Dave Stewart won his 10th game of the season against 7 losses, limiting Boston to one run on seven hits in seven innings.[12] The Oakland A's, who had struggled with sub–.500 teams since 1981, were building a powerhouse in Northern California, but they were still one year away. When they obtained slugger Dave Parker from the Cincinnati Reds on December 8, 1987, picked up 15-game winner Bob Welch from the Los Angeles Dodgers three days later, and completed the successful conversion of Dennis Eckersley from a starting pitcher to the major league's premier closer, they were ready to scale the heights.

Hershiser won his 10th game on July 6, defeating the Pittsburgh Pirates by a 6–1 score. "Bulldog," as Lasorda called him, and two relievers, held the Bucs to three hits, while Danny Heep and Mike Scioscia drove in two runs apiece. Hershiser faced a minimum of 15 batters, allowing a single hit over five innings before a stiff lower back forced him to retire with a 6–0 lead. On July 12, Bob Welch, struggling through a frustrating two-month period where his teammates gave him little offensive support, closed out the first half of the season by throwing a 12–0 complete game at the Chicago Cubs. By the 22nd of the month, the Dodgers' 41–53 record had Lasorda talking to himself. His team was ensconced in the cellar, 10½ games behind the Cincinnati Reds, and, as Hatcher noted, "Right now, there's a lot of frustration in this clubhouse. It's something I saw a lot with the Twins. It just seems like we can't get anything going, and we're losing a lot of games we should win."[13] Their record bore out Hatcher's claims, as they could do no better than 10–16 in one-run games. They were letting the close ones get away. Although their sterling pitching staff had the lowest ERA in the National League on July 22, their offense and their defense were both atrocious. They were last in batting average and runs scored, and next to last in fielding average. Hatcher was one of the few bright spots, hitting .337. Pedro Guerrero was stinging the ball at a robust .327 pace with 20 home runs, and Mike Marshall was hitting .282 with 10 home runs.

One of the Dodgers' bright spots in an otherwise dreary July was a 6–5 win over their hated rivals, the San Francisco Giants, in Dodger Stadium on the 28th of the month. Kelly Downs started on the mound for Roger Craig's Giants, and he was opposed by hard-throwing right-hander Bob Welch. L.A. sent Downs to an early shower with a three-run outburst in the first inning, but that was the extent of their offense until the eighth inning. In the meantime, San Fran kept nibbling away at Welch, scoring single runs in the first, second, and fifth innings, to deadlock the score at 3-all. Mickey Hatcher homered in the bottom of the eighth to give L.A. a 4–3 lead, but the bullpen couldn't protect it. Tim Crews made his major league debut in the eighth inning, and might have come away with a victory with better defense, but an error allowed the tying run to score. The two teams traded runs in the eleventh inning, with Steve Sax crossing the plate for L.A. The game finally ended in the bottom of the twelfth when Franklin Stubbs, who had gone 0 for 5 with 3 strikeouts, drove the ball out of the park against Scott Garrelts, sending 33,741 fans home happy.

Pedro Guerrero was voted the Dodgers' Most Valuable Player for the month of July after stroking the ball at a .415 clip, with 6 home runs and 16 runs batted in. He finished the month with a season average of .338, trailing only Tony Gwynn of San Diego.

On August 1, Welch defeated the Atlanta Braves 7–2 for just his second victory since June 7, bringing his record to 10–6. Four days later, the Dodgers had pulled themselves up to fourth place, their 48–59 record leaving them 9½ games behind the Reds and 4½ games behind the third place San Francisco Giants. The starting pitching was still strong, their 3.88 ERA just 0.12 behind the Houston Astros, but Fernando Valenzuela's health concerned Dodgers management. After racing to a 3–1 record early in the season, the talented southpaw could do no better than 6–8 in June and July with a near 6.00 ERA, raising fears that he was overworked and that he had a sore arm. Reporters noted that Fernando "had pitched an average of 267 innings during the last six seasons, and was coming off career highs for victories with 21 and complete games with 20.... Valenzuela said his arm is fine, but understands the concerns of the fans. "If I am not well I don't help the team," he said. "If I don't help the team, I won't go out there."[14] Fernando did win his next start on July 31 and, although he was touched up for five runs, he was unhittable over his last three innings of work.

The bullpen, the offense, and the defense were still the club's Achilles heels. The team was last in the National League in saves, last in batting average, last in runs scored, and last in fielding percentage.

Tommy Lasorda brought his team to New York on August 25 for a series against the Mets and, in the opener, they pushed the second-place Mets another game behind the St. Louis Cardinals. Dodgers ace Fernando Valenzuela stifled the New Yorkers on four hits, winning 3–1. The game was not as easy at it sounded, however, as the gutty Mexican southpaw fanned 13 men but walked a season-high eight and pitched out of trouble all night long, stranding 11 enemy baserunners. John Shelby cracked a two-run homer in the opening stanza, following a Franklin Stubbs double, and Fernando made it stand up the rest of the way. The Mets tallied one run in the bottom of the fifth, but missed a golden opportunity to send Fernando to a quick shower. Mookie Wilson opened the inning with a double, Keith Hernandez walked, and Darryl Strawberry was safe at first on an error by Valenzuela, loading the bases with no outs. Tim Teuffel knocked in Wilson with a single, but then Fernando took another hitch in his pants, fanned Kevin McReynolds, got Gary Carter to foul out to Mickey Hatcher at first base, and struck out Howard Johnson to end the inning.

Name	Pos	AB	R	H	Name	Pos	AB	R	H
Sax	2B	4	0	0	Wilson	CF	5	1	1
Stubbs	RF	4	1	1	Teufel	2B	3	0	2
Guerrero	LF	3	0	1	Hernandez	1B	3	0	1
Shelby	CF	4	1	1	Strawberry	RF	3	0	0
Hatcher	1B	4	0	0	McReynolds	LF	3	0	0
Landrum	RF	0	0	0	Carter	C	2	0	0
Scioscia	C	4	0	0	Johnson	3B	3	0	0
Woodson	3B	4	1	3	Santana	SS	4	0	0
Hoffman	SS	3	0	1	Cone	P	2	0	0
Valenzuela	P	4	0	1	Almon	PH	1	0	0
					Leach	P	0	0	0
					Mazzilli	PH	1	0	0
Totals		**34**	**3**	**8**			**30**	**1**	**4**

```
Los Angeles   2 0 0   0 0 0   0 0 1 — 3 — 8 — 2
New York      0 0 0   0 1 0   0 0 0 — 1 — 4 — 1
```

Doubles— Stubbs, Hernandez, Wilson.
Home Runs— Shelby

Name	IP	H	R	ER	BB	SO
Los Angeles						
Valenzuela (W 11-11)	9	4	1	1	8	13
New York						
Cone (L 3-3)	6	4	2	2	2	3
Leach	3	4	1	1	0	2[15]

John Shelby, another valuable addition to the Los Angeles pennant quest, joined the team on May 22, 1987 (author's collection).

A typical game, and one that exposed the frustration of the Dodgers field leadership, was played the following night. L.A. lost a tough 3–2 decision to the New York Mets in Shea Stadium, with Bob Welch taking the loss. Tommy Lasorda, in an attempt to keep the game close while he strove to unleash his pitiful offense, used a major league record eight pitchers in the game, including five pitchers in the eighth inning. Steve Sax, with three base hits, and Pedro Guerrero with two, accounted for five of the Dodgers' six hits in the game.

John Shelby, who was having one of his best all-around seasons in the major leagues, was voted the Dodgers' Most Valuable Player for August after hitting .327 with 18 homers and 61 RBIs. His home run total through August exceeded his highest single-season mark of 11, set with Baltimore in 1986.

As the stretch run began in the major leagues on September 5, the Dodgers were still in fifth place, one game ahead of San Diego and 2½ games behind fourth place Atlanta. Not much had changed in the team's performance since early August: the team's batting average of .249 was 12 points below Houston, their 512 runs scored was 42 runs less than Houston, their 130 errors were seven more than the Montreal Expos, and their 21 saves were three less than Atlanta. The team ERA of 3.71 was good enough for a first place tie with the Houston Astros.

Fred Claire obtained pitcher Tim Belcher from the Oakland Athletics on September 3, 1987, as the player to be named later in the trade of Rick Honeycut. Belcher had gone 9–11 with the A's farm team in Tacoma, walking 133 men in 163 innings. He came to the Dodgers with a reputation for having an excess of talent but no idea of where the plate was. Dodgers pitching coach Ron Perranoski was puzzled when he first saw Belcher. "His control was really excellent and I've been trying to figure out how he could be so wild in the minors."[16] He helped Belcher concentrate on every pitch, which, according to Belcher, was his undoing in the minor leagues. A lack of concentration may have resulted in numerous bases on balls in the minors, but in L.A. his bases on balls dropped dramatically. During the closing month of the season, Dodgers fans got a glimpse of the future when the 6', 3", 210-pound right-hander compiled a 4–2 record and a 2.38 ERA, walking just 7 men in 34 innings.

Once again, injuries played a part in the Dodgers' malaise. Bill Madlock was placed on the disabled list on April 10 after having arthroscopic surgery on his right shoulder. Mike Marshall was on the DL twice during the season for a total of five weeks, limiting his playing time to 104 games. He spent three weeks on the DL in May after undergoing surgery to remove warts and scar tissue from his left index finger. He also lost time for a back injury, food poisoning, and an ankle injury. Mike Scioscia spent 15 days on the shelf in early June after fracturing the tip of the middle finger on his left hand during batting practice. Franklin Stubbs lost most of August when he separated his shoulder. And Mariano Duncan was out from June 19 to July 4 with a laceration above his right knee, and again from August 17 to the end of the season with a torn ligament in his left knee. Alejandro Peña went on the DL on August 3 with a strained abdominal muscle. Dave Anderson (left hamstring pull) and Jeff Hamilton (sprained ankle) both went on the DL on August 13. And Len Matuszek lost most of the season with a nagging foot injury, and then retired after the close of the season.

The 1987 season, which came to a merciful end on October 4, seemed like déjà vu all over again, as Yogi Berra used to say. The season was forgettable; it was their second consecutive 73–89 season and a fourth place finish, 17 games behind the Western Division leaders, the San Francisco Giants. Their 155 errors were the most in the major leagues, and their .975 fielding average was the lowest. Their offense was just as bad as their defense as they finished dead last in the major leagues in runs scored with 635. On the positive side, Pedro Guerrero bounced back from injuries to compile a .338 batting average with 27 home runs and 89 runs batted in, and Mike Marshall batted .294 with 16 homers and 72 RBIs. Steve Sax hit .280 with 84 runs scored and 37 stolen bases, Mike Scioscia hit .265 and was a demon on defense, and the effervescent Mickey Hatcher chipped in with a .282 average, 7 home runs, and 42 RBIs in 287 at-bats. The rest of the offense was forgettable. Their lone bright spot was their pitching. With Hershiser, Welch, and Valenzuela leading the way, the Dodgers staff compiled an impressive 3.72 ERA, second best out of 30 major league teams. Hershiser went 16–16 with a 3.06 earned run average, Welch was a sensational 15–9 with a 3.22 ERA, and Fernando was 14–14 with a 3.98 ERA. Still, there was no indication that this team was on the verge of a world championship, or that it could even challenge for the Western Division title in the National League. They had too many holes in their lineup.

Several of the Los Angeles minor league hopefuls were called up during the season, but their performance didn't give Dodgers fans much cause for optimism. Jeff Hamilton, who was called up to replace Franklin Stubbs, hit just .217 with no home runs in 83 at-bats, and Mariano Duncan, who made two trips to the City of Angels, hit .215 with 6 homers in 261 at-bats. Tracy Woodson batted .228 with 1 homer in 136 at-bats. Other players who made short trips to the big club included Chris Gywnn (.219), Ralph Bryant (.246), Mike Ramsey (.232), and Mike Sharperson (.273).

Dodgers fans were hoping for Fred Claire to pull off a big trade during the winter meetings, but things moved slowly during the meetings. There were no blockbuster trades to report. Not even any minor trades. The media accused Claire of being indecisive. Several owners grumbled that Claire was not qualified to do his job. They were wrong. Major league executives were facing a thinking man for a change, not a hip-shooting wheeler-dealer. Unlike the verbose, cigar smoking windbags that frequented these types of meetings, Fred Claire was an introspective professional. Many owners felt that the Dodgers GM would be putty in their hands. After two successive disastrous seasons that saw the Dodgers go 73–89, Los Angeles was expected to be in a panic mode in Dallas, making numerous deals in an effort to reverse the trend. A rookie general manager, whose club just finished at 73–89, could be expected to be panicked into making bad deals. But not so Fred Claire. Claire was more than up to the task of filling the holes in his lineup. He was determined to take his time, carefully assess his alternatives, and make a trade if, and only if, it would help him fill the holes in his lineup. He had three major needs— a reliable shortstop that would plug the leaks in his infield, a stopper in the bullpen who could close out a Dodgers victory with consistency, and a power hitter to lend the offensive support the Dodgers so badly needed.

Fred Claire filled two of those holes with a blockbuster three-way trade involving the Oakland Athletics and the New York Mets on December 11, 1987. The Dodgers sent 31-year-old fireballer Bob Welch, who was 15–9 for the Dodgers in 1987, and relief pitcher Matt Young, who had 11 saves with L.A., to the A's, and Jack Savage to the Mets. In return they received shortstop Alfredo Griffin and closer Jay Howell from the A's and relief ace Jesse Orosco from the Mets. Griffin, at 30 years of age, was regarded as one of baseball's best all-around shortstops. He was an outstanding defensive shortstop with excellent range, and was adept at making double plays. The 5', 11", 165-pound switch hitter was also a pesky hitter, with a .258 career average, and had stolen 161 bases in 1372 games, including 83 stolen bases over the previous three years. And, in addition to his offensive and defensive contributions, Griffin was one of baseball's iron men, having played in all 162 games in four of the previous six seasons, with one run of 392 consecutive games. Orosco was coming off the worst year of his eight-year career. He had 16 saves in 1987, but went just 3 and 9 in decisions, and had a poor 4.47 ERA in 77 relief appearances. Obviously Claire was looking for Orosco to rebound, although some New York Mets experts said that the crafty lefty had lost his fastball, making his slider less effective. Howell was a throw of the dice for Claire, who was counting on the big right-hander to shut down the opposition in the ninth inning. On paper, Howell was just a mediocre closer whose eight-year major league career showed a 29–30 won-loss record, a 4.17 ERA, and 68 saves in 89 save opportunities, a so-so 68 percent save percentage, only slightly better than what Niedenfuer and Peña had provided in 1986. Four days later, on December 15, the Dodgers signed free agent Mike Davis, who had slugged 22 home runs for the A's in 1987. Claire and Lasorda were hoping that Davis, who at 28 years of age was entering his prime years, would have a breakout season, and be the five-point player they thought he could be. He was a good defensive outfielder with a strong throwing arm, and a left-handed power hitter with exceptional speed. Davis stole 32 bases in 1983 and, in his best overall season two years later, he slugged 34 doubles and 24 home runs, drove in 82 teammates, stole 24 bases, and hit .287. Lasorda was penciling Davis in for right field to take over for Mike Marshall, freeing Marshall up to play first base.

Public reaction to the trades from the Dodgers side was mixed. Fred Claire was quoted as saying, "I think in Alfredo Griffin, we have one of the outstanding shortstops in baseball. Jay Howell is a quality relief pitcher and we're confident that whatever physical problems he's had in the past have been taken care of. And in Jesse Orosco, we're receiving a premier left-handed relief pitcher. All three of these players have been All-Stars and I feel they're all in the prime of their careers." Dodgers manager Tommy Lasorda was excited about the trades. "As I told our team in many meetings, you could take Juan Marichal, Bob Gibson, Don Drysdale, and Sandy Koufax and put them all on the same pitching staff, but if you have to get four or five outs an inning, you're just not going to be able to win. Our defense was very shoddy last season, and Alfredo Griffin will help us immensely." He went on to say, "If [Howell's] healthy, he'll help in our bullpen. As will Jesse Orosco. Our bullpen has not done the job the last two years, and I think these two guys will do the job for us. I think the world of Jesse. He's a great competitor. On the other hand, I hate to see Bobby Welch go. You have to trade something good to get something good, but when I realized Bobby would have to go in the deal, I got sick to my stomach. I was up all night pacing at the hotel room. He's a great competitor who wore the Dodger uniform with a lot of pride. I'll miss him very much." Radio talk show callers in general did not like the trade with one caller asking, "What is he [Claire] doing? How can you trade a pitcher like Bob Welch for three question marks?"[17]

4

IN THE SPRING...

Fred Claire's talent hunt continued into the new year. Claire was determined to give Los Angeles Dodgers fans a pennant winner and a world championship team quickly. His first signing of 1988 took place on January 5 when he inked 22-year veteran Don Sutton to a one-year contract. The 42-year-old curveball artist had begun his professional baseball career with Los Angeles as a fuzzy cheeked 20-year-old in 1965. That year, he ran up an 8–1 record for Santa Barbara in the California League before making the jump to AA Albuquerque in the Texas League where he continued his pitching dominance, going 15–6 in 21 games. The precocious right-hander became a major league fixture the following year, compiling a 12–12 record with the pennant-winning Dodgers. He pitched in Los Angeles for 15 years, winning 233 games against 181 losses, for a .563 winning percentage, and a 3.09 earned run average. His best year was 1976 when he went 21–10. Overall, with the Dodgers, he set franchise records for wins, games pitched (534), starts (517), innings pitched (3728), strikeouts (2652), and shutouts (52). He pitched in three post-season classics, going 3–1 in the NLCS and 2–2 in the World Series. Sutton pitched for four teams between 1981 and 1987, with his career totals rising to 321 victories against 250 losses.

The most significant deal of the off-season for Claire was the signing of outfielder Kirk Gibson. The talented slugger, who played with the Detroit Tigers from 1979 through 1987, and who sparked them to a World Series championship in 1984 when he hit .333 with 2 homers and 7 RBIs in five games, was granted special free agency by the arbitrator on January 22, 1988. He subsequently signed with the Los Angeles Dodgers on February 1, 1988. Tigers owner Tom Monaghan said he was happy to see the last of Gibson. "His best talents, hitting home runs against right-handed pitchers, and stealing bases, are not worth a million and a half dollars a year. He has maybe one of the weaker arms in baseball for an outfielder, and can't field well."[1] Obviously Monaghan was a poor judge of talent who had forgotten about the 1984 world championship.

Kirk Gibson was just the man Fred Claire needed to bring a world championship to the City of Angels. Gibson was a winner. He had been a winner

Kirk Gibson, the man called the heart and soul of the 1988 Los Angeles Dodgers, was signed as a free agent on February 1, 1988 (courtesy of Los Angeles Dodgers).

all his life, an outstanding player and a great competitor. At Michigan State University, he had been an All-American flanker on the football team and an All-American outfielder on the baseball team. He holds several Michigan State football records for flankers including 112 receptions, 2,347 yards gained, and 24 touchdowns. On the diamond, he ripped the ball at a sizzling .390 clip with 52 runs batted in, in 48 games. He was drafted by the St. Louis Cardinals of the National Football League and by the Detroit Tigers in baseball. Gibson opted for baseball and, after two years in the minor leagues, he starred for the Tigers for the next nine years, sparking them to a world championship in 1984. He batted .282 that year with 23 doubles, 10 triples, 27 home runs, 91 RBIs, and 29 stolen bases, in 531 at-bats. He went on to lead the Tigers to a three-game sweep of the Kansas City Royals in the ALCS, hitting .417 with a homer and two RBIs, and followed that up by slugging .333 with two home runs and 7 RBIs as Detroit knocked off the San Diego Padres in five games. And Kirk Gibson put on a show for the home fans in the finale, scoring from third base on a fly ball to shallow right field that was caught by the second baseman, and blasting two home runs, a two-run shot in the first inning that gave Sparky Anderson's team a 2–0 lead, and a tremendous upper-deck poke with two men on base in the eighth inning that put the final nail in the San Diego coffin, cementing an 8–4 victory for the fans of the Motor City.

When Gibson was introduced to the Los Angeles fans at a press conference, he made it quite clear why he had joined the Dodgers. "I know the Dodgers have been one of the premier organizations in baseball. One thing I can assure everybody is that I play hard on every pitch of every inning ... and I hate to lose."[2] He went on to say, "I play to win. I don't see why you should play for any other reason. I'll do whatever it takes to win. I always give 100 percent. When I go to spring training, I go to win a pennant." Later he added, "When I step on the field, I may offend some with my actions, but to be quite honest with you, I don't step on he field to make friends. I'll be happy to fight for my teammates, I'll dig and claw, I'll fight if I've gotta fight." He went on to assure his new teammates about his friendly demeanor. "Contrary to what you've heard, I'm very easy to get along with. As long as you give 100 percent with me on the field, I would never have a quarrel and I'll be easy to get along with."[3] Gibson's internal fire was tested during spring training, and his response to that test ignited a fire in the bellies of his teammates, a fire that would culminate in a world championship for Los Angeles.

Pitcher Kenny Howell, for one, was happy to see the fiery Gibson join the Dodgers. "Hey, it's great to have somebody like him around here. After what's gone on around here the last two years with the losing and the bad attitudes and everything, having Gibson here will shake things up. And that's good. He won't take any (bleep) from anybody. I like that. Some people may not like him because of that, but he'll be like a breath of fresh air around here."[4]

The next addition to the Los Angeles squad, and another valuable one was Rick Dempsey, who was a member of the Baltimore Orioles from 1976 through 1986. He played with Cleveland in 1987, but was not offered a contract for 1988, so he called Fred Claire in Los Angeles and offered his services to the Dodgers. Claire said he would get back to him, but when Rick didn't hear anything after a few weeks, he went to the Dodgers' executive offices and sat in the receptionist's office for several hours to get to see Claire. The Dodger GM invited Dempsey to spring training, and on February 14, he signed Dempsey to a one-year contract. The 38-year-old backstop was Claire's type of guy, a hard-nosed, take charge individual, who gave 100 percent every game, and who was a respected and popular leader in the clubhouse. He was a 19-year veteran by the time the Dodgers signed him, having caught 1380 games with four major league teams. Although he was just a .236 career hitter, he was an outstanding defensive specialist, who was particularly adept at calling the game, blocking wild pitches, and throwing the ball. He also responded well to the pressures of post-season play, batting .273 in two ALCS and .324 in two World Series. He was the Most Valuable Player in the 1983 World Series when he pounded the ball at a .385 clip for the Baltimore Orioles, with five extra base hits including a home run in the Orioles five-game win over the Philadelphia Phillies. Dempsey was also a well-known character who, once during a rain delay, imitated a batter hitting a ball, then racing around the bases on top of the wet tarpaulin, and bringing the crowd to its feet, roaring its approval, with a sensational head-first dive across home plate, sending water flying in all directions. The Dempsey mentality fit in perfectly with Mickey Hatcher's.

The Dodgers made two other futile attempts at signing free agents, but both players eventually decided to stay with their original teams. Dave Righetti, a 29-year-old lefty, who had gone 8–6 with 31 saves in 60 games in 1987, was courted by Fred Claire to be the Dodgers' closer. Claire and Righetti's agent, Bill Goldstein, met several times in late December, but when the final

Rick Dempsey was a key member of the notorious Stuntmen (author's collection).

bell rang, Righetti re-signed wirh the Yankees, who had been his first choice all along. The other free agent target was Gold Glove third baseman Gary Gaetti of the Minnesota Twins. The 6', 200-pound right-handed power hitter would have been an ideal fit for Tommy Lasorda's squad. Hitting alongside such sluggers as Kirk Gibson, Pedro Guerrero, Mike Marshall, and Mike Davis, he would have given the Dodgers a dangerous Murderers Row to supplement their outstanding pitching staff. Gaetti, a seven-year veteran, had a combined batting average of .272 over the previous two years, with an average of 33 home runs and 108 runs batted in a year but, as it turned out, he was just testing the waters and when it came down to decision time, he opted to stay with the Twins even though the Dodgers offered him $4.8 million over three years, a cool $500,000 more than the Twins offered. Gaetti explained his decision by saying, "I didn't want to leave Minnesota. This is my home now and I want to win another championship for the Twins. Kent Hrbek said he would never talk to me again if I played for the Dodgers. I used to hate the Dodgers. I still do. I guess I can say that now. I hate the Dodgers." Fred Claire said he was not disappointed at Gaetti's decision. "We made a substantial offer. I felt they understood we were serious."[5]

Another important footnote to the winter season involved pitcher Tim Leary, who had a miserable year in 1987, with a 3–11 record and a 4.76 ERA. The 6', 3", 190-pound right-hander decided to go to Mexico in the off-season and pitch in the Mexican Pacific League to work on his repertoire. He pitched for the Tijuana Potros and helped them capture the league championship. As reported by *Baseball America*, "Tim Leary of the Dodgers, commuting from his home in Santa Monica, Calif., had a 9–0 record and 1.24 ERA for Tijuana. He used the work to develop a split-finger pitch."[6] When spring training got underway, a new, smarter, and better-equipped Tim Leary impressed pitching coach Ron Perranoski with his new weapon. Other Dodgers players who honed their skills in winter leagues around the western hemisphere included Alfredo Griffin who played with Estrellas Orientales in the Dominican Winter League, plus a bevy of minor leaguers.

Many of the Dodgers players began their 1988 workouts in Dodger Stadium on January 11, preparatory to leaving for Vero Beach. Players who participated in the workouts included new Dodgers Don Sutton, Mike Davis, and Alfredo Griffin, as well as about a dozen returning Dodgers. The workouts continued through February 14, when the players left for Florida. One of the attendees, Orel Hershiser, suffered a setback when he underwent an appendectomy on February 12, but he still showed up for practice with the rest of the pitchers on February 18, and he pitched in a Grapefruit League game less than three weeks later. Jay Howell, who had arthroscopic surgery on his elbow in August, recovered satisfactorily during the off-season, causing team physician Dr. Frank Jobe to say, "He has more range of motion now than he had before the surgery. He should be just fine. He's had plenty of time."[7]

The Dodgers' payroll for the 1988 season settled in at approximately $17.4 million, with Fernando Valenzuela receiving a $2 million contract, followed by

Kirk Gibson at $1.8 million, Pedro Guerrero at $1.7 million, Orel Hershiser at $1.1 million, and Mike Scioscia and Jesse Orosco at $1.0 million each. Bringing up the bottom end were Franklin Stubbs at $235,000, Ken Howell at $215,000, Mariano Duncan at $200,000, and Tim Leary at $190,000. The payroll was the highest in the National League, and second to the New York Yankees' $18.8 million payroll, in spite of the fact that the team released or traded many of its highest paid players during the 1987 season or in the off-season, including Jerry Reuss, Bill Madlock, Bob Welch, Ken Landreaux, and Tom Niedenfuer.

By the time the team assembled in Vero Beach to prepare for the upcoming season, Fred Claire believed he had the players in place to bring the Dodgers a National League pennant. Manager Tommy Lasorda's projected opening day lineup consisted of:

Catcher — Mike Scioscia, a tough-as-nails eight-year veteran who caught 138 games in 1987.

A strong starting staff of Orel Hershiser (16–16 in 1987), Fernando Valenzuela (14–14), Tim Leary (3–11), and Tim Belcher (4–2), with Alejandro Peña (2–7, 11 saves), Jesse Orosco (3–9, 16 saves), Brian Holton (3–2, 2 saves), Tim Crews (1–1, 3 saves), and Ken Howell (3–4) in the pen, to set up closer Jay Howell (3–4, 16 saves).

First base — Franklin Stubbs, 16 homers in 386 at-bats in 1987.

Second base — Steve Sax, .280 batting average, 37 stolen bases.

Shortstop — Alfredo Griffin, a defensive wizard with a .263 batting average in 1987.

Third base — Jeff Hamilton, a big, 6', 3", 207-pound right-handed hitter who tortured Pacific Coast League pitching to the tune of .360 in 1987, with 12 home runs and 48 runs batted in, in 65 games.

Left field — Kirk Gibson, the catalyst of the team, a nine-year major league veteran who batted .277 with 24 homers in 1987.

Center field — John Shelby, who batted .277 with 21 homers and 16 stolen bases for the Dodgers in 1987.

Right field — Mike Marshall, a big, strong right-handed batter standing 6', 5" tall and weighing 218 pounds, batted .294 with 16 homers and 72 RBIs in 104 games in 1987.

A strong bench, with Mickey Hatcher, Rick Dempsey, Dave Anderson, Mike Davis, Mike Sharperson, Tracy Woodson, and Danny Heep.

The big question marks were third base, first base, and right field. Hamilton had been penciled in at the third base position, but Lasorda wanted to take another look at Pedro Guerrero there, in spite of Pedro's disastrous experience three years before. Steve Sax was also being mentioned as a candidate for the hot corner with Mariano Duncan taking over second base. And Mike Marshall volunteered to learn the position, which would free up Guerrero to play first base, a position Pedro felt comfortable playing. Franklin Stubbs was listed as the first baseman, but he would have plenty of competition there during spring

training, with Marshall in the running also. And, depending on the final res-
olution of the first and third base problems, the identity of the right fielder
would be known. The Dodgers manager preferred to have Mike Davis in right,
but only if either Marshall or Guerrero could be moved to the infield.

As the spring training schedule progressed to intra-squad games, the
bench players began to see a fair amount of playing time, starting many of the
early games to protect the regulars by giving them time to work themselves
into playing condition. It also gave the substitutes some work, something they
might not see much of once the regular season began. This scenario was quickly
noted by the team's two clubhouse characters, Hatcher and Dempsey, who
decided to organize the group into a united fighting force. The two men
equated their position to that of a stuntman in the movies, someone who
would step in to replace the star in a dangerous scene when the director didn't
want the star to get hurt, and he would throw in somebody he didn't care
about, somebody who remained a nameless and faceless entity for much of
his career. As noted in *Dodgers Dugout*, Stuntmen are the non-starting position players who serve much of the time by sitting and waiting for their chance.

"And they must be angry about it," according to Captain Hatcher. "That's
a rule," he said. "You must be unhappy about sitting on the bench. Show me
a happy reserve and I'll show you a loser."[8]

Kirk Gibson's first impression of the Los Angeles Dodgers was one of disgust. He didn't think the players took the game seriously enough, particularly
when they worked on the fundamentals. "Soon after we began working on
fielding bunts, Pedro Guerrero, who was playing third base, picked up a bunt
and threw it into right field. Everybody began laughing at this silly throw that
rocketed out of the infield. I was stunned. These guys, this team, finished in
fourth and fifth place the last two seasons, and it's funny to throw a ball into
right field? This type of attitude made me burn inside. It was not how Kirk
Gibson wanted to play baseball, even at spring training."[9]

Several days later, the situation came to a head. Just prior to beginning
their Grapefruit League spring training exhibition game schedule, on March
3, an incident occurred that set the tempo for the entire season. Jesse Orosco,
a noted prankster throughout his career, put shoe polish on the inside rim of
Kirk Gibson's hat, and when Gibson began working out in the hot Florida sun,
beads of black sweat began to run down his face. The deadly serious outfielder
exploded, screaming, "No wonder this team finished fourth last year." He
then disappeared into the confines of the clubhouse, and refused to take part
in that day's exhibition game against the visiting Chunichi Dragons of the
Japanese Central League, a game the Dodgers won handily 14–0. Steve Sax hit
a grand slam homer to pace the Dodgers attack. John Shelby pitched in with
a three-run homer. Tracy Woodson also homered and Ralph Bryant hit a 450-
foot shot over the right field embankment. Rookie Ramón Martínez hurled
three scoreless innings in his spring debut.

Tot Holmes reported on the shoe polish incident in *Dodgers Dugout*.

"He (Gibson) shouted that he didn't want to become part of the team's (bleeping) comedy act, then stormed off the field as Lasorda's plea to stay was ignored. The manager later said, "I told him that the way he was feeling, it was best for him to go. He wasn't in a real good mood."

Gibson returned to the clubhouse and reportedly said, "Send the guy who did it into the clubhouse and then I'll play." He told a Michigan paper that the Dodgers were "clowns" and later told Lasorda that he could understand why the Dodgers finished fifth the past two seasons, because "They have their priorities wrong."

The next day, Jesse Orosco came forward defusing a potentially explosive clubhouse meeting to admit he was the guilty party. "It was just a little joke. I felt bad about what happened and I told him that. He said there was no problem," Orosco said.

But Gibson was still steaming. "I don't want to walk out on the field and have people laugh at me. I make enough mistakes. They can laugh at those. I told Lasorda that I don't play pranks and I don't accept them well. I like to have a good time, but a good time to me is winning. I did what I had to do to get my point across and that is that."

"Let's just say I won't be doing it again," Orosco said. "That's because I don't want to read my name in the obituaries."[10]

When Tommy Lasorda (shown here with his assistant) assembled his team in Vero Beach in the spring of 1988, he was committed to winning a world championship (author's collection).

The shoe-black incident might have been a blessing in disguise for the Dodgers, because it made the team realize that if they wanted to win a pennant and perhaps a World Series they were going to have to take the game seriously and work hard from the beginning of spring training to the final out of the season. As Kirk Gibson later remarked, "I go by the rules. This other bull is foreign to me."

Tommy Lasorda's cohorts got off the mark quickly when the Grapefruit League got underway. They knocked off the Minnesota Twins by the score of 6–5 in 10 innings on March 4 and the Stuntmen made major contributions to the win. Mickey Hatcher, the recognized leader of the Stuntmen, singled in the winning run in the bottom of the 10th inning, and backup catcher Rick Dempsey banged a two-run home run. Orel Hershiser, not long out of a hospital bed, pitched three scoreless innings and Shawn Hillegas gave up one run in three innings. The day did not go without some bitterness however. Mike Marshall, upset at what he considered to be a slight, sounded off to reporters, according to *Dodgers Dugout.*

> Marshall was angered at what he perceived to be his exclusion from the club's upper echelon: Guerrero, Gibson, Scioscia, and Griffin.
>
> "Maybe John Shelby and Steve Sax are in that group too," Marshall told reporters. "There are four guys to whom management has said this is what it's going to take, so take what you need to get ready. I need this time to get ready too. I told them if they were going to work in that way that I'd like to play somewhere else."
>
> Marshall's remarks upset Lasorda. "I am not going to manage the team for Mike Marshall," he said. "He's entitled to his feeling and I couldn't blame him. But I didn't tell Scioscia he wasn't starting. I didn't tell Duncan he wasn't starting. Did they say anything?"[11]

Several of the players admitted things were tense in the clubhouse, but said they would improve once the regular season starting lineup was decided, and everyone knew his role on the team. On March 4, there were probably at least 12 to 15 players who were fighting for a starting berth, and the pressure of that battle sometimes spilled over into the press. But it was nothing to worry about. It was just competition at its fiercest.

There were other unhappy campers in Dodgertown early on, including Pedro Guerrero and Jeff Hamilton. Guerrero was the subject of trade rumors over the winter. The Dodgers had received an offer from the Detroit Tigers of Kirk Gibson for Pedro Guerrero early in the off-season, but decided against it, choosing to wait until the arbitrator, who heard the 1985 free-agent collusion case, made his decision relative to the penalties to be imposed on the clubs. It was a good decision because the arbitrator made Gibson and 61 other major league players free agents. Guerrero, who learned about the possible trade from friends in Los Angeles, was bitter that the Dodgers didn't inform him of the situation. "They're the boss, and I'm just a piece of meat. I'm in good shape and I want to show everybody I can still play and run, that I'm the kind of player I used to be. But if they want to trade me, it's okay. I don't care anymore. And they don't have to call me if they do. I'll probably change my number so they can't call me."[12] Guerrero's tirade probably spelled finis to his L.A. career. He would be gone before the summer was over.

Jeff Hamilton was unhappy over the possibility of Guerrero moving to third base, leaving him out in the cold. The 24-year-old infielder, who had been in the Dodgers organization since 1983, seemed to be ticketed for a return to Albuquerque, a move he would rather not make. He said he would rather be traded than go back to the minors.

On the field, L.A. ran up a string of six straight wins before tasting defeat at the hands of the Houston Astros at Kissimmee on March 10, a 7–6 heartbreaker that ended when Bill Brennan balked in the winning run in the bottom of the ninth. Ralph Bryant had given the Dodgers a temporary 6–5 lead in the top of the inning with a two-run shot off the right field wall. Then, the roof caved in. Lasorda's troops quickly righted the ship however, and ran off another six-game winning streak with wins over Baltimore, Atlanta, Boston, Montreal, and the New York Mets.

In the Baltimore game, won by L.A. 10–8, Rick Dempsey slammed a pinch-hit double during a five-run eighth inning rally, Mike Davis hit a 400-foot homer, and Kirk Gibson legged out a triple. Don Sutton gave up one run in three innings, but Alejandro Peña and Brian Holton were roughed up. L.A. blanked the Braves 2–0 behind the stellar pitching of Hershiser, Ramón Martínez, and Jesse Orosco. Franklin Stubbs, making his play to win the first base job, doubled in both runs in the first inning. The next day, the Dodgers dumped the Braves again in another tight pitchers duel, this one going L.A.'s way 3–2 in 10 innings. Danny Heep, coming off the bench, slammed a pinch-hit homer in the bottom of the ninth to pull Lasorda's cohorts back from the brink of defeat to tie the game at two-all. Ralph Bryant singled in the game-winner an inning later. Mickey Hatcher, ever one to take advantage of a comic situation, came to the plate late in the game and with dusk falling, with a flashlight taped to his batting helmet. Atlanta manager Chuck Tanner just smiled and said, "There's no rule against that. And if he gets a hit with it on, he'll use it for all 162 games." One of the Dodgers players later taped a photo of Hatcher and the flashlight to his locker with the astute observation, "The lights are on, but nobody's home."[13]

The Big Blue Machine won two games on March 14, one, their second consecutive 10-inning, 3–2 game against the Boston Red Sox at home, and the other, a 6–1 victory over the Montreal Expos in San Juan, Puerto Rico. Tim Leary, looking sharp after his winter sojourn to Mexico, held the powerful Red Sox to four base hits during five scoreless innings of work in Vero Beach. José González saved the game for the Dodgers with a diving catch in the top of the ninth inning, and Mike Marshall hit an 0–2 pitch into left field to plate the winning run in the 10th. In San Juan, Fernando Valenzuela matched Leary's effort by zipping the Expos for five innings in the Dodgers rout. Tracy Woodson homered, doubled, and drove in three runs for L.A., and Bryant also contributed a homer to the attack. The win was not without its downside however. The team lost Mike Davis, who stepped into a hole in the outfield before the game, suffered a sprained ankle, and had to be carried off the field. He missed most of the next two weeks, playing in four of the last five games, and missing one game after receiving a shot for bursitis in his left shoulder. His Grapefruit League totals showed just 3 hits in 28 at-bats.

The L.A. brigade fell to the Expos 7–1 in Bayamon, Puerto Rico, on March 15, when Alejandro Peña was touched up for three runs in five innings, and then left the game with a pulled groin muscle. The game might have turned out differently except for the fact that the Dodgers played like Little Leaguers in the field. Catcher Alex Treviño committed three throwing errors, including an overthrow of third base on a botched squeeze play, with each error leading to an Expos run. He was also charged with a passed ball, allowing a fourth run to score. A fifth run came across when Ralph Bryant played a fly ball into a home run when the ball popped out of his glove and over the fence. The comedy of errors was topped off when Steve Sax, thinking there were three out, flipped the ball to the umpire instead of completing, what would have been, an inning-ending double play. In a postscript to the game, Alex Treviño was released on April 1, with Rick Dempsey winning the battle as Scioscia's backup.

The Dodgers lost their second straight game when they were unceremoniously dumped by the Kansas City Royals 10–2. And, once again, shoddy fielding was a determining factor in the loss. Right fielder Mike Marshall booted two balls in the seventh inning, and the Royals capitalized on the miscues by tallying 6 runs to convert a close 2–1 Kansas City lead into an 8–1 laugher. Orel Hershiser, who was touched up for two runs in four innings, took the loss.

Once again, Lasorda's resilient crew bounced back. They defeated the Philadelphia Phillies 6–5 on St. Patrick's Day before a raucous sellout crowd at Holman Stadium. Wearing green hats to celebrate the holiday, the L.A. crew opened up a 5–0 lead in the opening stanza on consecutive base hits by Sax, Griffin, Gibson, Guerrero, Marshall, and Shelby, but Dodgers starter Tim Belcher gave three of the runs back in his five innings of work, and Jesse Orosco yielded the tying run in the ninth when José González, trying to haul down a long fly ball, crashed into the chain link fence in center field, flattening the fence, and knocking the ball out of his glove and over the fallen fence for a home run. Kirk Gibson also flattened the fence earlier in the game, after making a sensational catch. Orosco became the winning pitcher when Mike Devereaux singled in the bottom of the ninth. After the game, the talented southpaw reliever just shrugged when reporters asked him about his 7.20 ERA. "I'm not worried, I've never had a spring with an ERA under seven, I'm about to turn it on."[14]

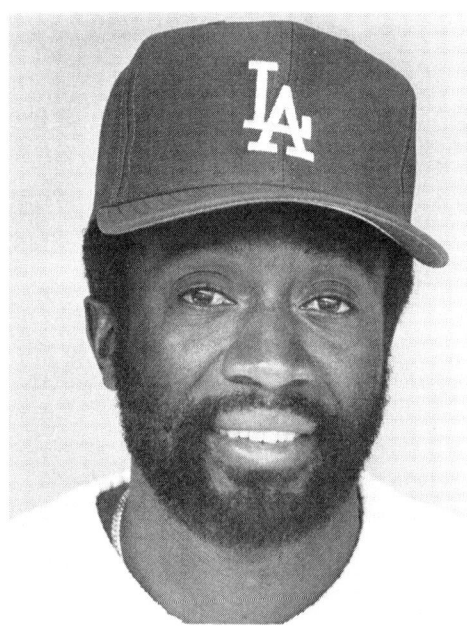

Alfredo Griffin, a slick fielding shortstop obtained in a trade with the Oakland Athetics, gave the Dodgers stellar infield defense (courtesy of Los Angeles Dodgers).

Lasorda's edition of Murderers Row jumped all over Minnesota the next day for a 12–0 rout that was mercifully called after 6½ innings because of rain. Righthander Tim Leary added another five scoreless innings to his fine spring, lowering his ERA to a microscopic 0.56. The Dodgers put the game out of reach in the second inning when they crossed the plate eight times, sparked by Shelby's bases loaded triple. The win gave Los Angeles a 14–3 record, their highest total since 1977 when they went 17–7, and they still had 15 games to play, essentially assuring themselves of a new spring training victory total. The game was costly for the Dodgers however, and may have ended the career of journeyman outfielder Len Matuszek. The big, hard-hitting left-hander was trying to come back after a season ending injury in 1987 when he re-injured his ankle at third base. "This might be the last chapter," he said. "I really tested it. I just can't do it. You have to run in this game and the bottom line is I just can't run."[15] Matuszek, who earlier in the game had cracked a three-run homer, subsequently retired.

Los Angeles suffered another serious blow to its roster when right-hander Ken Howell, recovering from off-season shoulder surgery, was unable to pitch in a simulated game because his shoulder was still not ready. Eventually Howell went on the disabled list and, except for a brief three-week period in late May and early June, and on September 28, when he pitched in a total of 4 games, he sat out the season.

With each Grapefruit League game, the team grew closer together, and their clubhouse chemistry improved. Mike Marshall and Jeff Hamilton were getting more playing time so they were happy. Gibson and Orosco had patched up their differences, and were focused on the job at hand. And Gibson came to appreciate the value of the off-field antics of Mickey Hatcher. The former Tigers outfielder was the catalyst that made the engine run on the field, and the players followed his lead and went all-out on every play. Mickey Hatcher and Rick Dempsey were the leaders of the Stuntmen, who provided relief in the dugout and in the clubhouse. Gibson, after watching the team in action for three weeks, said, "There's talent here, no question. How much character and how well it all comes together, I don't know yet."[16] Hatcher's locker-room antics gave the team a badly needed respite from the tension of the game, and would provide valuable comic relief during the pressure-packed pennant race to come. He kept the other players on their toes, with his propeller-topped beanies, and his mysterious bag of tricks. He kept two bins full of hats near his locker, one bin full of rally hats and another bin full of jinx hats, and he often reached into one bin or another prior to a game or during a game as the situation warranted. Occasionally he wore a jinx hat in the dugout to jinx the opposition if the game was going poorly, and at other times he wore a rally hat to spur his team into action. "He has a million hats," Dodgers catcher Mike Scioscia said, "and sooner or later he'll wear every one of them. He's got Army helmets, Stuntmen hats, batting helmets with pinwheels ... I don't think I've ever seen Mickey without a hat in his leisure time." Scott Ostler reported, "Hatcher loves his hats so much that when he goes to the barbershop for a haircut, he'll take along an old hat or two that are getting raggedy or threadbare and ask the barber to give the hats a trim, too." Even Kirk Gibson came to understand the team's loose cannon, and to appreciate his contribution to the pennant drive. "You may think he's funny, but he really isn't trying to be. That's just him." Hatcher reminisced on his life and his philosophy. "I've always been loose. I've always had fun. Things like running to first base on walks, that's something I always did. I've always played like that, hustled out to my position, that kind of thing. I know I'll never be a superstar. I just wanted people to know me for hustling, playing hard. You have to try not to let the pressures of the game get to you. A lot of times, this game gets tough. When guys are taking O-fers, you find a lot of them moving down the bench, further and further away from the manager, trying to climb in a corner and hide. My philosophy is not to let 'em hide. I want to get a relationship with a player where I can joke around with them, help them build their confidence back, so when things go bad they can count on me for a little laugh here and there. I hate to see a player make a big error, but he comes in the dugout and everyone just ignores him. You have to give him some encouragement or make a rude joke."[17]

Los Angeles ran into some rough times over the last two weeks of spring training, but they captured seven of their last 15 games, showed a strong balance between hitting and pitching, and finished the pre-season relatively healthy. They dropped three straight between March 19–21, dropping a 4–3 decision to Montreal, an 11–5 beating at the hands of the New York Mets, and a 9–4 loss to Philadelphia. In the Montreal game, Fernando Valenzuela proved he was only human by allowing his first runs of the year, two solo homers in six innings. Third base hopeful Tracy Woodson hit a three-run homer to win the B game 3–2, and Don Sutton was touched up for both runs in five innings of work. The March 20 game against the Mets was nationally televised, and did not show Lasorda's cohorts in their best light. Davey Johnson's sluggers hammered Orel

Hershiser for five runs in the top of the first inning and coasted to the victory. The next day, L.A. jumped out to a 4–1 lead, but Tim Belcher couldn't stand the prosperity and yielded all five Phillies runs in his five innings of work.

The Dodgers broke their losing streak against the Cincinnati Reds in Plant City when Mike Devereaux, battling for an outfield spot, singled in the eventual game-winner in the sixth inning, making a winner out of Tim Leary, who went the first $5\frac{2}{3}$ innings. Brian Holton escaped from a bases-loaded, one-out jam in the bottom of the eighth inning. The Dodgers clubhouse resounded with a Lasorda tirade after the game, resulting from the late arrival of Pedro Guerrero and Mariano Duncan to the park. The two players arrived four hours late for the game after Duncan suffered a migraine attack at the hotel. Dodgers trainer Bill Buhler told Duncan to stay in the hotel, but Guerrero also decided to stay at the hotel to take care of his friend. Later, after Duncan had recovered satisfactorily, the two players took a cab for the 40-mile trek to the park. They met in the clubhouse with Lasorda, apparently worked out their differences, and went to the dugout. Guerrero was then inserted into the Dodgers lineup as a pinch-hitter in the fifth inning and singled in the Dodgers' first run. After the game, reporters pressed Guerrero for details about the incident, and wouldn't accept his "no comment." The situation became heated between the reporter and Guerrero until manager Tommy Lasorda jumped into the fray and berated the men of the press for being so inconsiderate but, according to *Dodgers Dugout*, there seemed to be some unrest in Dodgerland.

> "Why don't they (management) stop protecting them (Duncan and Guerrero)?" asked one Dodger anonymously. But Fred Claire reacted sharply when asked if a double standard applied with Pedro. "We don't have two sets of rules," he said. He also didn't think that the dispute would have any long-term effect. "I don't see an incident like this pulling a team apart. We have to do all we can to pull together and I see this team coming together. Kirk Gibson would not criticize Guerrero specifically, but didn't defend his actions. "You're supposed to be here and there's never an excuse for not being here. It's your job. There's no excuse, barring a death in the family or something."[18]

Los Angeles dropped their next two games, 4–3 to Houston and 5–3 to the Boston Red Sox. The winds in Vero Beach contributed to the first loss as two, two-run homers, off Don Sutton, were assisted by the strong breeze. Steve Sax pounded out three base hits for the Dodgers, extending his hitting streak to 16 games. In the Red Sox game, Valenzuela was rocked for all five Red Sox runs in five innings. Jay Howell, rounding into form, threw two shutout innings, and Jesse Orosco fanned the side in the eighth.

Orel Hershiser got the Dodgers back on track on the 25th, tossing six shutout innings in a 4–0 whitewashing of the Atlanta Braves, the Dodgers' second shutout of the spring. Mike Marshall and Danny Heep hit dingers for Lasorda's troops. Tim Belcher bounced back from his poor performance against Philadelphia to limit the Houston Astros to one hit in five shutout innings as the Dodgers prevailed by a 7–2 count. Sax, with two singles, was in the middle of two Dodgers rallies, and was supported by long home runs off the bats of Guerrero, off the center field fence, and Ralph Bryant, who drove a 410 foot shot to center field.

Los Angeles frittered away several opportunities against Montreal and dropped a tough 3–2 decision. The West Coast team put together three base hits in the first frame but failed to score when Sax was thrown out on an attempted steal. Tim Leary, continuing his fine springtime effort, threw six scoreless innings. L.A. rebounded against the Expos the next day, winning 8–5 when backup catcher Rick Dempsey lashed a two-out, bases-loaded double in the eleventh inning to send the big Holman Stadium crowd home happy. The Dodgers were trailing the Expos 5–4 as the bottom of the eleventh inning got underway, but pushed across four runs to steal the victory from Buck Rodgers' team. On the 29th, L.A. defeated the Kansas City Royals 10–9 when former Dodgers pitcher Ted Power walked in the winning run in the bottom of the tenth inning. Jeff Hamilton hammered a three-run homer in the ninth inning to tie the game before Power's collapse. Fernando Valenzuela, who had gotten off to such a sensational start early in the spring, was pounded for seven big runs, increasing his futility index to 12 runs and 17 base hits allowed in his last eleven innings of work. In the Dodgers' final home game of the spring, they dropped a 6–1 lackadaisical effort to Montreal. Pedro Guerrero accounted for the Dodgers' only run with a homer. Hershiser, in his last warmup before the regular season opener, gave up single runs in each of the first three innings before settling down to throw four shutout innings. Sax, Scioscia, and Marshall all had doubles for L.A.

Following an off day, the Dodgers finished their Grapefruit League schedule with their usual three-game Freeway Series against the California Angels and rookie manager Cookie Rojas. Kirk Gibson was back in the lineup for L.A. after missing two games with a pulled quad.

The Dodgers finished their spring training schedule with a record of 21–11, a vast improvement over their 1987 record of 12–15 that pretty much mirrored their regular season performance. The 21 victories represented the most victories ever in Los Angeles Dodgers history, and their .656 winning percentage was the highest winning percentage since 1977. Over the years since 1958, there has been no correlation between spring training records and the performance of the team during the regular season. Still, it's always nice to finish the pre-season schedule on an optimistic beat. Some of the encouraging batting and pitching performances during the Grapefruit League games included:

Mike Devereaux who hit a resounding .414 in 21 games.

Jeff Hamilton who hit .405 with 2 home runs and 7 RBIs in 37 at-bats.

Danny Heep who scorched the ball at a .490 clip with 2 homers and 6 RBIs in 49 at-bats.

Mike Marshall who hit .366 with 2 homers and 12 RBIs in 82 at-bats.

Steve Sax who hit .404 with 23 runs scored in 89 at-bats.

Two of the new players, including Alfredo Griffin who hit .325 in 83 at-bats and Kirk Gibson who hit .291 with 1 home run and 10 RBIs in 55 at-bats.

Orel Hershiser who went 2–3 on the mound with a fine earned run average of 2.40.

Tim Leary who, following his excellent winter in Mexico, led the Dodgers staff in Vero Beach with a 3–0 record and a 1.71 ERA and struck out a team-high 22 batters in 32 innings while issuing just 6 bases on balls.

Don Sutton who went 2–0 with a 3.24 ERA.

New pitchers Jay Howell who pitched 10⅔ innings with a perfect 0.00 ERA, and Jesse Orosco who went 3–0.

Many of the Dodgers hopefuls, such as Mike Devereaux, José González, Mariano Duncan, Chris Gwynn, and Tracy Woodson, were optioned to Albuquerque as spring training drew to a close, but outfielder Ralph Bryant, at his request, was sold to the Chunichi Dragons of the Japanese Central League. The 26-year-old Bryant, who had batted .300 with a league-leading 31 home runs for San Antonio in the Texas League in 1984, had impressed Dragons' management enough with the towering home run he hit against them in the March 3 exhibition game that they signed him to a $200,000 contract.

Manager Tommy Lasorda, in an attempt to get the big bats of Pedro Guerrero, Mike Marshall, Kirk Gibson, and Mike Davis, all into the lineup, decided to play Marshall at first base instead of Franklin Stubbs, and Guerrero at third base in place of Jeff Hamilton, even though that strategy had failed five years earlier. His projected opening day lineup was:

C Scioscia
P Valenzuela
1B Marshall
2B Sax
SS Griffin
3B Guerrero
LF Gibson
CF Shelby
RF Davis

As opening day approached, two key players that general manager Fred Claire and manager Tommy Lasorda were counting on to carry the Los Angeles team to the promised land, Jesse Orosco and Jay Howell, looked like money in the bank. Orosco, a 31-year-old relief pitcher from Santa Barbara, California, was signed to a professional baseball contract by the New York Mets in 1978 and spent the next ten years in their organization, including eight years with the big club. The crafty 6', 2", 185-pound southpaw possessed a good moving fastball, a devastating slider, and a changeup, and he was a workhorse from day one. He appeared in 50 or more games every season from 1982 through 1987 with the New York Mets and, during his last five years, he was their bullpen ace, saving from 17 to 31 games every year. He compiled a 39–25 won-loss record, with earned run averages between 1.47 and 2.73, from 1983 through 1986, before experiencing an off-season in 1987. For some reason, Mets manager Davey Johnson lost faith in his closer in 1987 and turned the duties over to Roger McDowell and Randy Myers, leaving Orosco confused and dispirited. "There was a real cold war between Orosco and Johnson," Orosco's agent said. "Johnson wouldn't talk to him and I had to mediate." Orosco added, "It definitely wasn't a good situation for me to pitch under. I had no role. I didn't know whether I was going to be used long or short. When you aren't sure, you just have to make the most of it. If the Dodgers tell me what my role is, I'll make the most of it."[19] Fred Claire was hoping that the talented southpaw would return to his pre–1987 level when he was one of the top relief pitchers in the major leagues. His greatest year was 1986 when he was 8–6 with 21 saves and a 2.33 ERA during the regular season, and 3–0 with 2 saves in the post-season. In the NLCS, Orosco pitched in four of the six games, with a 3–0 record and a 3.38 ERA. He was the winning pitcher in game 6, pitching the final three innings of the sixteen-inning pennant clincher. A rapidly tiring Orosco was touched up for two runs in the bottom of the sixteenth inning but, with the tying and winning runs on base, he reached back one last time and put a back-door slider past Kevin Bass for the game-ending strikeout. He also pitched in four games in the World Series against the Boston Red Sox, with a perfect 0.00 ERA and 2 saves, including a perfect two innings in the world championship's seventh game.

Jay Howell was another matter. A hard-throwing, 6', 3", 220-pound righthander, Howell had a checkered eight-year career in the major leagues with the Reds, Cubs, Yankees, and Athletics. He had brief flashes of brilliance out of the bullpen with 61 saves between 1985 and 1987, but inconsistency and frequent arm problems made him a big question mark. He appeared in 61 games for the New York Yankees in 1984, pitching 104 innings and compiling a 9–4 record with 7 saves and a 2.69 ERA. The following season, with the Oakland Athletics, the two-time all-star won 9 games, lost 8, and saved 29, with a 2.85 ERA. Two injury-plagued seasons followed and, although he saved a total of 32 games during that period, he was sidelined for more than 16 weeks with various arm problems, including bone chips in his elbow. Once again, the Dodgers were expecting a complete recovery and were counting on Howell to be the closer they so desperately needed. According to the big right-hander, he was ready and able. "If you have questions about my arm, don't worry. I carried my wife's luggage to the airport today. If you don't think that is a big deal, you should see what she carries for two days."[20]

5

A FAST START

During the off-season, the baseball rules committee decided that the strike zone in use in the major leagues gave the hitters an unfair advantage. The official strike zone was from the armpits to the top of the knees but, in actual practice, the umpires usually called pitches above the belt balls. The rules committee, with the agreement of the Players Union and the owners, instituted a new strike zone that was identified as the area midway between the top of the shoulders and the top of the belt to the top of the knees. Although the new strike zone was officially smaller than the old strike zone, the general feeling was that the umpires would now call the high strike. The change didn't sit well with the hitters, naturally, who said it would be confusing for them since they were always told to lay off any pitch above the belt because it would be called a ball, and now they would have to swing at those high pitches. Pitchers, on the other hand, were looking forward to working with the new strike zone, hoping to improve on the ERAs that had reached 4.08 in the National League and 4.46 in the American League in 1987.

As opening day approached, baseball experts around the country, primarily from the media, after visiting major league spring training camps and reviewing teams' off-season player transactions, made their customary predictions as to where the teams would finish in their respective divisions, as well as who would win the National and American League pennants, and who would emerge as the ultimate world champion. Not many experts, it seemed, were overly impressed by the Dodgers' off-season machinations as they generally picked the West Coast entry to finish anywhere from third to fifth place in the National League Western Division pennant race, with most of the experts predicting another fourth place finish for Lasorda's charges. No one saw them winning the pennant, which was not surprising. After all, they had finished fourth in 1987 with a 73–89 won-loss record, and it was questionable how much they had improved their chances in the off-season compared to their opponents. *The Sporting News* picked the Dodgers to finish fourth behind San Francisco, Cincinnati, and Houston.

The 1987 division winners were Minnesota and Detroit in the American League and San Francisco and St. Louis in the National League. The Twins dumped the Tigers in five games to win the American League pennant and the Cardinals took the measure of the Giants in seven games to claim the National League crown. The World Series also went seven games with Minnesota edging St. Louis 4–2 in the finale behind the outstanding pitching of Frank Viola and Jeff Reardon. Viola recorded a 2–1 record in the Series while Kirby Puckett led the Twins' attack with a .357 average. The *Sports Illustrated* experts predicted the 1988 winners to be the Boston Red Sox and the Oakland Athletics in the American League and the New York Mets and the San Francisco Giants in the National League. The *Sporting News*' psychics gave the American League Eastern Division edge to the New York Yankees and the Western Division edge to the Kansas City Royals. They agreed with the *Sports Illustrated* experts that the Mets and Giants were the teams to beat in the National League.

The general consensus at *The Sporting News* was that the Yankees had strengthened themselves with the addition of slugger Jack Clark, who had 36 homers and 106 RBIs for the Cardinals in 1987, while the defending Eastern Division champion Detroit Tigers lost their sparkplug, Kirk Gibson, to free agency. The Tigers, in fact, were predicted to be in a free fall to fifth place. Kansas City, who had the league's best starting pitching rotation with Bret Saberhagen, Mark Gubicza, and Chuck Leibrandt, added 16-game winner Floyd Bannister in a trade with the Chicago White Sox, drawing the experts to their corner. *Sports Illustrated* experts felt that the Boston Red Sox, with the best starting pitching staff in the east, led by Roger Clemens and Bruce Hurst, would be enough to hold off a New York Yankees charge. They liked the Oakland Athletics in the west after the A's acquired another big bat, Dave Parker, who had 26 home runs and 96 RBIs with Cincinnati, to go along with monstrous sluggers José Canseco and Mark McGwire. Canseco, a muscular 6', 3", 230-pound right-handed batter, blasted 31 home runs with 116 RBIs in 1987, and his teammate Mark McGwire set a major league rookie record by sending 49 balls into orbit, breaking the old record of Al Rosen by 12. The pitching staff, that was already impressive with Dave Stewart (20–13), Curtis Young (13–7), Steve Ontiveros (10–8), and Dennis Eckersley (6–8 with 16 saves), got even better with the acquisition of Bob Welch (15–9) from the Dodgers.

Both publications were unanimous in their selections of the New York Mets and the San Francisco Giants. The Mets, according to the experts, had the best starting rotation in the National League with Dwight Gooden (15–7), Ron Darling (12–8), Sid Fernandez (12–8), David Cone (5–6), and Bob Ojeda (3–5), as well as Roger McDowell (7–5 with 25 saves), and Randy Myers (3–6 with 6 saves), in the bullpen. *Sports Illustrated* noted "the New York Mets are the best team in the National League East, with speed, power, fine defense, and great pitching, a team with a surfeit of talent that almost — but not quite — justifies its insufferable attitude."[1] The San Francisco Giants, who won the division in 1987, improved themselves in the off-season with the acquisition of Brett Butler, a 30-year-old speedster who swiped 33 bases for Cleveland in 1987 while batting .295 with 96 runs scored. Butler was also an outstanding defensive center fielder who had led the American League in fielding percentage in 1985.

Many baseball experts predicted that the Boston Red Sox would meet the New York Mets in the World Series, with the Mets capturing the crown in another down-to-the-wire battle.

Sports Illustrated had the Dodgers relegated to a fourth place finish, behind San Francisco, Houston, and Cincinnati, while *The Sporting News* saw them as no better than fifth, trailing San Diego as well as the four teams listed above. *SI*'s staff noted L.A.'s penchant for making errors, and with Guerrero at third, Sax at second, and Gibson and Davis in the outfield, the outlook for an improved defense was not good. They did say that the lineup, with Guerrero, Gibson, Marshall, Davis, Shelby, and Scioscia, might be the "most devastating batting order in the league — if everyone stays healthy. That's a big if, considering the medical histories of Marshall (back), Guerrero (knee), Griffin (thumb), and Gibson (wrist, ankle, and knee, not to mention hurt feelings)."[2] *The Sporting News* voiced concern about L.A.'s many question marks, such as, "Who plays third? Who plays second? Who's in right? Who plays short if Alfredo Griffin's thumb is still ailing? Who's in the starting rotation? How are Jesse Orosco and Jay Howell, etc.?"[3]

Opening day, April 4, was a mixed bag for the contenders, with the Mets and Giants victorious in the National League and the A's and the Yankees, who opened on the 5th, victorious in the American League. The Red Sox were edged by the Detroit Tigers, 5–3 in ten innings. The Mets took the measure of the Montreal Expos by the score of 10–6 with Darryl Strawberry going 4 for 4 with 2 homers. Oakland blanked Seattle 6–0 as Bob Welch scattered nine hits for the win, and the Yankees defeated Minnesota 5–3 on a two-run double by Rickey Henderson in the seventh inning. The start to the Dodgers' season was disappointing as they were beaten by the San Francisco Giants by a 5 to 1 score in Dodger Stadium. The day began on a high note for Dodgers fans when four of yesterday's stars, Steve Garvey, Ron Cey, Dusty Baker, and Reggie Smith, assembled at the mound and simultaneously threw four first pitches to four catchers. The euphoria continued when the bell sounded as Steve Sax hit the first pitch of the season into the left field stands for a home run, pumping the air with his right arm as he circled the bases, but shortly thereafter the game got out of hand. The defending National League champions jumped on Fernando Valenzuela for two runs in the top of the third inning, and added three more in the fourth, two of them coming on a triple by Brett Butler, who led the Giants' attack with three base hits. The Dodgers made two errors in the game, bringing back painful memories of 1986 and 1987. Still, the feeling was upbeat in the Dodgers' clubhouse. Mike Scioscia excused the errors as being the result of overaggressiveness, not sloppy fielding, and Kirk Gibson just shrugged and said, "Let's face it. We didn't play good. It may take us awhile to get going. This isn't the end of the world. Tomorrow is another day."[4]

L.A. got its second wind the following day when Orel Hershiser blanked San Fran 5–0, retiring the final 17 batters in succession. The Dodgers broke open a scoreless game with a single run in the bottom of the sixth on a single by Mike Scioscia, the Dodgers' first hit of the game, an error by Giants pitcher Kelly Downs on a pickoff throw, a balk, and a squeeze bunt by Hershiser. They iced the game with a four-spot in the eighth on two walks, a single by Scioscia and a double by Alfredo Griffin. Hershiser fanned six and walked two in his masterpiece. Lasorda's cohorts went on from there to run off five in a row, including a four-game sweep of the Atlanta Braves, to move into first place by ½ game. Los Angeles received a mild scare during the Atlanta series when general manager Fred Claire was carried from the team hotel on a stretcher, but the injury turned out to be nothing more than lower back spasms. Claire spent several days in the hospital before returning to the team as good as new.

The Stuntmen were called to action almost as soon as the season began. Danny Heep, one of the bench brigade, replaced center fielder John Shelby in the lineup when "T-Bone" was sidelined with an abdominal muscle pull on April 18. Mike Devereaux was recalled from Albuquerque to take Shelby's roster spot, and he shared the center field duties with Mike Davis during Shelby's absence. Devereaux, who had impressed the Dodgers brass by posting a .400 batting average in Grapefruit League games, was banging the ball to the tune of .395 with the Dukes at the time of his recall, with two homers and eleven runs batted in. The 5', 11", 185-pound southpaw swinging Heep took over in right field and scorched the ball at a .406 clip during Shelby's three-week absence.

The game of the eighteenth was won by the Dodgers 6–0 over the San Diego Padres, behind Tim Leary's impressive three-hitter, sprinkled with 11 strikeouts. The fireballing right-hander, who upped his record to 2–0, aided his own cause with a two-run single in the third inning. Steve Sax, who also batted in two runs, went two for three at the plate.

On April 23, after patiently waiting out three consecutive rainouts in Los Angeles and another one in the City by the Bay, Tommy Lasorda's Big Blue Machine defeated San Francisco 10–3 behind the pitching of Hershiser and the hitting of Alfredo Griffin and Mike Marshall. Hershiser hurled six innings, leaving for a pinch hitter in the top of the seventh, with the score deadlocked at one-all. The Dodgers ace had limited the Giants to four base hits, one of which was Will Clark's fifth home run of the young season in the fourth inning, pulling his team into a tie. L.A. made a winner out of Hershiser, upping his record to 4–0, when Griffin slugged a bases loaded triple in the big seventh.

Two innings later, after San Fran had narrowed the Dodgers lead to 5–3, big Mike Marshall put the game out of reach. Singles by Scioscia, Anderson, and Hatcher plated one run for the visitors, and then after a sacrifice by Griffin put runners on second and third, Giants manager Roger Craig ordered Guerrero walked intentionally, bringing up Marshall. The big right-handed slugger responded with a long grand-slam home run over the left field fence at Candlestick Park. The same situation had occurred in 1987, and that time Marshall ran around the bases clapping his hands and then, when he reached home plate, he stopped, pointed a finger at Craig and yelled at him. This time he was greeted at home by Mickey Hatcher who escorted him back to the dugout to prevent a repeat of that scene. Marshall just laughed when he was reminded of his previous actions. "All I can say is I ran around the bases today the way I always do. I was wrong what I did last year and I've said that before. That's not the type of player I am."[5] The victory, coupled with a 4–0 Houston defeat at San Diego, gave the Dodgers a one game lead in the National League Western Division. The next night, with the Padres shutting out Houston again, this time by a 3–0 count, and the Dodgers blanking the Giants 4–0 behind Fernando Valenzuela, the lead was up to two games.

The Dodgers continued hot through April, finishing the month with a 13–7 record that left them just ½ game behind the front-running Houston Astros. Jesse Orosco impressed the Dodgers brass by saving three of the Dodgers' first six victories. Orel Hershiser went a scintillating 5–0 during the month, yielding only ten runs. The year 1988 was destined to go down in Los Angeles Dodger lore as "The Year Of Hershiser" as a result of his overpowering pitching. Jim Murray in the *Los Angeles Times* said it best.

> Orel Leonard Hershiser IV does not intimidate the batter, although his nine hit batsmen last year indicated it's not entirely a good idea to lean over the plate looking to get at the curveball when he's on the mound.
> Hershiser throws ground balls. This is not to say his curve bounces but that his "out" pitch is a roller to shortstop. He throws a sinker, or what we kids in the old neighborhood used to call the drop. This is a pitch you hit on the top and it does exactly what a golf ball hit on the top does—it rolls along the ground until it hits something, usually an infielder's glove.
> Hershiser also throws a heavy ball—as did Drysdale. That's a ball that comes up to the plate like a 16-pound shot. It can break your bat—and your wrist along with it—if you meet it squarely. Which you seldom do."[6]

Some of the Dodgers players did not enjoy as successful a month as Hershiser did. Kirk Gibson hit just .246 with 2 homers and ten runs batted in. Mike Davis was at .183 with no homers and two RBIs. Alfredo Griffin's average was a miniscule .192, but he had batted in thirteen runs, six of them coming on a bases-loaded triple and a bases-loaded double. And John Shelby checked in with a .171 average and one RBI. On the other end of the spectrum, Pedro Guerrero sizzled with a .369 average, two homers and fifteen RBIs, and

Mike Marshall was at .267 with one homer and eleven RBIs. The pitching was keeping the team afloat during the early days of the season. In addition to Hershiser, Tim Leary was at 2–1 and the bullpen had recorded a perfect eight for eight in save opportunities.

While the Dodgers and Astros were fighting it out for the supremacy of the National League Western Division, the pesky Pittsburgh Pirates were giving the New York Mets a run for their money and held a ½ game lead over Davey Johnson's club on May 1. The American League Eastern Division was a crapshoot as the new month began, with Cleveland leading New York by ½ game, Boston by 1 game, and Detroit by 1½ games. The Western Division was somewhat different. The Oakland Athletics, behind the slugging of José Canseco (eight homers) and Mark McGwire (six homers), and the pitching of Dave Stewart (6–0 with a 3.00 ERA) and Bob Welch (3–2), had raced to a 17–7 record, opening up a four-game bulge over the Chicago White Sox.

L.A.'s performance was up and down during the first three weeks of May. They dropped a game to the Cardinals in Dodger Stadium by a score of 9–0 on May 1 in an unusual game. The St. Louis starter was southpaw John Tudor, who was returning to active duty after suffering a shoulder injury and was restricted to seventy-five pitches by manager Whitey Herzog. Tudor had held the Dodgers without a hit for six innings, but he was not allowed to pursue his dream, having reached his pitch limit. Reliever Scott Terry was touched up for a single by Kirk Gibson in the bottom of the seventh for the Dodgers' only hit of the game. The next night, Tommy Lasorda's troops welcomed the Pittsburgh Pirates to the friendly confines, and promptly swept the Buccos by scores of 6–3, 14–6, and 8–5 to claim first place by 1½ games over the Astros, who were drubbed by Philadelphia 7–1 and New York 8–0. Don Sutton was touched up for three runs in 4⅔ innings in the opener but the bullpen came to the rescue once again, blanking the Bucs over the last 4⅓ innings and the Dodgers held on for the win. Tim Belcher was roughed up for five runs in five innings on May 3, but was the recipient of a sixteen-hit Dodgers attack led by Mike Marshall who had a double and two home runs in four at-bats, good for five RBIs. Mike Scioscia also chipped in with three base hits while Sax, Davis, and Guerrero had two each. Orel Hershiser went 6⅓ innings in the finale, yielding two runs, for his sixth consecutive victory. He left with a 7–2 lead, but Jay Howell struggled to preserve the lead, finally persevering 8–5. Kirk Gibson clubbed a two-run homer in the first inning to give the Dodgers a lead they never relinquished.

The West Coasters took 2 out of 3 from St. Louis, winning 10–2 behind Fernando Valenzuela's complete game effort and Mike Marshall's two hits, one a homer, and two RBIs. Kirk Gibson electrified the crowd by scoring all the way from first base on a bloop hit-and-run single by Pedro Guerrero. Alfredo Griffin hit his second bases loaded triple of the season. The Redbirds took game two 2–1. John Tudor and Tim Leary were almost unhittable, although

Orel Hershiser, getting warmed up for his spectacular season, went a perfect 5–0 in
April (author's collection).

neither one figured in the decision. Leary gave up one run in seven innings, and Tudor, who threw seven no-hit innings, lost his 1–0 lead in the eighth when L.A. scored on a single by Marshall and a two-out single by Sax. The Cardinals pushed over the game-winner against Jesse Orosco in the bottom of the ninth on an infield single by Willie McGee, a hit-and-run single by Tom Brunansky, and a sacrifice fly by Terry Pendleton. L.A. took the getaway game 12–6, routing St. Louis starter José DeLeón in a seven-run seventh inning that broke open a tight 4–2 game. Mike Davis went 4 for 6 on the day with a double, a triple, and three RBIs. L.A.'s lead was now 2½ games as Hal Lanier's erratic club lost two of three to Montreal.

Tommy Lasorda's boys defeated the Chicago Cubs 6–5 in fourteen innings on May 10, after waiting through a rainout in the ninth. Kirk Gibson provided the winning margin with a home run. Brian Holton won in relief. When Houston dropped a 5–2 decision to the New York Mets, the Dodgers held a nice three-game lead, but they couldn't stand prosperity, dropping five of the next eight games.

The game played in Dodger Stadium on May 14 had historic significance attached to it, but the significance was not obvious at the time. Don Sutton defeated the Philadelphia Phillies by the score of 3–2, yielding two runs, one unearned, in 5⅔ innings. Alejandro Peña and Jay Howell, who recorded his third save of the season, shut down the Philly attack over the final 3⅓ innings. For Sutton, who struck out one man and didn't walk any, it was his third win of the season and 324th, and final, win of his illustrious career. He would make nine more starts in Dodger Blue, going 0–3, before retiring.

Philadelphia						Los Angeles				
Name	*Pos*	*AB*	*R*	*H*		*Name*	*Pos*	*AB*	*R*	*H*
Thompson	CF	4	1	1		Sax	2B	4	1	1
Bradley	LF	3	0	0		Davis	RF	4	1	2
Samuel	2B	4	0	1		Gibson	LF	3	0	0
Schmidt	3B	4	0	0		Guerrero	3B	2	0	1
Hayes	1B	4	0	2		Marshall	1B	4	1	1
Parrish	C	4	1	2		Shelby	CF	3	0	1
James	RF	4	0	2		Scioscia	C	3	0	0
Jeltz	SS	3	0	0		Griffin	SS	2	0	0
Young	PH	1	0	0		Sutton	P	2	0	0
Ruffin	P	2	0	1		Peña	P	0	0	0
G. Gross	PH	1	0	1		Heep	PH	1	0	0
Harris	P	0	0	0		J. Howell	P	0	0	0
Daulton	PH	1	0	0						
Totals		35	2	10				28	3	6

Philadelphia	0 0 1	0 0 1	0 0 0 — 2 — 10 — 1
Los Angeles	0 1 2	0 0 0	0 0 x — 3 — 6 — 2

Errors-Scioscia 2, Samuel
Doubles-Marshall, Parrish

Name	IP	R	ER	H	BB	SO
Philadelphia						
Ruffin (L 3-3)	6	3	2	5	2	1
Harris	2	0	0	1	0	1
Los Angeles						
Sutton (W 3-2)	5⅔	2	1	8	0	1
Peña	1⅓	0	0	1	0	2
J. Howell (Save 3)	2	0	0	1	0	4[7]

Los Angeles' lead was down to a mere ½ game over the Houston Astros on May 20 when they invaded New York to battle Davey Johnson's Mets, who held a 4½ game lead over the Pittsburgh Pirates. The red hot Mets swept L.A.'s best, three straight, to drop the stunned Californians 1½ games behind Houston. On Friday night, Sid Fernandez, the fireballing former Dodgers southpaw, bested Don Sutton 5–2. The next day, Dwight Gooden tossed a four-hitter at Lasorda's crew, winning 4–0. The game was particularly costly to the Dodgers, who lost their shortstop, Alfredo Griffin, after Gooden hit him with an inside fastball, breaking his right hand. Griffin went on the disabled list on May 27 and was lost to the team until July 25. The Mets completed the sweep on Sunday when David Cone upped his record to 6–0 with a 5–2 win. Dodgers starter Fernando Valenzuela didn't survive the second inning, being touched up for 3 runs in the opening stanza, and then knocked from the box during a two-run New York rally in the second. It was the shortest start of Fernando's career.

Once again L.A. fought back, winning five of their next six games to reclaim the top spot by 1½ games over the tenacious Astros. Tim Leary tossed a one-hitter at the Philadelphia Phillies on the 25th, winning 4–0. It was the best-pitched game of the year for the Dodgers. Leary, who upped his record to 4–3, struck out six and walked two in his masterpiece. Mike Scioscia gave Leary the lead with a two-run homer in the fourth inning, and Jeff Hamilton followed suit in the seventh to put icing on the cake.

Los Angeles					**Philadelphia**				
Name	*Pos*	*AB*	*R*	*HE*	*Name*	*Pos*	*AB*	*R*	*H*
Sax	2B	3	0	0	Thompson	CF	3	0	0
Davis	RF	4	0	0	Bradley	LF	4	0	0
Gibson	LF	3	0	0	Samuel	2B	4	0	0
Marshall	1B	4	1	1	Parrish	C	3	0	0
Shelby	CF	4	1	1	Schmidt	3B	3	0	0
Scioscia	C	4	1	1	James	RF	3	0	0
Hamilton	3B	4	1	2	Daulton	1B	3	0	1

Name	Pos	AB	R	HE
Anderson	SS	3	0	0
Leary	P	4	0	0
Totals		33	4	5

Name	Pos	AB	R	H
Jeltz	SS	2	0	0
Palmer	P	1	0	0
Ritchie	P	0	0	0
G. Gross	PH	1	0	0
Totals		27	0	1

Los Angeles	0 0 0	2 0 0	2 0 0 — 4 — 5 — 2	
Philadelphia	0 0 0	0 0 0	0 0 0 — 0 — 1 — 1	

Errors— Hamilton, Anderson, Daulton
Doubles— Shelby
Home Runs— Scioscia, Hamilton

Name	IP	R	ER	H	BB	SO
Los Angeles						
Leary (4–3)	9	0	0	1	2	6
Philadelphia						
Palmer (0–4)	7	4	4	5	1	6
Ritchie	2	0	0	0	2	3^8

The game the following day was one of the most important games of the season, with the Dodgers and Phillies battling for nine bloody innings before the Dodgers prevailed by a 10–8 score. Steve Sax had a career day at the plate with a double and two home runs, the only time in his career he would hit two homers in one game. L.A. held a 4–1 lead after 5½ innings but Lee Elia's team pushed over two runs off Dodgers starter Don Sutton in the sixth to trim the lead to 4–3. After L.A. added a run in the top of the seventh, the Phils came right back with a three-spot to take a 6–5 lead. Both teams scored two runs in the eighth inning, and Lasorda's never-say-die crew pushed over three more runs in the ninth for the win. Dave Anderson also had three hits for L.A., while Shelby, Hatcher, and Hamilton had two each. Jay Howell, with two scoreless innings, earned the victory. The win gave the Dodgers a ½ game lead over the Houston Astros, a lead they would never relinquish. After games of May 31, the Los Angeles record stood at 27–20, putting them in a flatfooted tie with Houston for first place in the National League Western Division. Orel Hershiser was setting the pace on the mound with a 7–2 record. He was followed by Tim Belcher at 3–2, Tim Leary at 4–4, and Don Sutton at 3–3. Fernando Valenzuela was no better than 3–5. The bullpen was contributing to the Dodgers success. Jesse Orosco had two wins against a single loss and had saved 4 games. Alejandro Peña and Jay Howell had identical records of two wins, one loss, and three saves. Brian Holton was one of the unsung heroes for the Dodgers in the early going. The middle-relief pitcher pitched in 14 of the Dodgers' first 46 games with two wins, one loss, and a 1.77 ERA. Pedro Guerrero carried the

Steve Sax had his only two-homer day on May 26, sparking the Dodgers to a 10–8 victory over the Philadelphia Phillies (courtesy of Los Angeles Dodgers).

big bat for Tommy Lasorda's sluggers, hammering the ball at a .317 clip with three homers and 26 RBIs. Mike Marshall was batting just .245, but he had six homers and 26 RBIs. Kirk Gibson had a timely .289 average with eight home runs and 26 RBIs. Steve Sax had pitched in with a .279 average, 28 runs scored and 12 stolen bases. And the famous Stuntmen were doing a sensational job filling in for the regulars. Mickey Hatcher was hitting .342, Dave Anderson was at .317, Rick Dempsey was at .281, and Danny Heep was at .333. For the Astros, Bob Knepper was beaten by the St. Louis Cardinals 9–7 for his first loss of the season after 6 wins. Nolan Ryan's record stood at 5–2, Jim Deshaies was at 4–2, and Mike Scott was at 6–1 after he also lost his first decision of the year. Glenn Davis, Houston's 6', 3", 210-pound right-handed cleanup hitter, had eleven home runs to his credit to pace the Houston attack

Experienced observers, as well as rival managers, kept waiting for the Dodgers to collapse, but they waited in vain. The Dodgers didn't collapse. They bent as the injuries mounted, but they never broke under the astute handling of manager Tommy Lasorda. As Stanley Cohen noted, "[The Dodgers] did not seem to have enough to keep them up there. Their hitting was still weak; they had little power. Their lineup was a patchwork affair that changed from day to day. But they remained a model of consistency, never losing more than three games in a row. Tommy Lasorda maneuvered his players with the dexterity of a magician and the foresight of a chess master."[9]

Mike Marshall had six home runs and 26 RBIs as May came to an end (author's collection).

In the other races, the Mets, Yankees, and A's were all making their supporters happy. Davey Johnson's club held a 4½ game lead over the Pittsburgh Pirates and were on the verge of blowing the race wide open. David Cone at 7–0, Ron Darling at 6–3, and Dwight Gooden at 8–1 were dominant on the mound. Gooden had run off eight straight wins before dropping a 5–2 decision to the San Francisco Giants on May 26. The game was tied at 1–1 after six innings, but Roger Craig's boys jumped on the Mets' ace for four runs in the top of the seventh, paced by Brett Butler's two-run double. The Mets hitting corps was led by Darryl Strawberry, who had eleven home runs, and Kevin McReynolds with five homers.

In the American League, the Yankees held a slim 2½ game lead over the Cleveland Indians in the Eastern Division behind the pitching of John Candelaria (7–2) and rookie Al Leiter (4–2), and the hitting of Dave Winfield (eleven home runs), Jack Clark (nine home runs), and Don Mattingly (four home runs). Both Winfield and Mattingly were stroking the ball at a plus .300 clip. The Boston Red Sox, under manager John McNamara, were bogged down in fifth place, seven games out of first. Roger Clemens at 8–2 and Bruce Hurst at 6–2 were the lone bright lights in Beantown. The rest of the pitching staff was in a shambles. The Oakland Athletics had opened up a huge nine game lead over the defending world champion Minnesota Twins in the Western Division, and were threatening to turn the race into a rout. Bob Welch at 8–2, Dave Stewart at 8–3, Storm Davis at 4–2, and Dennis Eckersley with 16 saves led the mound corps, while José Canseco (twelve home runs), Mark McGwire (eleven home runs), and Dave Parker (six home runs) were destroying enemy pitching, although McGwire was in the middle of a frustrating slump. He failed to connect for the circuit for 21 games, from May 17 through June 9.

Tommy Lasorda's hired guns had their biggest offensive outburst of the season on June 3 when they destroyed the Cincinnati Reds by a 13–5 margin, racking up 22 base hits, all singles. Steve Sax and Mickey Hatcher, batting 1–2 in the lineup each pounded out five base hits to lead the Dodgers attack. Pedro Guerrero and Mike Marshall each went three for four in support of Sax and Hatcher. Fernando Valenzuela started the game for L.A., and had a 6–1 lead after two innings, but was ko'd in the third when the Reds pushed across three runs to narrow the lead to 6–4. Tim Crews, who pitched 2⅓ innings for the win, Alejandro Peña, and Tim Belcher held Cincinnati to one run over the last 6⅔ innings.

Guerrero, who had to leave the June 3 game with a pinched nerve in his neck, eventually joined Griffin on the DL. José González was recalled from Albuquerque to fill Guerrero's spot on the roster. At the time of his recall, González was hitting .329 with the Dukes, with four home runs and 17 RBIs. Two of the Stuntmen were quickly rushed into action, and they responded to the emergency as any good Stuntman should. Dave Anderson filled in admirably

Pedro Guerrero hit a lusty .298 with five homers and 35 RBIs prior to his trade to
St. Louis (author's collection).

at shortstop for Alfredo Griffin, and Jeff Hamilton took over at third base for
Guerrero without losing a beat. Anderson, in particular, played spectacular
ball during Griffin's absence. He covered the left side of the infield with an
aggressiveness not seen before. His fielding covered the complete range from
routine to sensational and, over his last 48 games as the Dodgers' first-string
shortstop, he committed only one error, with a string of 29 consecutive errorless games. Ironically, Alfredo Griffin would make an error in his first game
back, on July 26. In addition to his slick defense, the 6', 2", 185-pound Anderson hit a respectable .265 in 189 at-bats, with 17 runs batted in, causing his
teammates to rave about his performance. Mike Marshall led the plaudits. "I
think he's been our MVP. Without him, who knows where we'd be. He's been
outstanding defensively, making all the plays, and he's helped us a lot with his
bat. He waited a long time for his chance and he's made the best of it." Anderson himself said, "I always had confidence that I could do the job, it's just that
a lot of people never had confidence in me. Not Tommy though. He's always
been in my corner. He's let me know that I helped the team when I've played,
and I appreciate his confidence. All I needed was a chance to play."[10] For the
record, when Griffin went down, the Dodgers were in second place, ½ game
behind the Houston Astros, with a 22–16 won-loss record. When Griffin
returned, the Dodgers led Houston by 5½ games, having won 37 games against
25 losses while Anderson was patrolling the left side of the infield. Perhaps,

as Mike Marshall suggested, Dave Anderson was the team's MVP during those ten weeks. At the very least, he was a major contributor to the team's success.

Jeff Hamilton was almost as solid as Anderson. He gave Lasorda some outstanding defense at third base and batted .256 with 44 base hits in 172 at-bats and 19 RBIs. The performances of Anderson and Hamilton focused attention on the Stuntmen, the brainchild of the creative minds of Mickey Hatcher and Rick Dempsey. When asked how the idea of labeling the reserves "The Stuntmen" got started, Hatcher said, "In spring training, we were always on a different field than the starters, until game time when we had to go in and play for them after they'd played their five or six innings. And we just came up with the idea to call ourselves 'The Stuntmen,' which really came from the TV show 'The Fall Guy' and we started having competition among ourselves during practice. The coaches would hit us 25 ground balls each, and we'd see who would make the most plays without an error, and we'd be battling and calling each other names, and we built a closeness that has carried over into the season."[11] Dempsey added that the Stuntmen "are a group of guys who are the backup players of this ballclub. It's tough to sit on the bench and watch all the time. It starts to work on your mind. So we created this thing called 'The Stuntmen' just to keep the players (the reserves) into the game. To keep them mentally and physically alert for when their time comes (to contribute). And if you do that, like we did out of spring training, magical things begin to happen and they have been happening for the Dodgers so far.... I definitely see something happening here," he said. "We're forming a good ballclub. Individuals don't win pennants. *Teams* win pennants. And this team is coming together. We're pointed in the right direction. We're *a team*."[12]

On June 8, Los Angeles, after dropping two games to the Astros and seeing their lead shrink to a mere ½ game, defeated Hal Lanier's team 11–1 to maintain their hold on first place. Fernando Valenzuela hurled the complete game victory and, for the first time in his career, he didn't strike out a batter. The game was important because, prior to the game, Fernando's home record was a pathetic 0–4 with an 8.28 ERA. Conversely, the talented southpaw had a 3–1 mark on the road with a 1.85 ERA. After the game, answering questions about his arm, Fernando said, "It's nice to win anywhere. Fortunately, we scored a lot of runs and I was able to pitch more comfortably. My arm feels fine. I felt the same as the last five games. The difference is that we won."[13] Kirk Gibson and Mike Marshall hit back-to-back home runs in the third inning to pace the Dodgers. Marshall, who was back in right field after playing first base for two months, ripped two doubles and a home run, scoring three runs and driving in one and, after the game, he had this to say: "All the work at first base has taken a toll on my back, and I didn't want to take myself out of the lineup later on. I can stay healthy and really help the club by being in the outfield."[14]

Orel Hershiser gave the Big Blue Machine a little more breathing room the next day by tossing a five-hitter at the Astros, beating Nolan Ryan 4–2 for his eighth win of the season. He fanned 4 and walked 3 in his 8 innings of work before turning the ball over to Jay Howell to close it out for Howell's sixth save. L.A. tallied one run in the fourth inning, cutting a two-run Astros lead in half, and then pounded Nolan Ryan for three more in the fifth for their final total. Marshall, Shelby, Scioscia, and Hamilton accounted for the Dodgers RBIs, with Marshall's and Shelby's coming on doubles in the big fifth inning uprising. The Dodgers' "Bulldog" had good vibes about his team as the season neared the halfway mark. "I think we may be a legitimate pennant contender. Maybe by the All-Star break, once we go around the league and see what happens. We haven't been through a real bad slump. Hopefully we won't go through one, but a slump can show a team's character. Character develops and expands and shrinks and goes through stages, but I like the chemistry on this team a lot. It believes in itself, believes it can come back, believes it can hold a lead."[15]

John Shelby had one hit in three at-bats in Hershiser's game, but went oh for four in a 4–3 loss to San Diego the following night, ending his 24-game hitting streak, the longest in the majors in 1988. During the streak that began on May 14, "T-Bone" punched out 32 base hits in 89 at-bats, for a blistering .360 average. The offensive assault raised his season's batting average to .291.

Another Dodgers slump that saw them drop six of eight games to the Padres and Braves was not as serious as it could have been because Houston went three and five over the same stretch, so Lasorda's club still clung to a one game lead. The Dodgers pitching and hitting collapsed simultaneously during their eight game hiatus, as they were outscored 42 to 29. Fernando Valenzuela accounted for one of the Dodgers' victories, defeating the Atlanta Braves 5–4 on June 14, evening his record at 5–5. He hurled seven strong innings, before turning the game over to the bullpen, who preserved the win with Jay Howell tossing two shutout innings to earn his seventh save. Some, if not all, of Fernando's recent pitching problems, as noted above, may be traced to distractions in his personal life. His father, Avelino Valenzuela, was suffering from cancer at his home in Mexico, and was becoming progressively weaker. Fernando left Atlanta immediately after the game, flew to Los Angeles to get his family, and then went on to Mexico be with his father. Avelino Valenzuela died the next day.

The Dodgers, as was their wont, turned things around quickly, beginning on June 18, when Tim Belcher and two relievers blanked the San Diego Padres 3–0. It was Belcher's first win in five weeks. A two-run homer by Jeff Hamilton over the 370-foot marker in left field in the second inning and a solo shot by Kirk Gibson in the eighth provided L.A.'s firepower. Tommy Lasorda's warriors went on to win 10 of the last 12 games in June, including two of three in the Astrodome. Los Angeles entered Houston on June 27 with a 3½ game lead, and they threw rookie Shawn Hillegas against former 20-game winner

Joaquín Andújar, whose career was in its death throes. The Dodgers right-hander, pitching perhaps the best game of his career, upped his record to 2–0 by throttling the Astros on two hits over six innings, with three strikeouts and a single base on balls. Andújar also enjoyed one of the best days he had seen in three years, yielding just two runs, one earned, over 6⅓ innings, but he came away a 4–0 loser to Hillegas. Mike Scioscia gave the Dodgers a start with a fourth inning home run, and they added an unearned run in the seventh and two in the ninth on a double by Dempsey, a single by Sax, and another double by Stubbs. Alejandro Peña pitched two innings for his sixth save. Hal Lanier's club kept the Astros in the fight by edging the Big Blue Machine 4–3 the next night. Al Knepper won his eighth game against one loss, holding L.A. to three runs on just two hits over 8⅓ innings. Brian Holton, in relief of Don Sutton, who was touched up for two runs in five innings, took his second loss against three wins. Billy Hatcher hit a tie-breaking sacrifice fly in the sixth inning and Billy Doran homered in the eighth. Unfortunately for Houston, they had to face Orel Hershiser in the finale, and the Bulldog shut them out on two hits. He fanned six and walked one in his overpowering effort, winning 2–0 and running his record to 12–3. Nolan Ryan was almost as overpowering in defeat. He struck out ten men, walked four, and gave up four hits, in 7⅓ innings, but Mike Marshall was a thorn in his side all night. The Dodgers right fielder knocked in both runs, one after Ryan plunked him in the ribs with the bases loaded in the third inning and the other on a single in the eighth. Sax, who scored the first run, noted, "Marshall was laughing when he got to first base after being hit (with a 94 miles per hour fastball) by Nolan Ryan with the bases loaded. He wasn't laughing because the run scored, but because he was still alive."[16] Hershiser's victory brought L.A.'s June record to 17–11, giving them a season mark of 44–31, and opening up a 4½ game lead over the struggling Houston Astros, who continued to run hot and cold during the first three months of the season.

An important series in the American League Western Division on the June 24th weekend matched the top two contenders in Oakland, and Tom Kelly's Twins sent a message to the A's that they were in the race till the end. They pummeled the league-leaders 11–5 on Friday night, breaking open a 5–5 game with a six-run outburst in the top of the ninth inning. Gene Nelson took the loss after facing just one batter in the big inning, but it was Rick Honeycutt who took the brunt of the attack, failing to retire any of the four batters he faced. Gary Gaetti was the top sticker for Minnesota, going three for five with two home runs, and driving in four teammates. The A's evened the series at one game apiece with a 4–3 win in game two. Bob Welch pitched 7⅓ innings to record his ninth win of the season against four losses. José Canseco drove in all four Oakland runs, three of them coming on a home run in the third inning. Minnesota answered back with a furious barrage in the Sunday getaway game, embarrassing Tony LaRussa's Bashers to the tune of 11–0. They drove Matt

Young to cover in less than five innings and continued the cannonading against Gene Nelson, while Charlie Lea posted his fourth win of the season against three losses with six solid innings of work. Every member of the Twins' lineup contributed to the fifteen-hit attack, led by Al Newman, who was three for five, and Gary Gaetti, who was also three for five, with another home run and 3 RBIs. For the series, Gaetti went six for fourteen with three home runs and seven RBIs.

The pitching continued to be Tommy Lasorda's secret weapon in June, led by Orel Hershiser, who went 5–1 in the month. Tim Leary compiled a mark of 2–1 during the month, bringing his season record to six wins against five losses. Tim Belcher raised his won-loss record to 5–4, Don Sutton stood at 3–5 and Fernando Valenzuela was even at 5–5. Brian Holton was the most pleasant surprise of the season. He was doing a sensational job out of the pen, giving the Dodgers inning after inning of outstanding middle relief, holding the opposition scoreless while his teammates scratched for runs. The talented curveball artist, who almost saw his career go down the drain after he was hit in the elbow with a line drive off the bat of Marvel Wynne of San Diego in 1986, was saved when Dr. Frank Jobe transplanted a ligament from his wrist to his elbow. Kirk Gibson (fourteen homers, fourteen stolen bases), Mike Marshall (nine homers), and Steve Sax (nineteen stolen bases) continued to pace the offense with a timely balance of hitting, base running, and slugging.

The Houston Astros, who went 14–17 in June bringing their record to 41–37, were just 4½ games behind the dogged Dodgers. The top performers for Hal Lanier were Bob Knepper, who had eight victories against a single loss; Jim Deshaies, who stood at 5–5; Juan Agosto, who had a perfect 5–0 record; and Dave Smith with fourteen saves, on the mound. Nolan Ryan, after a disappointing 0–4 mark in June, stood at 5–6 for the season. The Astros' top batsmen were Glenn Davis with seventeen home runs, Kevin Bass with six homers, and Gerald Young with more than thirty stolen bases. The San Francisco Giants went 14–11 in June to bring their record to 39–37, moving them within one game of the Astros. Rick Reuschel (10–4), Mike Krukow (6–4), and Mike LaCoss (5–5) paced the mound corps, while Kevin Mitchell with eight home runs, Will Clark with eighteen home runs and on his way to a league-leading 109 RBIs for the season, and Brett Butler, on his way to a league-leading 109 runs scored, and forty-three stolen bases, were the sparkplugs who made the Giants run.

In other races, the leaders were the New York Mets in the National League Eastern Division, Detroit in the American League East and Oakland in the West. The Mets at 49–28 held a comfortable six-game lead over Jim Leyland's Pittsburgh Pirates. Dwight Gooden (10–4), Ron Darling (8–5), Randy Myers (11 saves), and Roger McDowell (4–1 with eight saves) led the pitching rich Mets. Darryl Strawberry with nineteen homers and more than a dozen stolen bases, Davey Johnson with fourteen homers, and Kevin McReynolds with nine homers gave the high-scoring New Yorkers more than enough offense to support their outstanding pitching staff.

Sparky Anderson's snarling Bengals roared through June with an 18–9 record to pass both Cleveland and New York, eventually settling atop the American League Eastern Division with 46 wins and 29 losses. Billy Martin's frustrated New York Yankees were 1½ games back after struggling to a 12–15 mark in June. Cleveland, who held down second place at the end of May, and who enjoyed a two-game cushion over Detroit at that time, lost a full eight games to the Tigers after going 10–17 in June. The Boston Red Sox won 14 games against 12 losses in June, ending the month six games behind the league leaders. In the American League Western Division, the Oakland Athletics' record stood at 48–29 after a lukewarm 13–14 June, and Minnesota, who had been given up for dead a month earlier, hung tough with a 17–10 record that shaved four games off the A's once insurmountable nine-game lead. Bob Welch, 2–2 in June, Dave Stewart, 2–3, and Storm Davis, 1–1, couldn't get untracked, although Dennis Eckersley was still able to save seven games. José Canseco carried the only reliable bat during the month, accounting for seven home runs. But Mark McGwire still couldn't find the range, hitting only two dingers in 27 games, giving him just thirteen homers in 77 games.

Los Angeles got off to a slow start in July, going four and five in their first nine games, but fortunately the All-Star break came just in time, giving the Dodgers three days to regroup. The Fourth of July game, between the Dodgers and the St. Louis Cardinals, was nationally televised from Dodger Stadium, and Dodgers manager Tommy Lasorda, always the entertainer, and always aware of the spotlight, enchanted the TV audience by wearing one of Mickey Hatcher's favorite hats, a batting helmet with a red, white, and blue spinner on the top. And it must have been a good luck charm because the Big Blue Machine came from behind to defeat the Redbirds 5–3. John Shelby hit a two-out, two-run single in the eighth inning to break a three-all tie. Kirk Gibson punched out three base hits, including a double and his fifteenth home run, and drove in L.A.'s first three runs. One of his RBIs came on a perfect squeeze bunt. Tim Belcher, filling in, in the bullpen while Jay Howell was on the DL, pitched the ninth inning for his third save of the year.

The All-Star game was played in Cleveland Municipal Stadium on Tuesday, July 12, with the American League winning 2–1. Frank Viola of Minnesota was the winning pitcher while Dwight Gooden of the New York Mets was saddled with the loss. Terry Steinbach, Oakland's catcher, hit a game-winning home run in the top of the fourth inning. Orel Hershiser, L.A.'s only All-Star representative, pitched a scoreless eighth inning for Whitey Herzog's team.

When play resumed on July 14, the Dodgers broke from the gate like caged tigers, running off a six-game winning streak, five of them against the Chicago Cubs. Tommy Lasorda unleashed his Big Blue Machine on the inhabitants of the Windy City in a doubleheader on the fourteenth and came away with two victories when Tim Leary out-pitched Rick Sutcliffe 1–0 in the opener, and home runs by Mike Marshall (a two-run shot in the first inning) and Kirk Gibson (two solo home runs in the third and eighth innings), powered the Dodgers past the third place Cubs in game 2. Leary pitched seven strong innings in game one, and Alejandro Peña threw two perfect innings, with three strikeouts, for his seventh save of the season. Sutcliffe, who fell to 7–7, posted a complete game. In the nightcap, Shawn Hillegas was given a 4–0 lead after 2⅓ innings but didn't survive the third inning as Chicago cut L.A.'s lead in half. Brian Holton was touched up for one run in 2⅓ innings, but came away with his fourth win against two losses when Crews and Howell blanked Don Zimmer's club over the last four innings, with Howell recording his ninth save of the season.

The Dodgers made it three in a row the next day as Fernando Valenzuela held the Cubs to two runs in seven innings, leaving with a 2–2 tie. He was followed to the mound by Alejandro Peña, the eventual winner, who pitched two scoreless innings, and Jesse Orosco, who recorded his sixth save with one shutout inning. The Western Division leaders scored the winning run in the top of the tenth inning on a two-out single by Tracy Woodson, one of the Stuntmen. Wins, numbers four and five, were recorded on the seventeenth after rain washed out the contest the previous day with the score deadlocked at 2–2 after eight innings. Orel Hershiser and Jamie Moyer battled through the rain, with Moyer going 5⅓ innings and Bulldog recording seven innings. Once again, the Stuntmen played a big part in the game as Tracy Woodson's sacrifice fly scored Mike Marshall with the tying run in the sixth inning. Lasorda's troops emerged victorious in both ends of the makeup doubleheader. In the lid-lifter, Tim Belcher recorded his sixth win of the season with six strong innings. The game was tied at one run apiece when Franklin Stubbs, pinch-hitting for Belcher, smashed a three-run homer to put his team on top by a 4–1 margin. Alejandro Peña earned his eighth save of the season with three shutout innings. L.A. won the nightcap by a 5–2 score to complete the five-game sweep. Once again, the two teams were deadlocked after six innings, with both teams scoring two early runs, the Cubs runs coming in the opening stanza off Shawn Hillegas, and the Dodgers' runs coming in the second inning off Al Nipper. Steve Sax hit a tie-breaking single for the Dodgers in the seventh inning and Jeff Hamilton stroked a two-run single in the ninth for the winning margin. Brian Holton, pitching one shutout inning, was rewarded with his fifth win against two losses, and Jay Howell gained save number ten by throwing a perfect ninth inning.

Los Angeles moved on to St. Louis next to do battle with Herzog's embattled Redbirds, who were ensconced in fifth place in the Eastern Division, 16½ games behind the high flying New York Mets. The Dodgers and Cardinals squared off in an old fashioned pitchers duel in the opener of the three-game series, with Tim Leary out-pitching Bob Forsch and two relievers by the score of 1–0. The winning run crossed the plate in the top of the ninth against Todd Worrell on a leadoff homer by Mike Marshall. Leary, who ran his record to 9–6 with his fourth shutout of the season, had his split-fingered fastball working to perfection, forcing the Cards to hit into fifteen groundball outs. After the game, Leary, who was pitching on three days of rest, said, "I prefer to work on three days rest. I can stay sharper that way."[17]

Los Angeles victory opened up an eight game lead over both San Francisco and Houston. They had picked up 5½ games over the Giants and 2½ games over the Astros in the four days since the All-Star break.

LA	54	36	—
Houston	47	45	8
San Francisco	46	44	8

Giants manager Roger Craig was overly impressed with Tommy Lasorda's edition of Murderers Row, saying, "I don't want to say I told you so, but I told you so. The difference in the Dodgers is Kirk Gibson. When the going gets tough, he gets tough. He's made the difference there. They've played well without Guerrero and Griffin. I'm glad we've got fourteen games to play with them. They're a good ball club, we've got a good ball club. We'll find out who's best."[18]

Allan Malamud of the *Los Angeles Examiner* supported Craig's views. "Kirk Gibson has been the Dodgers most valuable player since opening day. Now it's time to upgrade him. At the halfway mark of the season, he's the most valuable player in the National League. Other hitters may have better numbers—not that there's anything wrong with a 30 homer, 90 RBI, .290 kind of year—but nobody has been more important to his team. Gibson has been to the Dodgers what Magic Johnson is to the Lakers or Larry Bird is to the Celtics—an intense competitor who makes everyone else play better. To watch him every day is the only way to appreciate him fully. I even like his style when he butchered that play in left field in Houston. Instead of making excuses, he blamed himself for the loss to the Astros. He's been responsible for enough wins to allow the Dodgers to lead at the All-Star break, despite a string of injuries that would have buried them in past years."[19]

6

HOUSTON CLOSES IN

The world looked bright and cheery to the Dodgers management and to Dodgers fans as the sun came up on Tuesday, July 19. Their beloved team enjoyed a huge eight game lead in the National League Western Division pennant race, thanks to some great pitching, solid defense, and contributions from the Stuntmen. Dave Anderson, in particular, stood out. Filling in for the injured Alfredo Griffin, Anderson had committed only three errors in 55 games, batted a cool .273, and drove in 16 runs. Mike Marshall was impressed with the 1988 edition of the Dodgers, as reported by Gordon Verrell. "For the most part, when Tommy (Lasorda) has had to go to the bench, he's been able to get experienced players," Marshall said after the Dodgers reeled off their longest winning streak by sweeping a five-game series in Chicago and taking the opener of a three-game set in St. Louis. "He's taking major league players off the bench — Danny Heep, Franklin Stubbs, Mickey Hatcher, and Dave Anderson who, right now, is probably our MVP. In the past he's had to go with youngsters." As starters, Heep and Hatcher had been sensational. Heep was hitting .384 (28 for 73), and Hatcher, who was put on the disabled list the first week in July, was at .344 (22 for 64). "Another key is our pitching," Marshall said. "We're not scoring seven runs a game, so the pitching has had to have been outstanding. I believe our pitching is the best in baseball." The Dodgers' 3.06 earned run average through July 18 ranked second in the majors to the New York Mets' 3.02. And the bullpen, that recorded only 32 saves all last season, had 30, the most in the National League. "And we're catching the ball," added Marshall, citing perhaps what was the biggest improvement. "You look at the box scores and, every day, it's no errors or one error, not three and four like we were making the last couple of years. When we limit the other team to three outs an inning, with our pitching staff, well, that's why we're playing so much better in close games." Last year the Dodgers were 19–32 in one-run games. This year, after a 1–0 victory on July 18 in St. Louis — on Tim Leary's five-hit pitching and Marshall's twelfth home run — the Dodgers were 14–13 in one-run games. Three of the victories in their six-game winning streak were by one run. "We're better in just about every area," said Marshall, "but it goes back to the bench. Last year, we didn't have one. It was that simple."[1]

Even San Francisco manager Roger Craig noticed the difference in the Dodgers team. "Last year, they were losing the 2–1 and 3–2 games. Now they're winning them."[2]

Things began to change after the 18th, however, slowly at first, and then more rapidly as the Houston Astros, who had been lurking in second and third place all year, suddenly awoke from their slumber and made a concerted effort to overtake Tommy Lasorda's confident crew. And the Dodgers helped them in their quest by winning only 8 of 21 games from July 19 through August 9. It all started quietly enough when Los Angeles was defeated by the St. Louis Cardinals by a score of 3–2 on July 19. Houston's 4–3 win over the Montreal Expos went unnoticed in the City of Angels.

The Astros, in many respects, were similar to the Dodgers in their makeup. They had strong starting pitching, a good bullpen, and a popgun offense that had to scratch for runs day after day. The Astro's starting pitching included Mike Scott (16–13 in 1987), Bob Knepper (8–17), Jim Deshaies (11–6), and Nolan Ryan (8–16 with a league-leading 2.76 ERA and 228 strikeouts in 220 innings in 1987). Their closer, Dave Smith, had saved 84 games over the previous three seasons and was at the top of his game. Their primary offensive contributors were first baseman Glenn Davis (27 homers in 1987), outfielder Kevin Bass (19 homers), and Gerald Young (26 stolen bases and a .321 batting average).

Houston followed up its 4–3 win over Montreal by winning the next two games, defeating the Expos 3–2 and the Philadelphia Phillies 2–0, on the 20th and 21st respectively, behind the stellar pitching of Jim Deshaies and Nolan Ryan. On the 20th, Deshaies won his seventh game of the season, allowing two runs in six innings, and Larry Anderson pitched 2⅓ innings to earn his fourth save. Home runs by shortstop Rafael Ramírez and Terry Puhl gave Deshaies all the run support he needed. The next day, Hal Lanier's troops rode Nolan Ryan's three-hitter to a 2–0 victory, despite a fine effort by the Phillies' Mike Maddux. Ryan struck out nine and walked four to record his seventh win of the season against seven losses. Third baseman Buddy Bell's RBI single in the sixth inning broke a scoreless tie and Terry Puhl gave Ryan an insurance run with a round-tripper in the eighth. The wins, combined with L.A.'s losses to St. Louis and Pittsburgh, cut the Dodgers' lead to five games, put the red-hot Astros within striking distance of the league-leaders, and gave the Texans renewed confidence.

Houston had the momentum now, and when that happens a team feels like it can win every game, no matter what the score is in the middle innings. They believe they will win every time they step on the field. Hal Lanier's fighters defeated Philadelphia 5–3 behind Bob Knepper on the 22nd and took a close 7–6 decision against the same team the next day, in a game that further increased their confidence. The Astros held a 4–2 lead after six innings, only to see the Phils bounce back with four runs in the seventh inning and another in the eighth to grab a 6–4 lead. But the never-say-die Astros struck for two runs in the bottom of the eighth to tie it and scored the game-winner in the ninth when Craig Reynolds doubled, reached third on an error, and scored on a wild pitch. Lee Elia's club finally snapped Houston's five-game winning streak the next day with a 6–4 victory behind Kevin Gross. At the same time, the Dodgers were winning three straight over Pittsburgh, by scores of 4–2, 6–2, and 2–1, behind the strong pitching of Tim Belcher, Tim Leary, and Shawn Hillegas, respectively, with Leary tossing a complete game five-hitter, with nine strikeouts against a single base on balls, on the 23rd. L.A.'s feeble offense managed thirty base hits in the three games, but only five of them went for extra bases, four doubles, and one triple. Davis, Sax, Marshall, and Hamilton all had two RBIs.

The Dodgers were still battling the injury jinx as the summer progressed. Don Sutton remained on the disabled list. Ken Howell came off the DL on July 8 and Mickey Hatcher was activated on July 24. Alfredo Griffin returned from the disabled list on the 25th, and was charged with two errors in his first game back, the first errors by a Dodgers shortstop since June 25th. Pedro Guerrero was activated on the 28th. And there were other players who were injured but were not placed on the disabled list, such as Mike Marshall, who was nursing a bad back, and John Shelby, who missed four games with an eye injury, then suffered through a two for eighteen slump upon his return. Eventually, however, the DL claimed another Dodgers victim when Jeff Hamilton went down with a separated muscle in his rib cage during the second game of a doubleheader against the San Francisco Giants in Candlestick Park on July 26. Third baseman Tracy Woodson was recalled from Albuquerque, where he was hitting .319 with 17 homers and 73 RBIs in 85 games. Hamilton had gone two for four with a double and home run in the opener, and was one for four in the nightcap before his injury.

The Dodgers swept the twin bill by scores of 7–3 and 6–5 in 11 innings. Rick Dempsey's two-run homer in the seventh inning of the opener broke a one-all tie, and the Dodgers scored four more in the ninth, two on Steve Sax's triple, to ice the decision. But game two exposed the soft underbelly of the Dodgers' bullpen when they blew leads of 4–2 and 5–4 before Giants reliever Scott Garrelts came to their rescue by balking home the winning run. The balk call set off a wild free-for-all in the stands as frustrated Giants fans, watching their heroes slowly drop out of the pennant race, began throwing punches at each other and throwing objects on the field in the direction of the Dodgers players and the umpires. Fifty or more fans in the left field stands climbed the chain link fence and had to be ejected by the park security personnel. Another seventy-five fans were ejected by San Francisco police officers, and eighteen were arrested for fighting. The situation was so dangerous that Dodgers general manager Fred Claire called National League president Bart Giamatti to alert him to the problem. San Francisco Giants general manager

Steve Sax gave the Dodgers solid defense as well as a tough bat and a pair of flying feet (author's collection).

Al Rosen was also concerned about the failure of security at the park and promised immediate action.

L.A. went in to another tailspin following their three-game winning streak, losing four of seven games to end the month with a 60–43 record, leaving them with a tenuous 4½ game lead over Houston, who had run up a 4–2 mark over the same period. The statistics of July 25 confirmed that Kirk Gibson, Steve Sax, and Mike Marshall were the team's offensive leaders, John Shelby led the defensive brigade, and Dave Anderson and Mickey Hatcher were the shining stars for the Stuntmen. The pitching staff was led by "Bulldog" Hershiser, Tim Leary, Tim Belcher, and Jay Howell. And the bullpen did a magnificent job. Unsung heroes like Tim Crews, who pitched in 25 of the Dodgers' 97 games with a 2.44 ERA, and Brian Holton, who pitched in 28 games with a 1.94 ERA, helped build L.A.'s lead. And Alejandro Peña, who had been a starting pitcher most of his career, was becoming more comfortable as a reliever. "I really like relieving. I come in, in close situations in the game, and it makes me concentrate more on the hitter. I have to throw strikes. I can't fool around with breaking balls. I'm throwing all heat. If they go out, they go out with the best pitch. I've put being a starter away. Far away. Real far. No question. I feel stronger now in the bullpen. I just do my job whenever they give me the ball."[3] Over a seventeen game stretch following the All-Star game, the pen allowed only seven earned runs in forty-three innings, for a 1.47 ERA.

Name	AB	R	H	D	T	HR	RBI	SB	BA
Kirk Gibson	350	68	105	20	1	18	53	17	.300
Steve Sax	392	49	119	11	3	5	37	27	.304
Mike Marshall	376	47	104	20	1	14	58	0	.277
John Shelby	278	43	78	18	2	5	37	12	.281
Dave Anderson	207	24	54	8	2	1	17	3	.261
Mickey Hatcher	94	14	31	6	0	0	11	0	.330
Jeff Hamilton	210	23	50	10	2	3	23	0	.238

Name	AB	R	H	D	T	HR	RBI	SB	BA
Rick Dempsey	88	16	20	7	0	4	15	0	.227
Alfredo Griffin	144	14	24	5	3	0	19	3	.167
Pedro Guerrero	158	19	50	4	1	3	30	1	.316
Mike Scioscia	261	22	72	14	0	2	26	0	.276
Franklin Stubbs	139	16	28	5	0	5	21	9	.201

Name	G	CG	IP	W	L	H	SO	BB	SVS	ERA
Orel Hershiser	21	6	154	13	5	123	100	46	1	2.69
Tim Leary	21	7	135	10	6	113	29	107	0	2.47
Tim Belcher	22	1	88	7	4	73	79	29	4	3.46
Jay Howell	30	0	39	2	2	29	38	16	12	2.09
A. Peña	37	0	59	4	3	42	49	21	8	1.53
Brian Holton	28	0	51	5	2	38	27	14	1	1.94
Tim Crews	25	0	48	3	0	46	20	10	0	2.44
S. Hillegas	7	0	41	3	2	35	21	10	0	2.83

Houston's enthusiastic charge continued in a three-game series against L.A.'s finest in Dodger Stadium on the weekend of July 29–31. On Friday night, Mike Scott, just back in the rotation after a three-week stint on the disabled list, needed only 90 pitches to beat Lasorda's cohorts 3–1. Scott tossed a four-hitter with five strikeouts and no walks as he improved his season record to 10–3. His opponent, Shawn Hillegas, pitched a creditable game himself but came up just short. Houston scored single runs in the first, sixth, and eighth innings, while the Dodgers' lone run came in the bottom of the fourth with Marshall driving in Sax. Buddy Bell was the batting star of the day with three base hits and two RBIs. The following day, the Astros pummeled the Dodgers on the NBC *Game of the Week*, coasting to a 14–6 triumph behind a 16-hit barrage aimed at Fernando Valenzuela and four relievers. The game was close for four innings, with the Dodgers holding a 2–0 lead, but in the fifth, the roof caved in on Mexico's answer to Carl Hubbell. He injured his shoulder pitching to the leadoff hitter, Billy Hatcher, but attempted unsuccessfully to pitch through the pain. After yielding a two-out single to Rafael Ramírez and throwing a home run ball to Alex Treviño, he was relieved by Brian Holton, who immediately surrendered two more runs for a 4–2 Houston lead. The Astros added five more runs in the sixth, three in the seventh, and two in the eighth, sending the Big Blue Machine reeling. Orel Hershiser temporarily stopped the bleeding with a 6–1 win in the finale, stretching L.A.'s lead to 4½ games. The Dodgers ace threw a complete game five-hitter for his fifteenth victory of the season, fanning three and walking two. John Shelby's two-run bloop single highlighted a three-run fourth inning for L.A., and they added single runs in the fifth, sixth, and seventh. Two Stuntmen contributed to the win. Rick Dempsey went one for three with two RBIs and Mickey Hatcher had two hits with a run scored and an RBI.

Fernando Valenzuela was placed on the disabled list as Hershiser was taming the Astros, causing him to miss a start for the first time in eight years. *The Sporting News* reported, "He stretched the anterior capsule of his left shoulder in an outing against Houston. 'We don't know the extent of the injury,' said Dr. Frank Jobe, the Dodgers team physician. 'But it is causing a slippage of the muscle away from the socket, and pitching can only make it worse. I insisted that he be taken out of the rotation.' Jobe said no operation was planned but would not predict when Valenzuela might pitch again. He did say he believed there was a 100 percent chance for full recovery."[4] Some Dodgers coaches and players felt that Fernando's problems were more involved than just his sore shoulder. He had been manhandled by the opposition since the middle of June, posting an 0–3 record in eight starts, with a 5.91 ERA. For the season he was 5–8 with a 4.41 ERA, yielding 138 base hits in 135 innings, and issuing 72 bases on balls. More telling, however, may have been his strike-out total that was just 60 strikeouts, an average of four strikeouts for every nine innings pitched, compared to his career average of 7.3 strikeouts per nine innings. Pitching coach Ron Perranoski felt that Fernando's problems were more mechanical and were related to his rhythm, "but what Fernando has to do is throw strikes earlier in the count. That way they have to chase the screwball or risk being called out." Catcher Rick Dempsey thought it was more involved than that. "He would get in a fastball situation and it was tough for him to rear back and pop it like he wanted to. What else can you say? He needs 5 to 10 miles per hour on his fastball to make the screwball effective."[5]

While the Dodgers were fighting off the charge of the Houston Astros, the New York Mets were still trying to put away the stubborn Pittsburgh Pirates. Jim Leyland's club, although still two years away from a division title, was loaded with young players like Barry Bonds (23 years old), Bobby Bonilla (25), Andy Van Slyke (27), Doug Drabek (26), Jim Gott (28), and John Smiley (23). Pittsburgh's young lions were pounding the ball with enthusiasm, with Bonilla hitting 18 home runs through July 31, followed by Van Slyke and Bonds at 17 homers each. Bob Walk, with an 11–6 record, John Smiley at 9–7, Doug Drabek at 9–5, and Jim Gott with 17 saves were making life miserable for Davey Johnson's club. Still, the Mets kept their composure and their lead. Dwight Gooden had won 13 games against only 5 losses by the end of July. David Cone was at 10–2, and Ron Darling was 11–7. Darryl Strawberry with 27 home runs, Howard Johnson with 18 home runs, and Kevin McReynolds with 15 homers helped New York maintain their position as the highest scoring team in the National League.

By far, the most interesting pennant race in the major leagues in July was the American League Eastern Division race where the favored Boston Red Sox were chasing the fired-up Detroit Tigers under Sparky Anderson, the man who guided the Cincinnati Reds to five National League pennants and two world championships during the 1970s. After the Red Sox sleep-walked through a tepid 14–12 month in June, leaving them 6 games behind Detroit, they were still lethargic as July got underway, and they managed just 4 wins against 8 losses by the time the July 10 All-Star break arrived. That was all the Red Sox ownership could take and, with Boston trailing Anderson's Bengals by 9 full games, they made a managerial change. They fired manager John McNamara and promoted Joe Morgan from their minor league system to right the ship. And, for whatever reason, whether it was a change in the manager's chair, or something else, Boston suddenly caught fire after Morgan took the helm and raced to a 17–1 mark through the end of the month, bringing them to within one game of first place and ½ game behind the New York Yankees. The major catalyst in the Red Sox charge was Roger "Rocket" Clemens, who improved his season record to 15–5 in six appearances, all of which the Red Sox eventually won. He threw three complete games with 4 wins and no losses. In 49⅓ innings the Rocket yielded just 36 base hits, struck out 69 batters with just 8 bases on balls, and had an earned run average of 1.64. In one game he left after 6⅓ innings with a 5–3 lead but the bullpen blew the lead. Bruce Hurst won two games against one loss, bringing his record to 11–4. And big Lee Smith, all 6', 6", 245 pounds of him, who came to the Red Sox from the Chicago White Sox in an off-season trade, had thirteen saves to his credit. Detroit hung tough into mid-September despite injuries to Alan Trammel, Lou Whittaker, Mike Henneman, and Jeff Robinson. The strong arms of Frank Tanana at 12–6, Jeff Robinson at 2–4, and Doyle Alexander at 10–5 kept the Tigers in the race, ably supported by the timely hitting of Chet Lemon (8 homers), Alan Trammel (11 homers), and Matt Nokes (11 homers), and the all-around play of Trammel and Lou Whitaker in the center of the diamond. Billy Martin's Yankees would also stay in contention until after Labor Day, but their pennant hopes realistically disappeared when Ron Guidry's season was short circuited because of elbow problems. "Louisiana Lightning" made three trips to the DL during the season, limiting his contribution to 12 games pitched and a 2–3 won-loss record. The New Yorkers struggled through July with a depleted pitching staff, and playing mostly the middle-of-the-road teams, Chicago, Texas, and Milwaukee, they won 15 games against 11 losses.

The Western Division still belonged to the Oakland Athletics, but Minnesota, like Pittsburgh and Detroit, did not make life easy for the league leaders. The two division leaders, Oakland and Detroit, met seven times during the month, and the A's showed the Tigers how to play the game, winning five of the seven. A four-game series in Detroit ended in a 2–2 deadlock, with the Tigers scoring 16 runs and the A's 15. But, when Oakland returned home to host the visiting Tigers, their pitching dominance surfaced. They outscored the visitors 9 to 2 in the three games, sweeping the series by scores of 4–1, 4–1, and 1–0. In the opener, the Tigers led 1–0 after 5½ innings, but Rickey Henderson smashed a three-run homer in the sixth, and José Canseco followed with a solo job to give Storm Davis all the runs he needed. In game two, Mark

McGwire lofted a three-run blast into the Oakland sky in the sixth inning, his sixth home run in July, breaking open a tight game. And in the finale, Bob Welch gave Detroit hitters nothing but trouble as he threw a six hitter at them, fanning eight and walking one, to beat Walt Terrell 1–0. José Canseco finished the month with 30 home runs, Mark McGwire had 19, and Rickey Henderson had 15. Bob Welch finished the month with 12 wins against 6 losses, Storm Davis went 10–4, Dave Stewart went 13–10, and Dennis Eckersley had thirty saves.

Manager Hal Lanier's cohorts, still determined to wrest the crown away from Lasorda's boys, took two out of three from San Francisco from August 1 through 3, before hosting the Dodgers in another weekend series, this one of four games. Houston dropped the opener in San Francisco 4–1 as southpaw Atlee Hammaker won his fifth game of the year with a neat five-hitter. Will Clark and Robby Thompson supplied the punch with home runs. Game two was a real donnybrook and a big confidence builder for Hal Lanier's team at a time when they needed it most. Roger Craig's sluggers KO'd Bob Knepper in the second inning and raced to a quick 6–4 lead, but it was short-lived as the Astros duplicated their first inning feat by scoring four runs in the top of the fourth inning for an 8–6 lead that they never relinquished. They added another four-spot in the eighth and closed out the scoring with a single run in the ninth, making the final score 13–10. Heroes were everywhere, except on the mound. Bill Doran had four base hits, including his seventh home run, and drove in four runs. Bell, Ramírez, and Puhl all had three hits, with Bell hitting a three-run homer in the eighth. Houston enjoyed a quieter game on Wednesday, as Mike Scott throttled the Giants for eight innings en route to a 3–2 win. Dave Smith pitched the ninth for his nineteenth save of the year.

While the Astros were doing battle with San Francisco, Tommy Lasorda's troops, who had lost 7 of their last 13 games, tried to recover their lost skills in a series at home against Cincinnati. In the opener, L.A.'s troubles continued as they blew a 3–0 lead in the eighth inning. Tim Belcher had a three-hit shutout after seven innings, but when he yielded a single and a base on balls to the first two batters in the top of the eighth, he was replaced by Jesse Orosco, who proceeded to walk Kal Daniels to load the bases. Closer Alejandro Peña was brought in to restore order, but instead he self-destructed, picking up a ground ball off the bat of Barry Larkin and heaving it into right field, allowing two runs to score. Chris Sabo, who was in a 1 for 32 slump, hit a seeing-eye ground ball back up the middle that went into center field, chasing two more runners across the plate. Tracy Woodson homered for L.A., and Steve Sax and John Shelby had two hits each. The next day, Tim Leary kept the Reds in check and his teammates scored two runs in the bottom of the first, good for a 2–0 win before a crowd of 44,091 ecstatic Dodgers fans. Leary, now 11–6 on the season, held the Reds to six hits, struck out three and walked two. Gibson's double drove in Steve Sax with the first run and Pedro Guerrero's single scored Gibson, who had three base hits in the game, and added a stolen base for good measure. The good feeling in the City of Angels disappeared in a flash on Wednesday as the bullpen blew another game and the Dodgers lost another game off their lead over Houston. L.A. starter Shawn Hillegas lasted only four innings against Pete Rose's team, leaving with a 3–3 tie. Brian Holton, the most reliable of the Dodgers bullpen corps over the last two weeks, blanked the Reds for three innings, and left with a 4–3 lead, but Jay Howell quickly gave up the tying run. The two teams battled into the eleventh inning when Cincinnati hammered Alejandro Peña for three runs, two of them unearned after a comedy of errors opened the door for the visitors. Peña failed to touch first base after taking a toss from Pedro Guerrero, to open the inning. Later in the inning, an error by left fielder Kirk Gibson, a passed ball by catcher Rick Dempsey, and singles by Jeff Reed, Ron Oester, and Herm Winningham scored three runs, giving the Reds a 7–4 victory.

Tommy Lasorda's boys, still reeling from the Cincinnati fiasco, left on a seven-day, two-city junket. Their first stop was Houston where they entered the lion's den on August 5 and proceeded to drop three of four, cutting their lead to just 1½ games. Tim Belcher, who beat Nolan Ryan 5–3, was the only winner for L.A. Hershiser dropped the opener 6–4 as he was raked for five runs in five innings, yielding 8 base hits and walking five men in an uncharacteristic performance. Glenn Davis knocked in the go-ahead run in the sixth inning, breaking a 4–4 tie. Rick Dempsey hit home run number 9 and Kirk Gibson deposited number 21 over the fence in a losing effort. Tim Belcher prevented a complete collapse with his win over Ryan. Actually, Belcher was in control throughout the game as he was staked to a 5–0 lead after seven innings, with Tracy Woodson driving in the first two runs with a fourth inning single. Steve Sax with three hits, and Kirk Gibson and Mike Marshall with two hits each, led the Dodgers' attack. Ryan gave up eight hits and five runs although only three of the runs were earned as the Astros committed two errors, one by Ryan. Kevin Bass' three-run homer in the eighth ended Belcher's day. Manager Hal Lanier rallied his troops for the next game and they responded with a tough 4–2 decision. Bob Knepper raised his record to 12–3 with 7⅓ strong innings, allowing only one run and five base hits. His counterpart, Tim Leary, was as wild as a hare, yielding three runs in six innings, throwing two wild pitches and balking home a run. Then relief pitcher Brian Holton balked home another run in the seventh inning. Billy Hatcher and Kevin Bass drove in runs for the Astros, while Mike Marshall, who pounded out three hits, slammed his 15th homer for L.A. Shawn Hillegas started the get-away game but he was routed by the Astros before he could retire a batter. Two base hits, including a double by Billy Doran, and two walks, brought Tim Crews into the game. The Dodgers bullpen, with Crews, Holton, and Orosco, kept Houston at bay after the four-run first inning, but L.A. couldn't do anything with hard throwing Mike Scott, who fanned six and walked one in tossing an eight-hit shutout. A six-run outburst against Alejandro Peña by the fired-up Astros in the bottom of the eighth inning made the final score 10–0. Mike Marshall was one of the few Dodgers to rise to the occasion during the series, going 9 for 15 with a double, a home run and two RBIs. Conversely, Pedro Guerrero suffered through a 0 for 14 drought.

The Dodgers moved on to Cincinnati the next day, but things didn't get any better as Danny Jackson, on his way to a brilliant 23–8 season, shut down the Dodgers' attack for a convincing 6–0 victory. Don Sutton, who started on the mound for L.A., was pummeled for six runs in seven innings. It was Sutton's last game in a Dodgers uniform. Kirk Gibson said after the game, "Maybe it will do us some good to get out of first place. Then maybe we'd have something to fight for. I've talked about character all year. Now we're going to see how much character we've got." Other players echoed Gibson's feelings. Mike Marshall said, "Maybe after an eight-game lead, we lost some intensity. We're not the type of team who can just throw our gloves out there and win. Maybe other teams can get by like that, but we can't." And Rick Dempsey added, "We're not the best team. We know we're not the best team. We're playing very well. On paper, you can probably find a couple teams better than the Dodgers. But we're playing well together as a club and that's when you become ... I won't say unbeatable, but we're going to win more than other teams."[6]

After games of August 9, L.A. held a slim ½ game lead over the surging Houston Astros. During the 22-day period beginning on July 19, Houston won 15 games against 5 losses, outscoring the opposition 94 runs to 70 runs, or 4.7 runs per game against 3.5 runs per game. But those totals are somewhat misleading. The Astros' pitching was better than the totals indicate, but their hitting was overstated. They had three games that significantly affected the totals. They defeated the Dodgers 14–6 on July 30, edged the San Francisco Giants 13 to 10 on August 2, and shut out L.A. 10 to 0 on August 8. In the remaining 17 games, Houston outscored their opponents 3.4 runs per game to 3.2 runs per game. Obviously, Hal Lanier's team had to scratch and claw for almost every victory. And they did it with great pitching, timely hitting, and by turning the rabbits loose on the base paths. Bob Knepper led the pitching brigade with a 3–0 record. He was followed by Mike Scott at 4–1, Danny Darwin at 2–0, Jim Deshaies at 2–2, Nolan Ryan at 2–2, and Dave Smith and Juan Agosto at 1–0 each. Kevin Bass hit 3 homers during the surge and Glenn Davis hit 2. On the base paths, Gerald Young and Terry Puhl stole seven bases apiece, Kevin Bass and Billy Hatcher stole three each, Billy Doran stole two, and Glenn Davis and Alex Treviño stole one each, for a total of 24 stolen bases in 20 games.

On the other side of the coin, Tommy Lasorda's Dodgers won only 8 of 21 games during that 22 day period, being outscored 90 runs to 71 runs, or 4.3 runs per game to 3.4 runs per game. Tim Belcher was the only Dodgers pitcher with a winning record during the slump, going 2–0. Orel Hershiser could do no better than 2–2, bringing his record to 15–6. But Bulldog was about to get his second wind. He would go 8–2 from August 9 to the end of the season, finishing his Cy Young year with 23 victories against 8 losses. Brian Holton had a 1–1 record over the three-week period, Tim Leary was 2–2, Shawn Hillegas was 1–1, while Fernando Valenzuela and Alejandro Peña lost two games each. The offense, as skimpy as it was, was led by Kirk Gibson who tried to keep the team fired up during the tough times by doing whatever was necessary to score runs. He hit 4 home runs in the 21 games, scored 10 runs, drove in 11, and stole 5 bases. Mike Marshall, one of the unsung heroes of the pennant drive, slugged 3 homers, scored 7 runs, and drove in 12. Steve Sax scored 9 runs, batted in 7, and stole 9 bases. In all, L.A. stole 16 bases in 21 games.

As a team, the Dodgers were still running second to the Mets in ERA with 3.06. They were third in complete games with 17, second in shutouts with 11, second in strikeouts with 617, and they were still setting the pace in saves with 33, five more than Houston and San Francisco. They had the second highest team batting average in the National League, hitting .259 to .263 for the Chicago Cubs. They were fifth in runs scored with 429 runs in 101 games, ninth in home runs with 64, and seventh in stolen bases with 82.

Kirk Gibson rallied the team from their late summer slump with his fiery temperament, his aggressive base running, and his clutch base hits (courtesy of Los Angeles Dodgers).

Finally, on August 10, Don Robinson hurled San Francisco to a 5–0 victory over Houston while the Dodgers fought off a three-run Cincinnati rally in the bottom of the ninth inning to whip Pete Rose's Reds by an 8–5 score, awarding the victory to Orel Hershiser and stretching the Dodgers' lead to 1½ games. Kirk Gibson rejoiced in the clubhouse after the game, screaming, "How sweet it is, the fruits of victory. What a team. What a bleeping team." The Dodgers ace was touched up for a Ken Griffey home run in the second inning, but watched as his teammates roared back with a four-spot in the top of the fifth, sparked by Mike Marshall's leadoff homer, to give him a 4–2 lead. In the top of the ninth, Mickey Hatcher, the leader of the Stuntmen, ignited a four-run rally with a pinch-hit single, driving in a run. He later scored himself, extending the L.A. lead to 8–2, but Bulldog apparently didn't know how to pitch with such a big lead, and manager Tommy Lasorda rescued him after he had thrown a home run ball to Kal Daniels, Daniels' second homer of the game, and put Chris Sabo on base with nobody out, in the bottom of the inning. Dodgers closer Jay Howell made it a bit interesting before recording the final out, as he was touched up for Paul O'Neil's two-run homer, cutting the lead to 8–5.

Los Angeles					Cincinnati				
Name	*Pos*	*AB*	*R*	*H*	*Name*	*Pos*	*AB*	*R*	*H*
Sax	2B	4	0	0	Daniels	LF	4	2	2
Anderson	2B	1	1	1	Sabo	3B	5	1	1
Scioscia	C	5	1	1	Larkin	SS	5	0	1
Gibson	LF	4	0	0	E. Davis	CF	4	0	1
Guerrero	1B	4	0	0	O'Neil	RF	5	1	3
Stubbs	1B	0	0	0	Griffey	1B	5	1	2
Hatcher	PH-1B	1	1	1	Díaz	C	1	0	0
Marshall	RF	4	1	3	Winningham	PH	1	0	0
Shelby	CV	4	1	1	Murphy	P	0	0	0
Woodson	3B	4	1	1	Collins	PH	1	0	0
Griffin	SS	4	1	2	Birtsas	P	0	0	0
Hershiser	P	4	1	1	St. Claire	P	0	0	0
J. Howell	P	0	0	0	Treadway	2B	3	0	0
					Rijo	P	2	0	0
					Dibble	P	0	0	0
					Reed	PH-C	2	0	1
Totals		39	8	11			38	5	11

Los Angeles	0 0 0	0 4 0	0 0 4 — 8 — 11 — 1
Cincinnati	0 1 0	0 1 0	0 0 3 — 5 — 11 — 3

Double-O'Neil
Triples-Shelby, Marshall
Home Runs-Marshall, K. Griffey, Daniel (2), O'Neil

Name	IP	R	ER	H	BB	SO
Los Angeles						
Hershiser (W 16-6)	8	4	4	10	3	2
J. Howell	1	1	1	1	0	0
Cincinnati						
Rijo (L 11-8)	5	4	3	6	3	6
Dibble	1	0	0	0	0	2
Murphy	2	0	0	1	0	1
Williams	⅓	2	0	2	0	0
Birtsas	⅓	1	0	0	0	1
St. Claire	⅓	1	0	2	0	1[7]

There was a sad note to report on August 10. Don Sutton, one of the Dodgers' all-time greats, was released after failing to regain his form at the age of 43. He won 3 of his first five decisions for L.A., but could do no better than 0–3 over his last 9 starts, including his last start on the 9th, a 6–0 loss to Cincinnati. Sutton's career numbers showed 324 victories against 256 losses for a fine .559 winning percentage. He had 178 complete games in 23 years, with 58 shutouts and a 3.26 earned run average. At the time of his retirement, he was number three all-time in games started with 756, trailing only Cy Young and Nolan Ryan. He was number ten in shutouts, number seven in innings pitched, number five in strikeouts, and number twelve in victories.

The National League Western Division standings at the end of the day, August 10, were:

LA	63	49	—
Houston	62	51	1½
San Francisco	60	53	3½

The fire that burned in Kirk Gibson's belly exploded after the game of August 11, sending a message through the Dodgers clubhouse that the team was everything and the individual was nothing. The goal of the organization was to win a world championship, and nothing less was acceptable. The Dodgers had led the Cincinnati Reds 8–6 after eight innings, but the bullpen let it get away when the Reds scored two runs in the bottom of the ninth to tie it, and then pushed over the game-winner an inning later when Eric Davis hit a two-out single. The reporters, as usual, crowded around Gibson's locker looking for a story, and one of them, noting that he had gone 4 for 5 on the night, with 3 doubles, a home run, 4 runs scored, and 3 batted in, said he was the batting star of the game. "Big deal," he snapped. "We lost didn't we?" When it was mentioned that he was in the running for the National League MVP title, he barked, "People talk about the MVP, but I want to be World Champion. That's the only title I want."[8]

Apparently, Dodgers players got Kirk's message loud and clear because from that game on, they gradually pulled away from their challengers. They won 14 of the next 18 games, stretching their lead over Hal Lanier's scrappy club to 6½ games by the end of the month. Tim Leary got the rally started by stopping the San Francisco Giants in Candlestick Park by a 7–3 score, for his 12th win of the season. And his sacrifice fly in the sixth inning broke a 3–3 tie. Mike Scioscia went 3 for 5 in the game with 2 RBIs and Pedro Guerrero had a solo home run. The Astros, who made a courageous run at Los Angeles, just fell short, and they would never again challenge for the Western Division title. In fact, they would win just 20 games while losing 30 the rest of the season. Their fall from grace would leave them floundering in fifth place, 12½ games behind the high-flying Angelinos.

Shawn Hillegas was sent to the bullpen after his ugly outing of August 8, and right-hander Ramón Martínez was recalled from Albuquerque. The Dodgers, reportedly, decided to go with a four-man rotation temporarily, with Martínez joining Hershiser, Belcher, and Leary, a move that Hershiser relished. "I think this puts a heavier weight on us. A move like that is made because we're in a pennant race. I think we can be equal to the task. This is where we earn our checks."[9] Martínez, the tall, skinny, 20-year-old right-hander, who stood 6', 4" tall and weighed a wispy 165 pounds, hailed from Santo Domingo in the Dominican Republic. He was armed with a 94-mile-per-hour fastball that overpowered minor league batters in Texas where he started the season, but he also possessed a wicked curveball and a deceptive change of pace. Pitching for San Antonio in the Class AA Texas League, he went 8–4 with a 2.46 earned run average, fanning 89 batters in 95 innings, before being promoted to the Class AAA Albuquerque Dukes of the Pacific Coast League. His performance with the Dukes, a 5–2 record, a 2.76 ERA, and 49 strikeouts in 59 innings, convinced the Dodgers brass that the precocious flamethrower was ready for the big time.

Ramón Martínez made his major league debut on August 13, facing the San Francisco Giants in the friendly confines of Dodger Stadium. The fearless Dominican was sensational as he blanked Roger Craig's team on four hits over seven innings, before giving way to Jesse Orosco after issuing a two-out base on balls in the eighth. Orosco subsequently gave up a run-scoring single to Will Clark before retiring the side. L.A. had scored first on a double by Pedro Guerrero and an RBI single by Mike Marshall in the sixth inning. Both bullpens shut down the opposition over the next three innings, before the Big Blue Machine unlimbered its big guns in the bottom of the 11th. After Alejandro Peña had completed his two-inning chore, the Dodgers sent the fans home happy, thanks to pitcher Tim Leary. Guerrero led off the inning with a double off Giant left-hander Joe Price. Two outs and two walks later, Leary, who had knocked in the winning run in his 7–3 victory over the Giants the previous night, ripped a game-winning single to center field. It was Leary's 16th base hit of the year in 51 at-bats, giving him a .314 batting average.

Jesse Orosco, who was unhappy when manager Tommy Lasorda replaced him with two men out in the ninth inning of the August 13 game against the Giants, depriving him of a save, told his manager that he wanted the opportunity to save games. Two days later, he replaced Tim Belcher with one man out in the eighth inning, and set down the next five men, two by strikeout, to preserve Belcher's ninth victory, 1–0 over the Giants. It was Orosco's seventh save of the season. After the Giants series, in which the Dodgers took three out of four, Roger Craig had nothing but praise for Mike Scioscia, who he called the best all-around catcher in the league. Scioscia, who batted .313 during the series on a 5 for 16 series, tagged out two Giants at the plate, and threw out three would-be base stealers in four attempts.

Pedro Guerrero, one of the Dodgers' most dangerous hitters and their top offensive threat of the 1980s, was suddenly traded to the St. Louis Cardinals on August 16 for pitcher John Tudor, a slick southpaw finesse pitcher who owned a 6–5 won-loss record and a league-leading 2.29 earned run average for the Cards at the time of the trade. L.A. did not like to lose Pedro, but with Fernando Valenzuela out indefinitely, they felt they needed a left-hander in the starting rotation. Rick Dempsey had predicted the move some weeks back when he said, "I would think that at this point they would probably go out and make an acquisition for a left-hander. We're going to need a left-hander against Pittsburgh and the Mets. These decisions are up to Fred and Tommy, but that is my personal hope, that they go out and buy a good lefty."[10] According to the press, Tudor was apprehensive about his new assignment. "I don't relish the idea of going over there as the guy who's going to pick it up for them. I'm not going to be the one to do that. It's got to be a team effort." But *St. Louis Post-Dispatch* columnist Kevin Horrigant

Mike Scioscia was hitting .276 at the All-Star break, and was doing a brilliant job handling the pitching staff (author's collection).

disagreed. "He's a gamer, and more. A hundred percent was never enough for John Thomas Tudor. His left shoulder went south on him in 1986, but he gutted it up for 13 victories. The New York Mets' Barry Lyons crashed into him in the dugout early in 1987, but Tudor willed himself back early from the broken leg he suffered in that collision and pitched the Cardinals to another pennant."[11]

Tudor's first start for Tommy Lasorda's club was on August 17 at home against the Philadelphia Phillies, and the cagey veteran gave Lasorda and the L.A. fans more than they expected. He pitched a complete game 7–2 victory, holding Lee Elia's team to just two runs, one earned, and scattering eleven base hits. After Franklin Stubbs hit a two-run double in a three-run L.A. first inning, the Phils came back with two runs off Tudor in the second. John Shelby restored the Dodgers' three-run lead by hitting a two-run homer in the third inning and that was all Tudor needed. He blanked the Phils over the final seven innings, and his teammates pushed over two more runs in the seventh to complete the scoring.

Ramón Martínez made his second start on the 18th and, like the first one, he pitched an outstanding game, holding the Phils to one run on four base hits in seven innings, with seven strikeouts and four walks. But, like the first game, his team couldn't score any runs for him and he left with the game tied at 1–1. After Jay Howell shut down Philadelphia in the eighth inning, the Dodgers pushed over the game-winner. Tracy Woodson led off the inning with a single, advanced to second on a sacrifice by Alfredo Griffin, and came across on a single by Dave Anderson.

The next night, with Montreal in town, Orel Hershiser threw a 2–0 five-hitter at them, bringing his record to 17–7. The Dodgers defeated Buck Rodgers' team again on the 20th, in a game that Kirk Gibson showed the L.A. fans what he's all about — winning. With the Expos nursing a 3–0 lead in the seventh inning, Gibson and Marshall doubled to cut the lead to 3–1. Then, with the Dodgers trailing 3–2 in the bottom of the ninth inning, after Tracy Woodson's eighth inning homer, L.A.'s one-man army took over. He hit a two-out single to score Dave Anderson with the tying run, and then proceeded to steal second base, putting the winning run in scoring position. When Expos pitcher Joe Hesketh uncorked a wild pitch, Gibson took off with one thought in mind — to score the winning run. Running with abandon, while Montreal catcher Nelson Santovenia chased the ball, he surprised the entire Montreal team when he rounded third base at full speed and headed home. The screams of the crowd alerted Santovenia to the danger that was unfolding before him. He grabbed the ball and threw it to Hesketh, who was covering the plate, but the ball popped out of Hesketh's glove as Gibson slid across home plate with the winning run. L.A.'s leader immediately bounced to his feet, pumping the air with his arms like a boxer, as 46,743 Dodgers fans screamed themselves hoarse and Gibson's teammates, led by manager Tommy Lasorda, overwhelmed their hero.

Jay Howell gave the Dodgers outstanding relief throughout the season, saving 21 games with a 2.08 ERA in 65 games (author's collection).

Tim Leary won his 14th game against 8 losses with a 4–0 shutout over the listless Expos on August 21, his 6th shutout of the season. The big right-hander, using his new split-fingered fastball, a cut fastball, and a 95 mph heater to perfection, fanned 12 and didn't walk a man in his latest gem. For the season, he had struck out 146 men in 183 innings pitched while walking only 39.

Los Angeles had stretched its lead over the Houston Astros to 5½ games by August 22, and the Astros were in danger of falling out of second place as San Francisco had moved into a tie with them. In the Eastern Division, the pesky Pittsburgh Pirates had chipped a game and a half off the New York Mets' lead, and now trailed Davey Johnson's club by just 3½ games.

On August 22–24 Tommy Lasorda team ran into a buzz saw in the guise of Davey Johnson's New York Mets. The L.A. team was brimming with confidence as the series got underway in Dodger Stadium, because they were riding a seven-game winning streak while the Mets were in the throes of a lingering slump, having lost eight of their last eleven games. But the fresh air of the West Coast seemed to work wonders for the Eastern Division leaders and they embarrassed their Western Division counterparts in the three-game series by scores of 7–1, 5–1, and 2–1. In a likely preview of the National League Championship Series, Dwight Gooden (15–6), David Cone (13–3), and Ojeda, Leach (6–1) and McDowell (fourteenth save) shut L.A.'s finest down with just three runs on 24 base hits in 27 innings. It ran the Mets' record against the Dodgers to eight and one with a three-game series remaining in New York on the Labor Day weekend. In the finale, Ojeda, with help from Leach and

McDowell, out-pitched Orel Hershiser, who protected a 1–0 lead into the eighth inning when the Mets erupted for two runs on a single by Keith Hernandez and a sacrifice fly by Kevin McReynolds. It was Hershiser's eighth — and last — loss of the season. He would go on to win his last six decisions.

The Mets series left L.A. fans in the doldrums, but their grief didn't last long. The game of August 27, that was more than of passing interest in the City of Angels, brought smiles back to their faces. After the Dodgers had recorded the final out in a 4–2 victory over the Philadelphia Phillies, manager Tommy Lasorda had the 1000th victory of his major league career. The 61-year-old former pitcher became the third Dodgers manager to record 1000 or more victories, trailing only Walter Alston who won 2040 games and Wilbert Robinson who won 1375. Lasorda, who had spent the last 38 years in the Dodgers organization as a player, coach, minor league manager, and major league manager, was a decent minor league pitcher who once struck out 25 men in a 15-inning game for Schenectady, and who still owns the International League record for most career victories with 125, but his wildness short-circuited his major league career after 26 games with the Brooklyn Dodgers and the Kansas City Athletics, leaving him with an 0–4 record. Following his playing career, Lasorda embarked on a career as a manager, beginning with Pocatello in 1965, and climbing his way up the Los Angeles managerial ladder through Ogden, Spokane, and Albuquerque. When Walter Alston retired after the 1976 season, Lasorda was given the helm, and he has led Los Angeles to three National League pennants and one world championship in his twelve years at the Dodgers' helm. His milestone victory came at the expense of Elia's cellar dwellers, compliments of Tim Leary and the entire Dodgers team. Leary, with relief help from Peña and Jay Howell, who recorded his sixteenth save, won his fifteenth game, yielding two runs on five hits in 5⅓ innings. The Dodgers scored three runs in the 3rd inning on a sacrifice fly by Gibson and RBI singles by Marshall and Hatcher. They added their final run in the eighth inning on an RBI by Griffin.

7

THE MONTH OF THE BULLDOG

Three days after manager Tommy Lasorda's historic 1000th major league victory, Orel Hershiser embarked on a historic journey of his own, one that would produce a record that, under today's pitching philosophy, may never be broken. The quest began innocently enough on August 30 in Montreal, where the Dodgers' sinkerball specialist defeated the Expos by the score of 4–2 in a complete-game effort in which he held the home team to six hits while striking out nine and walking two. L.A. roughed up right-hander Brian Holman for three runs in the second inning on a two-out single by Alfredo Griffin that scored Franklin Stubbs, and a double by Hershiser that sent John Shelby and Griffin scurrying home. It was Griffin's second consecutive game-winning RBI. And he scored the Dodgers' fourth and final run in the fifth when he doubled, went to third on a sacrifice by Hershiser, and came home on a ground ball by Steve Sax. Buck Rodgers' team was not about to quit however, and they touched Hershiser up for a deuce in the bottom half of the fifth, cutting the Dodgers' advantage to 4–2. But that was all they would get as the Bulldog shut them down over the last four innings, a feat that didn't seem particularly important at the time, but would prove to be crucial in Hershiser's record-breaking effort later in the season.

The next day the Dodgers lost to the Expos by the score of 4–3 when Peña gave up a two-out, game-winning single to Tim Wallach. The loss gave Lasorda's troops a 77–55 record at month's end, and a 6½ game lead over the Houston Astros, who held a one game lead over the San Francisco Giants. The Mets were still maintaining a safe lead over the Pittsburgh Pirates in the Eastern Division, thanks to the Bucs' sorry 13–17 record in August. Even though the Mets' record for August was only 15–14, they still increased their lead over Pittsburgh another 2½ games, giving them a 7½ game cushion. And pitching was still leading the way in the New York pennant drive. Dwight Gooden was sporting a 15–6 record, Ron Darling was at 13–9, Randy Myers had saved 20 games, and Roger McDowell had saved 14. Even though their sluggers had not produced any home runs for several weeks, Darryl Strawberry still had 30 round-trippers to his credit and Kevin McReynolds had 20. Strawberry's home run drought lasted 20 days until he hit number 31 on September 5. McReynolds went 19 days without touching them all.

The Oakland Athletics were on fire during August, reeling off twenty victories against just nine losses. That performance allowed them to pick up another 3½ games over Tom Kelly's Minnesota Twins, who won 17 games in August against 13 losses. During the A's August romp, Mark McGwire, breaking out of his summer doldrums, whacked 8 home runs. José Canseco hit 4 homers and Rickey Henderson hit 6. Storm Davis won all four of his decisions during the month, upping his record to 14–4; Bob Welch went 3–1 to bring his record up to 15–7; and Dave Stewart, who also went 3–1, boasted a 16–11 record. Dennis Eckersley, who had suddenly become the most overpowering closer in the major leagues, saved 6 games, giving him 36 saves for the season. Tony LaRussa's ball club demonstrated their proficiency in all phases of the game when they swept the Boston Red Sox in a three-game series in the Oakland Coliseum between August 29 and 31. Bob Welch out–pitched Mike Boddicker in the opener, winning 3–1. Dennis Eckerlsey got the final out for his 36th save of the year. Mark McGwire's two-run home run in the home sixth provided the winning margin. The next night, Dave Stewart and Roger Clemens squared off in a classic battle, with Stewart emerging the victor, 1–0, when Glenn Hubbard squeezed Carney Lansford home in the sixth inning. Stewart, in winning his 16th game, held the Red Sox to five hits, while fanning eight and walking three. Roger Clemens, who lost for the 10th time against 15 wins, struck out 9 and walked 2, while scattering nine base hits in 6⅓ innings. Oakland completed the sweep on Wednesday, pummeling 6', 8", sinkerball specialist Mike Smithson for six runs in six innings en route to a 7–2 win. Storm Davis was the recipient of the outburst, registering his 14th victory of the season. Mark McGwire's three-run homer in the first inning set the pace for the A's, who added two more runs in the second inning, and single runs in the fifth and seventh. McGwire, Henderson, and Weiss, all had two hits for the A's.

The three-game debacle in Oakland left Boston with a 13–16 August mark, 73–59 overall, dropping them two full games behind Detroit in the American League Eastern Division. The New York Yankees, who had a horrendous 9–20 month, slipped into third place, 5½ games behind Sparky Anderson's club, who had a losing month of their own. They could do no better than 14–16, but they still picked up ground on their challengers.

Orel Hershiser made his first September start on the 5th of the month against the Atlanta Braves in Georgia, and he found his groove as the game progressed. He said he felt too strong when the game began, being touched for three base hits and one walk in the first three innings, but he was tough when he had to be, and the Braves left three men stranded over that stretch. The Dodgers, meanwhile, were having better luck against Rick Mahler, nicking him for two runs in the opening stanza on an RBI single by Mickey Hatcher and an error by left fielder Dion James that allowed the fiery Gibson to score all the way from first base. They scored another run in the third on an error by catcher Ozzie Virgil. Meanwhile, as Hershiser noted, "I found my rhythm after that and pitched five perfect innings. Until I gave up a leadoff single in the ninth, I had retired sixteen straight hitters, five on strikes."[1] Jeff Blauser, who opened the ninth inning with a base hit, was stranded as Hershiser ended with a flourish, fanning Dale Murphy for the fourth time, his eighth strikeout of the game.

The Dodgers welcomed Hal Lanier's Houston Astros to Dodger Stadium for a two-game series on September 7, with L.A. holding a five game lead over the Texas team. In the series opener, two sinkerball specialists faced each other with Houston's ace, Mike Scott (13–5), taking the mound against Dodgers right-hander Tim Leary (15–9). The game, as expected, was a pitchers duel with each team crossing the plate once over the first seven innings. L.A. scored first, in the third inning, when Alfredo Griffin doubled, went to third on a fielder's choice, and scored on a sacrifice fly by John Shelby. The Astros tied the game with a run in the fourth inning, with Kevin Bass driving in Gerald Young. In the Dodgers eighth, Steve Sax whistled a single to left field and was bunted to second by Griffin. After Kirk Gibson was passed, Scott retired Mickey Hatcher, bringing Shelby to the plate. The Dodgers centerfielder jumped on a 1–0 pitch, and drove it into the right field stands for a three-run, game-winning home run. Houston came back to take game two by a 2–1 score, with Nolan Ryan defeating John Tudor, but time was running out for the Astros. They still trailed L.A. by five games with twenty-three games remaining in the season.

The Dodgers were beaten by the Cincinnati Reds 5–2 in Dodger Stadium on September 9, when Danny Jackson, Hershiser's competition for the National League Cy Young award, won his 21st game against 6 losses by throwing a complete game nine-hitter, with eight strikeouts and a single walk. Eric Davis and Paul O'Neil both hit two-run doubles in the fourth inning to hand Ramón Martínez his second loss against one win. L.A. had lost three of four by the time Hershiser, looking for his 20th victory of the season, took the mound the next night. He was opposed by southpaw Norm Charlton, just up from Nashville in the American Association where he had compiled a record of 11–10. A crowd of 42,393 filed through the turnstiles to see Bulldog try to tame the big, bad Reds, who were on a hot streak, having won 11 of their last 16 games to move into third place, 5½ games out first. Cincinnati threatened to score in the top of the third inning, but Hershiser, whose scoreless inning streak hadn't yet progressed to the point where it had become a topic of conversation, was more concerned with winning his 20th victory and keeping the Reds off the Dodgers' backs. "Nineteen–3 was the best I had ever done, so 20 would be nice. More important, of course, was beating the Reds and keeping them in third place. That's why when I faced Eric Davis with two outs and the bases loaded in the third inning, I was just trying to keep him in the park. He had already hit 25 dingers in 1988, and he led the league in game-winning

RBIs with 16. We hadn't scored yet, and I figured a single would mean only two runs. I couldn't let Davis hit one out."[2] And Davis didn't hit one out. Hershiser fanned him on a sinker that Davis tried to check his swing on, but couldn't do it. Tommy Lasorda's cohorts made their threat pay off in the fourth inning when Kirk Gibson walked, raced to third on a hit-and-run single by Mickey Hatcher, and scored when John Shelby hit a sacrifice fly to left field. The ball looked like a home run when it left the bat, but Kal Daniels reached into the stands to snare it, robbing Shelby of four bases. Later in the inning, Hatcher came across on a wild pitch, upping the Dodgers' margin to 2–0. Charlton hit Gibson with a pitch in the fifth inning, and balked him to second before Hatcher, who had two hits in the game, drove him home with a single. And Rick Dempsey closed out the scoring with a two-run homer in the eighth inning, his seventh of the season. Hershiser kept the Reds in check after the third inning, yielding a total of seven base hits, while striking out eight men and walking three, but it wasn't as easy as it sounds. Eric Davis hit into two double plays to choke off Cincinnati rallies in the sixth and eighth innings, and Hershiser induced Ken Griffey to pop out with runners on first and third and only one out in the seventh, and then struck out Barry Larkin to retire the side. All in all, it was a hard fought shutout for the Dodgers ace, but when the dust settled, he had his 20th victory of the season against 8 losses, and he had extended his shutout streak to 21 innings.

The next day, the West Coasters trailed the Cincinnati Reds 3–2 in the bottom of the ninth inning. The two Dodgers runs had come on home runs by starting pitcher Tim Belcher, his first major league home run, and Kirk Gibson, his 25th of the season. John Franco, who had recorded 32 saves for the year in 34 opportunities, came on to preserve the victory for 15-game winner Tom Browning. Franco retired Steve Sax, but Kirk Gibson singled to put the tying run on base. Then, with two out, John Shelby hit a hard shot to third base that Chris Sabo made a diving stop on, but then threw wild past Dave Concepción at first base, bringing 40,635 screaming Dodgers fans

Tim Belcher pitched well down the stretch and even hit his first major league home run in a 4–3 win over Cincinnati (courtesy of Los Angeles Dodgers).

to their feet. Gibson, who was off with the crack of the bat, scored all the way from first base to knot the game at three-all. And Jeff Hamilton ended the suspense when he drove a 3–2 screwball into the left field pavilion, to give the undefeated Tim Crews his fifth win of the season. Tommy Lasorda led the charge out of the Dodgers dugout, yelling "Oh yeah! Oh yeah!" as Hamilton was swallowed up by his teammates as soon as he crossed home plate. And, in a season-long ritual following a win, Kirk Gibson, half undressed, stood by his locker in the clubhouse after the game, cupped his hands to his mouth, and yelled, "How sweet it is, to taste the fruits of victory."

John Tudor threw a two-hit shutout against the Atlanta Braves in Dodger Stadium on the evening of September 13, winning 2–0 on Mike Scioscia's two-run home run in the fifth inning off Braves rookie John Smoltz, whose record dropped to 2–5. Tudor pitched five innings, yielding two hits, and he was followed to the mound by Ramón Martínez and Jay Howell, who pitched two hitless innings each, with Howell notching his 19th save. Kirk Gibson had two hits in the game, but neither one figured in the scoring. The shutout began a streak where Dodgers pitchers threw five shutouts in seven games, two by Tudor, two by Hershiser, and one by Tim Belcher. Their only loss came as a result of Tom Browning's classic.

Orel Hershiser continued his pitching magic against Atlanta, shutting Chuck Tanner's team out for the second time in ten days, both coming at the expense of hard-luck Rick Mahler, who was beaten by the Dodgers ace 3–0 the first time, and was victimized 1–0 this time. The only run scored in the bottom of the ninth inning when Kirk Gibson walked to open the inning and scored all the way from first when Mike Marshall ripped a Mahler fastball into the left field corner for a double. It was a tough loss for Mahler, whose record fell to 9–15. The big righty held the Dodgers to five hits and two walks while striking out three men. Hershiser, in winning his 21st game, pitched a six-hitter with eight strikeouts and two bases on balls. The game was his 13th complete game of the season, and his sixth in a row, during which his earned run average was 0.67. His only trouble came in the seventh inning, as he said, "when Andres Thomas led off with a double to the gap in left-center. Dion James grounded to first, but Franklin Stubbs' throw pulled me off the bag and Thomas went to third. Ozzie Virgil, always a potential menace, grounded to Stubbs, who made the putout himself and held Thomas at third, James advancing to second. With first base open and only one out, I pitched carefully to Jerry Blocker, going to 2–0 before intentionally walking him to load the bases and face the pitcher, Rick Mahler. I struck him out but then had to face Ron Gant. I threw a curve and as soon as it left my hand I shouted, "No!" I had hung it. Gant lifted a long fly to left, and I held my breath. Gibson crashed into the wall but hauled it in, and I was out of my third jam in the game."[3]

Hershiser left the team immediately after the game to be with his wife, Jamie, who was due to deliver a baby any time. And, the next day she deliv-

Mike Marshall continued his outstanding play down the stretch, finishing with a .277 batting average, 20 homers, and 82 RBIs (author's collection).

ered as promised, presenting her husband with a beautiful baby boy named Jordan. While Orel was enjoying his wife and his new son, and celebrating his 30th birthday, his quest for immortality was put on hold, but a 28-year-old left-hander named Tom Browning, on his way to an outstanding 18–5 season with the Cincinnati Reds, claimed his own niche in Baseball's Hall of Fame in Cooperstown by pitching a perfect game against Tommy Lasorda's team in Crosley Field, winning 1–0 over Tim Belcher, who limited the Reds to just three base hits. The winning run scored in the bottom of the sixth inning on a throwing error by third baseman Jeff Hamilton that brought in Barry Larkin, who had doubled. The only hits in the ballgame belonged to Ron Oester, Chris Sabo, and Larkin. Browning's masterpiece, the rarest feat in baseball, was the 14th perfect game in major league history, and the first one in Cincinnati's glorious 119-year history. And there was only one close play in the game. It came in the fifth inning when Mike Marshall hit a high bouncer over third base, but Chris Sabo backhanded the ball and rifled it to Nick Esasky at first base in time to retire Marshall. The game was delayed by rain for two hours, twenty-seven minutes, but once it started, Browning required only one hour and fifty-one minutes to dispatch Lasorda's hitless wonders. As reported in *The Sporting News*, "'The only guy who gave us trouble all night was Rick Dempsey,' said Reds catcher Jeff Reed. 'Browning kept getting ahead with good first-pitch fastballs, but Dempsey is a first-pitch fastball hitter and he hit the ball hard his first two times up.' Dempsey got a change-up, fastball inside and flied to the warning track in right on another change-up. Steve Sax then sent a shot over second base, but shortstop Barry Larkin snatched the ball and threw him out."[4] Tracy Woodson was the Dodgers' last hope in the top of the ninth. "'I threw a fastball about forehead high,' Browning said. 'I was surprised he swung.' When Woodson missed, the Reds swarmed over Browning before carrying him off the field. 'The game was over and I knew I'd won 1–0. I looked at Reed and pumped my fist (three times). Then the dogpile hit,' Browning said. 'When they lifted me on their shoulders, I felt a tear come to my eye.'"[5]

The Dodgers retained their seven game lead in the Western Division as Houston dropped a 5–4 decision to the San Francisco Giants in the Astrodome when Roger Craig's troops plated five runs after two men had been retired in the sixth inning. Atlee Hammaker was the recipient of the outburst, recording his eighth victory of the season against the same number of losses. Houston's slide continued the next day, when Rick Reuschel (19–8) defeated Jim Deshaies (10–13) by the score of 4–2 in a complete game effort. Shortstop José Uribe, who had two hits in the game, homered for the Giants in the seventh inning. Will Clark and Robby Thompson also had two hits for San Francisco. At the same time the Astros were biting the dust, L.A. was taking the measure of the Cincinnati Reds to the tune of 4–3. Tim Leary struggled through five innings, yielding three runs and leaving with a 3–3 tie. Ricky Horton, Alejandro Peña, Jesse Orosco, and Jay Howell followed Leary to the mound and shut the Reds down over the last four innings. Orosco picked up his third win of the year against two losses and Howell earned his 20th save with a perfect ninth.

John Tudor continued his fine work with L.A. when he blanked the Reds 2–0 on September 18, with help from Alejandro Peña. Tudor pitched the first six innings and was awarded the victory, his 10th against 8 losses, when Lasorda's opportunists erupted for two runs in the top of the seventh inning, breaking a scoreless tie. Peña pitched three scoreless innings for his 11th save. The winning runs crossed the plate on a single by John Shelby, who had two of the Dodgers' five base hits, a stolen base, an RBI double by Jeff Hamilton, and consecutive walks to Scioscia, pinch-hitter Danny Heep, and Alfredo Griffin. The Dodgers lead was up to nine games when San Francisco pounded Houston 10–3, driving Mike Scott to cover under a barrage of base hits in his 3⅔ innings of work. Will Clark got the Giants off on the right foot when he hit a two-run homer in the first inning. They added a run in the second inning and three in the fourth, two of which came on a home run by winning pitcher Don Robinson.

Hershiser was back at it on the 19th, facing Nolan Ryan in the Astrodome. Unfortunately for Ryan, his day was a short one, as he had to come out after two innings. He was replaced by Danny Darwin, who matched Hershiser pitch for pitch over the next four innings. In the top of the seventh, John Shelby, in a horrendous 6 for 54 slump that had him batting just .111, hit a tremendous home run into the orange seats in right-center field, over 400 feet from home plate. That was the only run of the ballgame as the Dodgers could muster only three hits off Houston's pitching all day, a testament to L.A.'s .189 team batting average for the first 19 days of the month. Hershiser was almost as stingy as his opponents, holding the Astros to four hits, while striking out five with no walks. In the Houston ninth, after the leadoff batter reached base, Glenn Davis hammered a ball into the hole between third and short that looked like a base hit. But Alfredo Griffin gobbled it up and flipped it to Sax, who relayed it to first to complete a pretty double play. When the next batter, Buddy Bell, fouled out, Hershiser had his fourth consecutive shutout, bringing his scoreless inning streak to 40 and bringing national attention on himself. Now the media coverage became more intense, the number of reporters following the games increased, and the number of them looking for interviews rose ten-fold. ESPN was on the scene for every game now that Hershiser's streak had reached impressive numbers, and also because the Dodgers' magic number for clinching the National League Western Division title was down to five.

Tim Belcher blanked Houston 6–0 on the 20th, the Dodgers split with San Diego the next day, losing the opener 9–3 and winning the nightcap 6–5 in ten innings on an RBI single by rookie Mike Devereaux, and they lost to San Diego again on the 22nd by a 5–4 score. Now it was Orel time again, and Big O had to face the always-tough San Francisco Giants in Candlestick Park, where the wind blows in uncertain directions causing excitement on every fly ball hit to the outfield. Atlee Hammaker started for Roger Craig's Giants and he was on top of his game. With the game scoreless in the bottom of the third, San Francisco threatened. José Uribe led off with a single and Hammaker laid down a perfect sacrifice bunt, but Hershiser slipped while fielding the ball and both runners were safe. The next batter, Brett Butler, hit a ground ball to Jeff Hamilton at third base that looked like a potential double play ball. Hamilton rifled the ball to second to force Hammaker, but Butler beat the relay, putting runners on first and third with one out. Third baseman Ernest Riles stepped in to face Hershiser, and Bulldog, realizing he needed a double play ball to preserve his scoreless inning string, threw Riles nothing but sinkers. Riles finally hit a ground ball to Sax who flipped it to Griffin for one out, but Griffin's relay to Tracy Woodson at first sailed wide, with Uribe crossing the plate with the run that apparently broke Hershiser's streak. Hershiser remembered the feeling. "I grimaced and let out a huge breath. It's disappointing to come so close and a real letdown to see it all end, but now we're trailing 1–0 and I have to face Will Clark. I was rubbing up the ball and turning back toward the mound when I saw second base umpire Paul Runge signal that both Butler and Riles were out. I headed straight for the dugout before he changed his mind. I knew exactly what he was saying. Butler had apparently slid outside the baseline at Griffin and was called for interference.... When I got to the dugout, both Tommy and Perry were laughing. 'Drysdale got his break,' Tommy said. 'Now you got yours.'"[6] Hershiser settled down after that near miss, and retired the next nine batters in a row. The Giants' lefty matched Bulldog, goose egg for goose egg, inning after inning, and the game remained scoreless when the top of the eighth rolled around. Tracy Woodson led off the inning with a single, went to second on a sacrifice by Hershiser, and stayed there as Alfredo Griffin walked. Both runners held as Steve Sax was retired for out number two. Then, Mickey Hatcher, who was 6 for 44 in September, and who had not hit a home run in 172 at-bats during the season, rectified that failing by lofting the ball over the fence to give the Dodgers a 3–0 lead. And that was that. Hershiser gave up singles in both the seventh and eighth innings, but never was in serious trouble. He retired the Giants without incident in the ninth inning, finishing with a five-hitter, with two walks and two strikeouts. He was now within 9⅔ innings of Don Drysdale's scoreless innings streak.

The Dodgers defeated the Giants again the next night 7–3 but were shut out in the get-away game 2–0 when Dennis Cook threw a two-hitter at them. On Monday, the 26th, manager Tommy Lasorda led his troops into San Diego to tangle with Larry Bowa's Padres, with the Big Blue Machine leading Cincinnati by seven games with just seven games remaining on the schedule. It was pennant-clinching time, and Fernando Valenzuela was given the honor of starting the potential pennant-clinching game, opposed by the Padres' 15-game winner, Dennis Rasmussen. Bowa's club drew first blood when they nicked Fernando for two runs in the bottom of the first inning on an error by the Dodgers lefty and a two-run homer by Randy Ready. L.A. drew even on homers by John Shelby in the fourth inning and Tracy Woodson in the fifth. In the Dodgers' eighth, Alfredo Griffin reached second base on Dickie Thon's throwing error, moved to third on a sacrifice bunt by Sax, and carried home the tie-breaking run when Mickey Hatcher singled through the drawn-in infield. With Jay Howell on the mound in the ninth, trying to nail down the pennant, the crowd was on its feet in anticipation of witnessing a history-making event. Dodgers players were standing nervously in the dugout, eyeing the action with taut faces. Howell went to 3–2 on Marvel Wynne before Wynne hit a ball to short right. Sax, backing out under it, waved everyone else off the play. As the Dodgers second baseman squeezed the ball, the Dodgers bench exploded in unison. They raced across the field like madmen, knocking pitcher Jay Howell to the ground in a frenzied charge to the mound. High-fives were everywhere as Dodgers players congratulated each other on the successful completion of an impossible dream. Tommy Lasorda and Fred Claire left the park arm in arm and proceeded down the runway to the locker room where the victory celebration was getting underway, and where, already, the bubbly was flowing like water.

The Dodgers were a team that had finished fifth and fourth the previous two years, and were picked to finish way down in the division again in 1988. But they confounded the experts by racing to the front of the pack almost from the start of the season, and by holding on to first place for 123 days from May 26 on. They had rebounded from a fourth place finish in 1987 to become the National League Western Division champions. It had been a great season, a dream season, but it wasn't over yet. They still had to meet the Eastern Division champion New York Mets in the National League Championship Series, starting in about nine days. Lasorda's team wouldn't be given much chance against the mighty New York Mets machine, having lost ten of eleven meetings to them during the regular season, but they still had their secret weapon, Kirk Gibson, and they remembered what their fiery leader said some seven long months ago during spring training. "I came to L.A. to win. That's my number one goal every day. When I leave spring training, I'm leaving to be a World Champion."[7] The Michigan native was without question the heart and soul of the 1988 Los Angeles Dodgers and, as he admitted, "I am a madman at times." That was never more obvious to the paying customers than when he struck out in a crucial situation. Gibson hated to strike out, and he was known to crack himself in the batting helmet with his bat when he fanned. When he got particularly upset with himself, he would heave his bat toward the bat rack and sling his helmet into the dugout. And if he thought he got a bad call from the umpire, he would yell and scream at the ump from the dugout. At times like that, the other players kept their distance from him. No one would talk to him. No one would sit near him. No one would even look at him.

With the pennant clinching behind them, the team now focused its attention on ace hurler Orel Hershiser and his quest to break the all-time consecutive scoreless innings record, held by former Dodger Don Drysdale. The night after the pennant-clincher, the listless Dodgers fell to the Padres by the score of 8–4, with San Diego scoring in each of the first five innings, driving Tim Leary to cover in the fourth after he had been raked for seven runs on eight hits. Dave Anderson had two hits for the Dodgers and Franklin Stubbs had a double and two RBIs.

The big day arrived with incredible fanfare, as literally hundreds of media vultures swept down on Jack Murphy Stadium in San Diego, trying to get an audience with Orel Hershiser, his manager, or his pitching coach. But the crafty right-hander stayed pretty much to himself prior to the start of festivities, concentrating on the task at hand and trying to prepare himself mentally. He felt confident pitching against the Padres because his career statistics against Bowa's club showed a record of seven victories against four losses, with four shutouts and a 1.90 ERA. Everything was fine during batting practice and in the clubhouse, but as soon as he went down to the bullpen to warm up, with pitching coach Ron Perranoski observing, the magnitude of the event struck him.

I threw a few pitches and turned to him. "You know, I'm really pretty nervous. I can even feel it in my stomach."

"You'll be all right once you get out there and get the first couple of outs," Perry said.

I continued to throw.

"Did you hear that?" he said suddenly.

"No."

"That was *my* stomach. I think I'm nervous too."[8]

After the Dodgers were retired in the top of the first inning, the San Diego bench jockeys unlimbered their lungs and kept up a steady stream of unsettling remarks in the direction of the Dodgers pitcher. The 22,596 die-hard fans who turned out for the game joined in the Hershiser-baiting also, letting the Dodgers pitcher know that his days (or innings) were numbered, and that he would be taking his shower early today. But that wouldn't happen in the first inning as Bulldog set them down without a problem, even retiring the pesky Tony Gwynn on a ground ball to Steve Sax at second base. It was the first of four consecutive times that Gwynn would ground out to second. San Diego right-hander Andy Hawkins, a big 6', 3", 223-pound fireballer, had little trouble with Lasorda's would-be hitters, setting them down without a whimper inning after inning. Hershiser was gaining confidence as his scoreless streak continued. By the fifth inning, he had left his nervousness behind, but now he was becoming excited as the big moment when he would approach 59 consecutive scoreless innings neared. At the end of six innings of play, Bulldog had thrown a modest 65 pitches, and had limited the Padres to just four base hits.

Both Hawkins and Hershiser breezed through the seventh inning, and then the eighth, and the ninth. By now, the leather-lunged fans had changed their loyalty and were fiercely behind the quest. When Hershiser left the dugout for the mound to start the seventh inning, the fans gave him a standing ovation. And their cheering never stopped. They cheered every out, and even followed him back to the dugout at the end of the inning. His streak now stood at 56 consecutive scoreless innings, surpassing Walter Johnson's old mark of 55⅔. Another play for the highlight reel occurred in the eighth inning when Roberto Alomar hit a two-out single but, while he was jockeying to get in position to steal second base, Hershiser picked him off. Inning number 57 had gone by the boards. The ninth was a surprisingly easy inning for Big O as he set Bowa's boys down in order. After he had returned to the dugout, he asked Lasorda to take him out of the game if he retired the first two batters in the tenth inning because he didn't want to break Drysdale's record. He wanted to share the record with Big D. Lasorda wouldn't buy that idea however, and he told Bulldog he had to complete the inning. "Drysdale laughed when he heard of Hershiser's plan. 'I'd have kicked him in the pants if I'd known that,' Drysdale said. 'I'd have told him to get his buns out there and get them.'"[9]

The Dodgers ace walked to the mound at the start of the tenth inning. He tipped his hat in the direction of the press box where Don Drysdale was broadcasting the game, and vowed to get three more outs. The San Diego lead-off man, Marvel Wynne, reached first base on a strikeout when Hershiser's curveball hit the dirt and bounced away for a wild pitch. He moved to second on a sacrifice, and advanced to third on a ground ball by Randy Ready. Two men out. One to go, for the record. The next batter, Gary Templeton, walked and stole second, but Hershiser finally ended the suspense by retiring Keith Moreland on a 1–2 can of worms to José González in right field. He remembered the moment. "My teammates on the field and from the bench mobbed me, and Don Drysdale met me at the end of the dugout. We embraced. "'It couldn't have happened to a nicer kid,' he said with a smile. 'I can't believe you didn't win that game — just like the sixties.' He interviewed me right there for KABC radio while the game was still going on."[10] Later, baseball's newest Dr. Zero would admit, "I had so much pressure on me out there. That's probably the most nervous I've ever been in my career. It's also probably the sharpest I've been mentally in my career."[11]

Orel Hershiser retired at the end of the tenth inning with his new record. He had pitched 10 shutout innings, holding the San Diego Padres to four base hits, while striking out three and walking one. His 59 consecutive scoreless innings record will probably never be broken if today's pitching philosophy remains unchanged, nor will his September pitching record, shown below.

G	CG	IP	W	L	H	SO	BB	ERA
6	5	55	5	0	30	34	9	0.00

Orel's opponent, Andy Hawkins, was just as good as his more famous adversary in this game. He also held the enemy to four hits in ten innings, and he struck out six and walked two. Orosco, Crews, and Ken Howell followed Hershiser to the mound, throwing another six shutout innings at the Padres. And the Padres relievers did likewise. In the top of the sixteenth inning, L.A. broke through when Mickey Hatcher, the leader of the Stuntmen, singled, moved around to third on two ground balls, and came home when José González's ground ball was bobbled for an error. But the Dodgers pen couldn't stand prosperity. Ken Howell walked Carmelo Martínez with two men out in the bottom of the sixteenth, and southpaw Ricky Horton was brought in to face the left-handed hitting Marvel Wynne. But Wynne didn't bat. Manager Larry Bowa sent Mark Parent, a big right-handed slugger, up to face the Dodgers lefty. Parent, who already had five home runs to his credit in 106 at-bats during the season, hit the biggest one of his career, a two-run, game-winning shot off Horton to send the San Diego fans home happy.

Orel Hershiser broke Don Drysdale's consecutive scoreless inning streak in San Diego on September 28 (author's collection).

Los Angeles

Name	Pos	AB	R	H
Sax	2B	5	0	0
Sharperson	2B	2	0	0
Stubbs	1B	5	0	0
Hatcher	PH-1B	1	1	1
Gibson	LF	5	0	1
Orosco	P	0	0	0
Woodson	3B	2	0	1
Shelby	CF	5	0	1
C. Gwynn	LF	1	0	0
Mi. Davis	RF	4	0	0
González	RF-LF-CF	3	0	0
Scioscia	C	4	0	0
Dempsey	C	3	0	0
Hamilton	3B	5	0	0
Crews	P	0	0	0
Heep	PH	1	0	0
K. Howell	P	0	0	0
Horton	P	0	0	0
Griffin	SS	5	0	1
Hershiser	P	3	0	1
Devereaux	RF	2	0	0
Totals		56	1	6

San Diego

Name	Pos	AB	R	H
Alomar	2B	7	0	1
Flannery	3B	4	0	1
Roberts	PR-3B	1	0	0
T. Gwynn	CF	5	0	0
Jefferson	CF	1	0	0
Martínez	1B	5	1	0
Wynne	RF	5	0	2
Parent	PH	1	1	1
Santiago	C	5	0	0
Ready	LF	6	0	0
Templeton	SS	5	0	0
Hawkins	P	3	0	0
Moreland	PH	1	0	0
Ma.Davis	P	0	0	0
Nelson	PH	1	0	0
McCullers	P	0	0	0
Brown	PH	0	0	0
Thon	PR	0	0	0
Leiper	P	0	0	0
		50	2	5

| Los Angeles | 0 0 0 | 0 0 0 | 0 0 0 | 0 0 0 | 0 0 0 | 1 — 1 — 6 — 1 |
| San Diego | 0 0 0 | 0 0 0 | 0 0 0 | 0 0 0 | 0 0 0 | 2 — 2 — 5 — 2 |

Double-Griffin
Triple-Woodson
Home Run-Parent

Name	IP	W	L	H	SO	BB
Los Angeles						
Hershiser	10	0	0	4	3	1
Orosco	1	0	0	0	0	4
Crews	2	0	0	0	2	0
K. Howell	2⅔	0	0	1	3	3
Horton (L 1-1)	0*	0	1	1	0	0
San Diego						
Hawkins	10	0	0	4	6	2
Ma. Davis	2	0	0	0	4	0
McCullers	3	0	0	1	4	0
Leiper (W 3-0)	1	1	0	1	0	0

* Pitched to one batter in the sixteenth inning.[12]

The rest of the season was routine except for the game of September 30 in which John Tudor suffered a muscle spasm in his right hip in the second inning and had to leave the game against the San Francisco Giants. He injured it while pitching to Dennis Cook and, after trying to take a warmup throw, he walked off the mound with trainer Charlie Strasser and pitching coach Ron Perranoski. The Dodgers won the game 6–4 with Horton (7–3) picking up the win and Alejandro Peña earning his 12th save. L.A. ended the season with a two-game series against the San Francisco Giants at home. They won the first game 2–1 as Tim Belcher captured his 12th win against 6 losses. Fernando Valenzuela earned his first save of the year, and his first save since his rookie season of 1980. The Giants won the season finale 1–0 with Don Robinson picking up his 10th win of the year, out-dueling Tim Leary.

The final standings gave Tommy Lasorda's team a big lead over their challengers in the Western Division of the National League. The most shocking story of the season was the late collapse of the Houston Astros, who plummeted all the way to fifth place by season's end. They trailed the Dodgers by only ½ game after the games of August 9, but they won just 20 of 50 games after that date, going 9–12 over the last three weeks of August and 11–18 in September.

Name	W	L	GA/GB
Los Angeles	94	67	—
Cincinnati	87	74	-7
San Diego	83	78	-11
San Francisco	83	79	-11½

Name	W	L	GA/GB
Houston	82	80	-12½
Atlanta	54	106	-39½

Los Angeles finished strong, winning 17 games in September against 11 losses. The team batting average during the month was a barely visible .203, but fortunately, the Dodgers' pitching was sensational down the stretch, compiling a 2.02 earned run average, with eight shutouts. The leader of the pack, naturally, was Orel Hershiser who went 5–0 with a perfect 0.00 ERA. Tim Belcher was 2–1 with a 1.06 ERA, and John Tudor was 2–2 with a 2.08 ERA. Tim Leary, who was 2–2, had a 5.14 ERA. The bullpen crew was led by Brian Holton (11 innings) and Jay Howell (7 innings) both of whom had perfect 0.00 ERAs. Jay Howell finished the year with a flourish. After blowing the lead and eventually losing the August 11 game to Cincinnati, the Dodgers' closer was perfect the remainder of the season. He appeared in 15 games, with two wins and seven saves. He pitched 20⅔ innings, allowing no runs and only four base hits. Alejandro Peña had a 0.49 ERA in 18 innings, Tim Crews was at 0.77 in 12 innings, and Jesse Orosco was at 0.92 in 9 innings. Ricky Horton had a 5.00 ERA covering 9 innings. Alfredo Griffin was the big sticker on offense with a batting average of .247. He was followed by Kirk Gibson at .242, Mike Scioscia at .240, John Shelby at .239, Steve Sax at .232, Mike Marshall at .228, Jeff Hamilton at .217, Mickey Hatcher at .206, and Franklin Stubbs at .156.

Their regular season statistics are even more revealing of their strengths and weaknesses. L.A., as a team, was average in runs scored, average in home runs, and average in stolen bases. They were ninth out of twelve teams in fielding average and errors, but they were second in ERA and second in opponents runs scored. Their pitching staff led the league in complete games, shutouts, and saves.

Los Angeles Pitching Statistics-1988 Season.

Name	G	CG	IP	W	L	ERA	Saves
Orel Hershiser	35	15	267	23	8	2.26	1
Tim Leary	35	9	229	17	11	2.91	0
Tim Belcher	36	4	180	12	6	2.91	4
John Tudor	30	5	198	10	8	2.32	0
Brian Holton	45	0	85	7	3	1.70	1
Alejandro Peña	60	0	94	6	7	1.91	12
Jay Howell	50	0	65	5	3	2.08	21
Jesse Orosco	55	0	53	3	2	2.72	9
Tim Crews	42	0	72	4	0	3.14	0
Fernando Valenzuela	23	3	142	5	8	4.24	1

Los Angeles Batting Statistics-1988 Season

Name	AB	R	H	D	T	HR	RBI	SB	BA
Kirk Gibson	542	106	157	28	1	25	76	31	.290
Mike Marshall	542	63	150	27	2	20	82	4	.277
John Shelby	494	65	130	23	6	10	64	16	.263
Mike Scioscia	408	29	105	18	0	3	35	0	.257
Steve Sax	632	70	175	19	4	5	57	42	.277
Alfredo Griffin	316	39	63	8	3	1	27	7	.199
Jeff Hamilton	309	34	73	14	2	6	33	0	.236
Mike Davis	281	29	55	11	2	2	17	7	.196
Dave Anderson	285	31	71	10	2	2	20	4	.249
Mickey Hatcher	191	22	56	8	0	1	25	0	.293
Rick Dempsey	167	25	42	13	0	7	30	1	.251
Tracy Woodson	173	15	43	4	1	3	15	1	.249
Franklin Stubbs	242	30	54	13	0	8	34	11	.223
Danny Heep	149	14	36	2	0	0	11	2	.242

The Los Angeles Dodgers players were among the league leaders in several individual categories. Kirk Gibson, the leader of the L.A. pack, was second in runs scored with 106, and was fourth in on base percentage with .381. And he was unquestionably the league leader in intangibles, leading by example day after day, showing his teammates how to win. Orel Hershiser, another player who led by example, led the league in victories with 23 (tied with Danny Jackson), in complete games with 15 (tied with Jackson), in shutouts with 8, and in innings pitched with 267. He finished third in ERA with 2.26, and third in winning percentage with .742. Tim Leary was second in shutouts with 6. John Tudor was fourth in ERA at 2.32.

Tim Leary was the biggest surprise of the season, rebounding from a dismal 3–11 mark in 1987 to a sensational 17–11 mark, with a 2.91 ERA, in 1988. He credited his success to a new split-finger pitch that he developed in the Mexican Pacific League over the winter.

The Dodgers, as a team, stole 131 bases in 177 attempts for an outstanding .740 percentage. The team leaders were Kirk Gibson, who stole 31 bases in 35 attempts for a .886 stolen base success rate; Steve Sax, who stole 42 bases in 54 attempts for a .778 stolen base percentage; John Shelby, who had 16 stolen bases in 21 attempts for a .762 percentage; and Franklin Stubbs, who had 11 stolen bases in 14 attempts for a .786 percentage.

The Dodgers bullpen set a team record by recording 49 saves, breaking the old mark of 46, set in 1962.

The other division races ended as shown below.

National League Eastern Division

New York Mets	100-60	—
Pittsburgh	85-75	-15

Franklin Stubbs was a valuable member of the 1988 Dodgers, handling most of the first base duties down the stretch and in the postseason (author's collection).

The New York Mets captured several individual honors during the season. Darryl Strawberry led the National League in home runs with 39, and in slugging percentage with .545. He was second in runs batted in with 101. David Cone, with 20 wins against just 3 losses, led the league with an .870 winning percentage. He was third in victories, second in strikeouts with 213, and second in ERA with 2.26. John Franco led the league in saves with 39.

American League Eastern Division

Boston	89-73	—
Detroit	88-74	-1
Milwaukee	87-75	-2
Toronto	87-75	-2
New York	85-76	-3½

Boston Red Sox players won several individual honors. Wade Boggs led the American League in batting average with .366, his fourth consecutive batting title and his fifth title in seven years. He also led the league in runs scored with 128, in doubles with 45, in on base percentage with .480, and in bases on balls with 125. He was second in base hits with 214. Roger Clemens led the league in shutouts with eight, in complete games with 14 (tied with Dave Stewart), and in strikeouts with 291. Bruce Hurst was second in winning percentage with .750, winning eighteen games against six losses.

American League Western Division

| Oakland | 104-58 | — |
| Minnesota | 91-71 | -13 |

Oakland players led the league in several individual categories. José Canseco led the league in home runs with 42, and he became the first 40–40 player in major league baseball history after stealing 40 bases. He also led the league in runs batted in with 124, and in slugging percentage with .569. He was second in runs scored with 120, and second in total bases with 347. Mark McGwire finished third in home runs with 32. Dave Stewart led the league in complete games with 14 (tied with Clemens), and in innings pitched with 275⅔. He was second in victories with 21. Dennis Eckersley led the league in saves with 45.

8

FACING THEIR NEW YORK
METS NEMESIS

The New York Mets were the Los Angeles Dodgers' worst fear during the regular National League season. The Western Division champions were completely mesmerized by Mets pitching, losing ten of eleven games and scoring only 18 runs to 49 for the New Yorkers. Dwight Gooden was the main antagonist, sending the Dodgers down to defeat three times without a loss and allowing only 6 runs in 35⅓ innings for a 1.53 ERA. Doctor K, as he was called, threw two complete games with one shutout, and fanned 22 batters in 35⅔ innings while allowing only 25 base hits and issuing 5 bases on balls. David Cone and Ron Darling were almost as good, with Cone registering a 2–0 mark with a 1.32 ERA and Darling taking the measure of the Dodgers twice without a loss while posting a 1.02 ERA. Orel Hershiser faced Davey Johnson's team only once during the regular season, dropping a tough 2–1 decision when the Mets crossed the plate twice in the eighth inning, wiping out a 1–0 LA lead. It was Hershiser's last loss of the season. He went on to win his last six regular season decisions.

The summary of the 1988 regular season NY-LA confrontations are listed below.

Date	Location	Score	WP	LP	Home Runs
5/20	Los Angeles	NY 5 LA 2	Fernandez (2-3)	Sutton (3-3)	H. Johnson
5/21	Los Angeles	NY 4 LA 0	Gooden (8-0)	Belcher (3-2)	
5/22	Los Angeles	NY 5 LA 2	Cone (6-0)	Valenzuela (3-5)	D. Strawberry
5/30	New York	NY 3 LA 2	Darling (6-3)	Leary (4-4)	J. Shelby
5/31	New York	NY 5 LA 4 (11)	Myers (3-0)	Peña (2-2)	K. Gibson, K. Elster
6/1	New York	NY 3 LA 4	Holton (2-0)	Fernandez (2-5)	K. McReynolds

Date	Location	Score	WP	LP	Home Runs
8/22	Los Angeles	NY 7 LA 1	Gooden (15-6)	Tudor (7-6)	K. Hernandez, K. McReynolds
8/23	Los Angeles	NY 5 LA 1	Cone (13-3)	Martínez (0-1)	
8/24	Los Angeles	NY 2 LA 1	Leach (6-1)	Hershiser (17-8)	
9/2	New York	NY 8 LA 0	Darling (14-9)	Leary (15-9)	K. Elster (2), G. Jeffries, M. Wilson
9/3	New York	NY 2 LA 1	Gooden (16-6)	Tudor (8-7)	

New York finished the year with a record of 100–60, giving them a fifteen game bulge over the Pittsburgh Pirates. Davey Johnson's team was a well-balanced group with no apparent weaknesses. Their big bats led the National League in runs scored (703) and home runs (152), and their strong arms led the league's pitchers in ERA (2.91) and strikeouts (1100), while holding opposing batters to the fewest runs (532), the fewest bases on balls (404), the fewest home runs allowed (78), and the lowest team batting average (.235). The Dodgers, with 94 victories against 67 losses, enjoyed a seven game advantage over second place Cincinnati. They were a middle-of-the-road offensive team, finishing sixth in the league in runs scored, tenth in home runs, and sixth in batting average. Their pitching was excellent, however, as they finished second to the Mets in ERA (2.96), third in strikeouts (1029), second in fewest home runs allowed (84), and second in opponents batting average (.237), while leading the league in saves (49), complete games (32), and shutouts (24). The Dodgers also had several other strong points: they had the best road record in the major leagues at 49–31, their longest losing streak was only three games, and they were 4–1–1 in doubleheaders.

It was obvious, based on the statistics presented in the previous chapter, that pitching would have to carry Los Angeles through if they were to win the NLCS. In addition to outstanding pitching, they would also need their defense to step up, and their offense to make timely, if not numerous, base hits. The media promoted the series as a David and Goliath matchup, and they weren't giving David much of a chance. Most baseball experts called the series a gross mismatch, and made the Mets 2–1 favorites to win the series in no more than five games—maybe even four straight.

The two managers were a study in opposites. Davey Johnson had been an outstanding second baseman who enjoyed a 13-year major league career. He was flawless in the field with three Gold Gloves to his credit, and he was a decent hitter with above average power. In 1973 with the Atlanta Braves, he set the single-season home run record for second basemen with 43 round-trippers. He began a managerial career in 1979, winning pennants in his first three minor league seasons. He was named the New York Mets manager in 1984, winning a world championship in 1986, and finishing second three times. In his five years at the Mets helm, he averaged 98 victories a year. As reported in *The Ballplayers*, "Johnson, who earned a mathematics degree from Trinity (Texas) University, gained immediate attention for his use of computers to compile player data. His attention to batter-pitcher matchups for platooning and in-game switches was learned from Earl Weaver. Johnson's strategy owes much to his former manager. He dislikes the bunt and manages according to the credos of 'pitching and three-run homers' and 'play for one run, lose by one run.'"[1]

Johnson's counterpart on the Los Angeles Dodgers, Tommy Lasorda, started out as a wild, 17-year-old southpaw pitcher with Concord, where he compiled a record of 3–12 with 100 bases on balls in 121 innings pitched. His most memorable pitching experience occurred when he struck out 25 Amsterdam batters in a 15-inning game while pitching for Schenectady in 1948. Two years later, he pitched for the Montreal Royals of the International League, the Brooklyn Dodgers' top minor league club. He still holds the I.L. record for career victories with 125. His major league career consisted of just 26 games, with Brooklyn and the Kansas City Athletics, with a 0–4 record. Lasorda began his managerial career with Pocatello in the Los Angeles Dodgers minor league system. After eight years learning his new trade, he was brought up to Los Angeles as a bench coach under Walt Alston in 1973. When Alston retired after the 1976 season, Lasorda was handed the reins of the Big Club. He won National League pennants his first two years on the job, but lost the World Series to the New York Yankees in six games each time. In his first 13 years as manager of the Dodgers, Tommy Lasorda won six division titles, three National League pennants (prior to 1988), and a world championship in 1981. He is noted as a great motivator, a rah-rah manager who is the club's leading cheerleader. He probably wouldn't know a computer if he fell over it.

The NLCS opened in Dodger Stadium on Tuesday, October 4, with a healthy Mets team ready to take on a slightly injured Los Angeles outfit. Kirk Gibson was still hobbled with a hamstring injury, and John Tudor was nursing a hip injury. But true to his persona, Gibson was in the starting lineup. Dwight "Doc" Gooden, the Mets ace, took the mound against Dr. Zero, Orel Hershiser, who was last scored upon 35 days previous, on August 30. Since that day, the man called Bulldog had thrown 59 consecutive scoreless innings, compiling a perfect 6–0 record. Gooden, a 6', 3", 198-pound right-hander from Tampa, Florida, was one of the top pitchers in the National League, having won 91 games against 35 losses, for a dazzling .722 winning percentage, over his brief five year career. He went 24–4 in 1985 at the tender age of 20, and in the regular season just ended he won eighteen games against nine losses with a 3.19 ERA. Hershiser, at 29 years of age, went 23–8 in the regular season, with eight shutouts and a 2.26 ERA. The game was expected to be a pitchers duel, and it didn't disappoint. It was fitting for a National League Championship Series opener. After Hershiser disposed of the Mets easily in the top of the first inning, for his 60th consecutive scoreless inning, Steve Sax led off the home half with a single and promptly stole second as 55,582 excited Dodgers fans screamed their approval. Kirk Gibson moved Sax to third base with an infield grounder, and Mike Marshall drove him in with a two-out single. The game remained a 1–0 Dodgers advantage until the seventh inning when Tommy Lasorda's opportunists struck again. Mike Scioscia opened the seventh with a double and came across on Alfredo Griffin's single. The game entered the ninth inning with L.A. in front 2–0. Hershiser, who had increased his scoreless innings streak to 67, had limited the Mets to four singles and one walk, with six strikeouts, over eight innings. In the top of the ninth, Gregg Jeffries, who already had two hits off the Dodgers ace, punched a single for a three-hit night. After Jeffries advanced to second on a grounder by Keith Hernandez, Darryl Strawberry ripped a double into right-center field scoring Jeffries with New York's first run, and the first run off Hershiser in 68 innings.

Lasorda, figuring that his pitcher had run out of gas, brought Jay Howell into the game to put the lid on it. The Dodgers closer walked Kevin McReynolds, then struck out Howard Johnson for out number two. With the count 0–2 on catcher Gary Carter, Howell threw him a low, outside curveball that Carter just managed to put the bat on. The ball, a dying quail, sailed over the infield. Center fielder John Shelby raced in, dove for it and caught it in his glove, but when he hit the turf, the ball fell out and Strawberry crossed the plate with the tying run. McReynolds, who was off with the crack of the bat, also headed home, and he bowled Scioscia over to score the go-ahead run. Randy Myers, who had come on to pitch in the eighth inning, set the Dodgers down in the bottom of the ninth to record the victory. The Dodgers clubhouse was like a

Former Expo Gary Carter was the leader of the New York Mets as they raced to 100 wins and a 15 game lead over second place Pittsburgh (courtesy of the Montreal Baseball Club).

funeral parlor as the Dodgers couldn't believe what had just happened to them. Protecting a 2–0 lead in the ninth inning with Hershiser, he of the 67 score-less innings, on the mound, the game seemed like a lock. And the ending happened so suddenly it all seemed like a bad dream. *The Sporting News* reported it. "The Dodgers looked like the world just stopped turning. 'It was as tough a loss as I've ever suffered professionally,' said Gibson. 'We didn't want to get beat again on a blooper.'"[2]

New York	0 0 0	0 0 0	0 0 3-3-8-1
Los Angeles	1 0 0	0 0 0	1 0 0-2-4-0

WP-Myers
LP- J. Howell

The world looked bleak indeed for Tommy Lasorda and his valiant warriors after their crushing loss in game one. They had fallen to the Mets for the eleventh time in twelve meetings, and they lost with their unbeatable pitcher on the mound. Their confidence was at an all-time low. But just when things looked darkest, a rescuer appeared on the horizon, and from an unexpected source. David Cone, the New York Mets' starting pitcher in game two, had contracted with the *New York Daily News*, to write a daily column about the Series. The column was to be ghostwritten by beat writer Bob Klapisch based on short interviews. After game 1, Cone swears, he gave thoughts about the Dodgers in a facetious tone. But they came out as serious journalism. Oh, did Los Angeles take offense. Under Cone's byline was a story that said Hershiser "was lucky for eight innings," and that "as soon as we got Orel out of the game, we knew we'd beat the Dodgers.... We saw Howell throwing curveball after curveball and we were thinking, 'This is the Dodgers idea of a stopper?... Seeing Howell and his curveball reminded us of a high school pitcher.'"[3]

Los Angeles Dodgers manager Tommy Lasorda, always on the lookout for something to give his team an edge, found the ideal target. Author David Cone, who had gone 20–3 with a 2.22 ERA during the regular season, was designated as the New York Mets starting pitcher in game two, and Lasorda took dead aim at him. He made copies of the Cone article and made sure every player on the team had a copy. He also unleashed a tirade at Cone, inciting his players to show Cone just how good they were. By the time the Dodgers made their way down the tunnel and into the dugout at Dodger Stadium, they were in a frenzy, and anxious to grab a bat and step into the batters box to face the harried Mets pitcher. And Cone, for his part, was a nervous wreck by game time.

Lasorda also decided the Dodgers needed a sparkplug to light a fire under the team. And he had just the man for the job. He inserted Mickey Hatcher into the lineup to make something happen, and the leader of the

Stuntmen did just that. After Tim Belcher, L.A.'s starting pitcher, who was 12–6 during the season, had set the Mets down without incident in the first inning, David Cone faced his jury. Mickey Hatcher, playing first base in place of Franklin Stubbs, who drew an O-fer in the opening game, drew a one-out walk, was balked to second by the Mets pitcher, and scored on a single by Mike Marshall. When Hatcher slid home with the first run, he immediately bounced up and raced to the dugout like a crazy man, throwing high-fives at everyone he met, from his teammates to the batboy. Cone escaped the inning without further damage, but in the second inning, he was not as lucky. He plunked Jeff Hamilton in the ribs with a two-strike pitch with one out. It looked like he might get out of the inning when he fanned Alfredo Griffin, but Tim Belcher kept the inning alive by punching out a base hit, and then the roof caved in on Cone. Steve Sax singled to score Hamilton, and Hatcher followed with a line drive inside third base and down the left field line into the corner. As Kevin McReynolds chased down the elusive pellet, pitcher Tim Belcher scored easily and Sax raced around third under a full head of steam. The relay from McReynolds to Johnson to Carter was executed perfectly, but the speedy Sax slid across home plate a split second ahead of the ball. Cone then walked Kirk Gibson intentionally, but Marshall upset the apple cart by singling in Hatcher. David Cone was gone after two innings, having given up five earned runs on five base hits and two bases on balls. The Mets trimmed the lead to 5–2 in the top of the fourth inning, when Keith Hernandez unloaded a two-run homer into the right-field seats, scoring Jeffries, who had walked, ahead of him. Griffin knocked in the Dodgers' sixth run with a fielders choice grounder in the fifth, and Hernandez, who had two of the Mets' six hits, closed out the scoring with single, driving in Len Dykstra, who doubled to lead off the ninth inning. Tim Belcher pitched 8⅓ innings for L. A., holding the Mets to five hits and striking out ten men.

Keith Hernandez, one of the game's greatest defensive first basemen, drove in five runs in seven games in the NLCS (Jay Sanford).

New York	0 0 0	2 0 0	0 0 1-3-6-0
Los Angeles	1 4 0	0 1 0	0 0 x-6-7-0

WP-Belcher
LP-Cone
SV-Peña

The Dodgers clubhouse was in a festive mood after their convincing victory over David Cone and the Mets. Hatcher, who had been inserted into the lineup by Lasorda to liven up the game, went 1 for 3 with a double, scored two runs, and drove in two. They never got him out of the lineup again. He played the final six games in the NLCS and all 5 games in the World Series, batting a combined .300. A downhearted Cone said his biggest mistake was hitting Hamilton. "That led to everything," he said.[4] He also promised, in his column, "This is my first and — I'm announcing today — my last attempt at tabloid journalism."[5] And he went on to apologize to those Dodgers players he had offended by name. But it was too little, too late. His poor judgment had given Lasorda and his team a new momentum, and it would eventually carry them through to a world championship.

Game three was scheduled for New York on Friday evening, October 7, but when it was rained out, it was rescheduled for the next afternoon at 12:20 P.M., much to the chagrin of New York management. Mets owner Nelson Doubleday, angered that Game 3 couldn't be played at night, which would have allowed for more drying time for the Shea Stadium field, was quoted by *Newsday* as saying that television was "screwing the national pastime." He threatened to have his team report late for the start of game 3. "'This is the Fall Classic,' said Doubleday, 'and we have to change things because the networks want to make money off us and off college football and pro football? When do we start making sense? They should come to us and ask us when we are going to play the games. I don't want my guys playing on a soggy field. I don't want a game decided because somebody's outfielder slipped on wet grass. TV shouldn't want it either.'"[6]

Game three went on as scheduled, beginning at 12:20 P.M., but the conditions were still miserable. The chilly rain made play almost impossible, and resulted in some vaudeville-like maneuvers on the field. The steady downpour kept the players on their toes all afternoon, and even that wasn't enough to avert disaster. Dodgers manager Tommy Lasorda took advantage of the postponement to juggle his starting assignments so Orel Hershiser could pitch game three, putting him in position to pitch game seven if necessary. John Tudor's start was pushed back to Sunday. This game would also present Los Angeles with another challenge, another test of their resilience. Davey Johnson gave his starting assignment to Hawaiian-born Ron Darling, who had a season record of 17–9. After a scoreless first inning, the West Coasters landed on Darling for two runs in the top of the second inning. Darling, who struggled with his control all day, walked Mike Marshall and John Shelby to open the inning. Then an attempted sacrifice bunt by Mike Scioscia turned into a single when he legged it out. An error by the usually flawless Keith Hernandez and a groundout by Jeff Hamilton gave L.A. two runs. They added a run in the third on a single by Steve Sax, a stolen base, and groundouts by Mickey Hatcher and Kirk Gibson. The Mets countered in their half of the third after Hershiser had struck out Ron Darling. He also fanned Mookie Wilson on a 55-foot sinker, but the ball eluded catcher Mike Scioscia and Wilson reached first. He went to third on a single by Gregg Jeffries and brought home the Mets first run on a double by Darryl Strawberry. The wet field continued to play havoc with the course of the game over the next two innings, but no damage was done. In the fifth inning, Mookie Wilson sliced a ball to left field that would have been a routine out on a normal day. But on this day, as Kirk Gibson was in pursuit toward the left field corner, he stumbled on the mushy turf, beginning a slow descent to the ground. Amazingly, as he started to fall, the never-say-die Gibson kept his eye on the ball all the way and, with glove outstretched and his right knee touching the ground, the former Michigan State flanker made one last lunge and caught the ball in the webbing of his glove just before he crashed to the Shea Stadium turf.

The score remained 3–1 until the home half of the sixth inning when New York scored two unearned runs, but as Mets owner Nelson Doubleday feared, the wet field had an effect on the outcome. Hernandez and Strawberry singled. Hernandez stopped at second base to watch Gibson field the ball, and when Gibson bobbled it, Hernandez tried to turn on the gas, but he stumbled in the mud, dropping to his hands and knees. He crawled a few feet in the mud, then got back up, took two more desperate steps, stumbled and fell again, and finally crawled into third, only to be tagged out by Hamilton when he touched Hamilton's shoe instead of the base. The next batter, Kevin McReynolds, was safe on a throwing error by Hamilton. After Howard Johnson hit into a fielders choice, Gary Carter and Wally Backman followed with run-scoring singles. The game was still tied in the top of the eighth inning, when fate once more intervened. Roger McDowell struck out the first two batters, Mike Marshall and John Shelby. Mike Scioscia followed with a tapper in front of the plate, but when McDowell tried to field it, he slipped and fell on the wet field and then made a wild throw to first, allowing Scioscia to reach base. The Dodgers took advantage of the error to load the bases on a single by Hamilton and a walk to pinch hitter Mike Davis. Danny Heep, batting for Hershiser, was sent up to face McDowell, but Davey Johnson retaliated by bringing in his southpaw closer, Randy Myers, to face the left-handed hitting Heep. Lasorda then replaced Heep with a right-handed pinch hitter, Mike Sharperson, who worked Myers for a walk to force in the tie-breaking run.

The lead was short lived, however, as the Mets roared back with a five-run outburst against four Dodgers pitchers, once again with the help of the gods. Jay Howell relieved Hershiser, intending to pitch the last two innings for a save, but....

When Howell fell behind 3 and 0 to leadoff batter McReynolds, Mets coach Bill Robinson was fixing him with a suspicious stare. Robinson thought he had seen something unusual about Howell's mannerisms on the mound in L.A.—something about the way he tugged at the strings of his glove as if it were a good luck charm. Robinson suggested to Johnson that he, too, keep an eye on Howell. Sure enough, Howell went to his glove again, and Johnson went straight to plate umpire Joe West and suggested he take a look.

Umpire crew chief Harry Wendlestedt trotted in from his post in left field and the two umps fingered the glove. Although nothing rubbed off on their hands, they told the two managers they detected something sticky there. Howell, they said, was in violation of baseball rule 8.02 (b), which prohibits the use of a foreign substance by a pitcher and calls for immediate ejection of the offending party." According to Howell, it was the weather that led him to use pine tar on the ball. "I use pine tar to get a better grip on the ball in cold weather. I don't us it to change the flight of the ball. Let's face it, it's illegal. But I don't feel I've done anything wrong. This is not on the same level as scuffing the ball."

Lasorda, quite naturally, bemoaned (National League president Bart) Giamatti's initial three-day sentence as "unjust." And Hernandez agreed. "Howell should not be suspended from the playoffs," he said before the judgement was announced. "Pine tar may give an edge, but it's not cheating. We're not choirboys here. These two teams have come too far. We should be able to play with our best."[7]

Jay Howell was ejected from the NLCS when the umpires discovered pine tar on his glove (courtesy of Los Angeles Dodgers).

Following Howell's departure from the game, the Mets went to work on his replacements, Alejandro Peña, Jesse Orosco, and Ricky Horton. After Peña threw ball four to McReynolds, he quickly disposed of the next two batters, retiring Howard Johnson on a popped-up bunt, and getting Gary Carter on a fly ball. Then Wally Backman banged a double to right field, sending McReynolds home with the tying run. After Lenny Dykstra walked, Jesse Orosco was brought in to face Mookie Wilson, but Wilson greeted him with a run-scoring single. Before Orosco could regain his composure, he hit Gregg Jeffries with a pitch and walked Keith Hernandez to force in another run. Darryl Strawberry welcomed reliever Ricky Horton to the mound with a looping single to left field that sent two more runners across the plate. That was the game. David Cone shut down Lasorda's team, one two three, in the top of the ninth, preserving the win for Randy Myers.

| Los Angeles | 0 2 1 | 0 0 0 | 0 1 | 0-4-7-2 |
| New York | 0 0 1 | 0 0 2 | 0 5 | x-8-9-2 |

WP–Myers
LP–Peña

As crazy as game three was, game four was a classic. It matched L.A.'s classy southpaw, John Tudor, against the New York Mets ace, Dwight Gooden. Surprisingly, the West Coast contingent clipped Gooden for two runs in the top of the first. Steve Sax, the Dodgers plate-setter, singled to open the frame and immediately stole second. Mickey Hatcher then coaxed a walk from Doctor K., and both runners advanced on a ground ball by Kirk Gibson. After Gooden took care of Mike Marshall, John Shelby came through with a base hit to drive in both runners. Tudor held the 2–0 lead until the bottom of the fourth inning, when Davey Johnson's sluggers found the range. In short order, Keith Hernandez singled and scored ahead of Darryl Strawberry's booming home run, and then Kevin McReynolds took Tudor downtown himself to give New York a 3–2 lead. They added a run in the sixth inning when McReynolds doubled and Gary Carter tripled him home on a ball that John Shelby turned the wrong way on and then watched it sail over his head. Manager Lasorda yanked Tudor in favor of Brian Holton at this point, leading to the first critical turning point in post-season play. The underrated Holton struck out Wally Backman, walked Kevin Elster, and then threw a double-play ball to Doc Gooden, 6–4–3, leaving Carter stranded at third base. In the meantime, Gooden was coasting along, limiting the Dodgers to one hit between the first inning and the ninth, and sending nine of them back to the bench dragging their bats behind them. Thanks to a shutout inning of relief by Brian Holton and two by Ricky Horton, L.A. trailed by only two runs entering the ninth.

The Dodgers bench was tense and quiet as Gooden readied himself for the last challenge. A nervous Mickey Hatcher stood hatless watching the action, but when Gooden's pitch sailed high and away to John Shelby for ball four, to open the ninth, Hatcher began to talk it up in the dugout. Mike Scioscia, who had three home runs all year, stepped in to face his destiny. With a count of 0–2, Gooden tried to throw a fastball by Scioscia, but the man with warning-track power was ready for it. He jerked it to right field, a high drive that sailed over Strawberry's head and disappeared over the 358 foot sign in front of the bullpen, for a game-tying home run. The Dodgers dugout erupted in a wild

Mike Scioscia had the biggest hit of the NLCS when he smashed a dramatic two-out, two-run homer off Dwight Gooden in the ninth inning of Game 4 (author's collection).

celebration, as the burly catcher ran his home run home. He said the guys in the dugout were kidding him about his home-run trot but he told them he was running as fast as he could. Shea Stadium fell deathly silent as the guaranteed Mets victory disappeared in a New York minute. Suddenly it was a new ballgame and Gooden was on his way to the shower. Three innings later, after Alejandro Peña had stifled the Mets for three innings, Kirk Gibson golfed an 0–1 pitch from Roger McDowell to right-center field. Gibson knew the ball was gone as soon as he hit it. Lenny Dykstra, in center field, gave chase, but he too knew the ball was gone. A quieter and more confident Dodgers dugout welcomed their leader back. But the Mets, like the Dodgers, were resilient, and they didn't quit. With Tim Leary on the hill, Mackey Sasser and Lee Mazzili both singled before Leary retired Gregg Jeffries on a fly to left. Jesse Orosco relieved Leary, and when he walked Keith Hernandez to load the bases, manager Tommy Lasorda bolted from the dugout like a frightened fawn, and raced to the mound, screaming at Orosco. "You said you wanted to be a closer. Well, prove it. Throw some damn strikes." Jesse got the message and forced Darryl Strawberry to pop up weakly to Sax. At this point, Lasorda decided to go with his best. He had Orel Hershiser in the bullpen. Bulldog, who had pitched seven innings the night before "had told Lasorda he would be ready if he needed him" and in the 11th inning, coach Mark Cresse called from the bullpen and said,

"Hershiser is down there. What should I do with him?" A delighted Lasorda shouted, "Warm him up."[8] Hershiser came on for his second relief appearance of the year, to face Kevin McReynolds, who hit a soft liner to short center field on a 1–1 pitch. John Shelby raced in at full speed and made a last-second knee-high catch to end the game.

Los Angeles   New York

Name	Pos	AB	R	H	Name	Pos	AB	R	H
Sax	2B	5	1	1	Wilson	CF	4	0	0
Hatcher	1B	4	1	0	McDowell	P	0	0	0
Peña	P	0	0	0	Mazzilli	PH	1	0	1
Stubbs	PH	1	0	0	Jeffries	3B	5	0	0
Leary	P	0	0	0	Hernandez	1B	5	1	2
Orosco	P	0	0	0	Strawberry	RF	6	1	1
Hershiser	P	0	0	0	McReynolds	LF	5	2	2
Gibson	LF	6	1	1	Carter	C	4	0	2
Marshall	RF	5	0	0	Myers	P	0	0	0
Shelby	CF	4	1	2	Dykstra	CF	1	0	0
Scioscia	C	4	1	1	Teufel	2B	3	0	0
Dempsey	PH-C	0	0	0	Backman	2B	1	0	0
Hamilton	3B	4	0	0	Elster	SS	2	0	0
Sharperson	PH-3B	1	0	0	Johnson	PH-SS	2	0	0
Griffin	SS	4	0	1	Gooden	P	3	0	1
Tudor	P	2	0	0	Sasser	C	2	0	1
Holton	P	0	0	0	Darling	PR	0	0	0
Heep	PH	0	0	0					
Horton	P	0	0	0					
Davis	PH	0	0	0					
Woodson	PH-1B	2	0	1					
Totals		**42**	**5**	**7**			**44**	**4**	**10**

Los Angeles	2 0 0	0 0 0	0 0 2	0 0 1-5-7-1
New York	0 0 0	3 0 1	0 0 0	0 0 0-4-10-2

Errors-Hatcher, Elster (2)
Double-McReynolds
Triple-Carter
Home Runs-Strawberry, McReynolds, Scioscia, Gibson

Name	IP	R	ER	H	BB	SO
Los Angeles						
Tudor	5	4	4	8	1	1
Holton	1	0	0	0	1	1
Horton	2	0	0	0	0	1
Peña (W)	3	0	0	0	3	1
Leary	⅓	0	0	2	0	0

Name	IP	R	ER	H	BB	SO
Orosco	⅓	0	0	0	1	0
Hershiser (S1)	⅓	0	0	0	0	0
New York						
Gooden	8⅓	4	4	5	5	9
Myers	2⅓	0	0	1	1	0
McDowell (L)	1⅓	1	1	1	0	1[9]

In game five, the Dodgers came out scratching and clawing. Tim Belcher, the winning pitcher in game two, squared off against former Dodgers farm-hand Sid Fernandez. The game was scoreless through three, but in the fourth, Lasorda's cohorts caught up with the Mets' husky southpaw. After Kirk Gibson lined out to left, Mike Marshall singled through the box. John Shelby, with the help of a favorable call from the plate umpire on a 2–2 pitch, eventually drew a walk. Rick Dempsey hit a line drive down the left field line. The ball landed about six inches fair and bounced into the corner with McReynolds in hot pursuit. Marshall coasted home with the first run and Shelby was right behind as the Dodgers jumped out in front 2–0. When Alfredo Griffin followed with another two-bagger, Dempsey raced home with the third run of the inning. Steve Sax led off the next inning with a single, and Mickey Hatcher followed suit. With Kirk Gibson up, Fernandez threw him a 2–1 fastball, and Gibson hammered it into the upper deck down the right field line just inside the foul pole, and suddenly the Dodgers were on top 6–0. That was all for Fernandez, who left before he could retire a man in the fifth inning. Once again Davey Johnson's team fought back. They jumped on Belcher for three runs in the bottom of the fifth, cutting the deficit in half. Howard Johnson singled, Wally Backman beat out a bunt, and Lenny Dykstra belted a home run into the right field bullpen. New York put another run on the scoreboard in the bottom of the eighth, and threatened more before Brian Holton could shut the door. Lenny Dykstra led off with a double into the right field corner and raced home on a single by Gregg Jeffries. That was all for Belcher. Ricky Horton came on in relief and struck out Keith Hernandez, but Darryl Strawberry clipped him for a soft single to left field, bringing Brian Holton into the game. Kevin McReynolds hit a slow grounder toward shortstop, but the ball hit Jeffries on the foot when he tried to jump over it, for out number two. Catcher Rick Dempsey said it was the biggest break of the series. When Gary Carter flied out, the threat was over. The Dodgers added a run in the top of the ninth, but it was a costly run. After Roger McDowell retired the first two batters, Kirk Gibson singled to keep the frame alive. He then stole second base, but he felt his left hamstring pop when he approached the base. It was the same hamstring that had troubled him down the stretch. Mike Marshall tripled to the wall in right-center field, scoring José González, running for Gibson. When Horton got into trouble in the eighth, Brian Holton came to the rescue and retired the last four batters, although the last batter was an adventure. Lee Mazzilli hit a fly ball to short right-center, and Marshall, Shelby, and Sax all converged on the ball. At the last instant Shelby dove and snared the ball just inches off the ground. Manager Tommy Lasorda led the charge to the mound to congratulate Holton, as L.A. assumed command of the series.

Los Angeles	0 0 0	3 3 0	0 0 1-7-12-0
New York	0 0 0	0 3 0	0 1 0-4-9-1

WP-Belcher
LP-Fernandez
SV-Holton

The Dodgers returned to Los Angeles surprisingly in the lead in the Series after taking two out of three in New York. Games four and five gave the entire Dodgers team immense confidence. The Dodgers were no longer snake-bit. They had gotten the specter of a 1–10 season record against New York off their back. From now on, they would be tough to beat. When game six started, Kirk Gibson, injured hamstring and all, was in the starting lineup, having taken a cortisone shot prior to stepping on the field. Unfortunately for Gibson and the rest of the Dodgers, David Cone, the Mets starter, was determined to make amends for his newspaper columns that had revitalized the Los Angeles team, and for his failure in game two. This time, Cone didn't let his team or his manager down. He kept the Dodgers off balance all day, and his teammates pounded Tim Leary unmercifully during his four-inning appearance. New York tapped the Dodgers starter for a run in the opening frame. Lenny Dykstra got the ball rolling by reaching first on an error by first baseman Mickey Hatcher. Wally Backman followed with a perfect hit-and-run single, sending Dykstra to third from which he scored on a sacrifice fly by Kevin McReynolds. Cone got off to a rocky start himself, walking the first two batters to face him, Steve Sax and Hatcher. Kirk Gibson, attempting to bunt, popped the ball up and Cone caught it. That was all the Mets ace needed. He retired Mike Marshall and John Shelby, leaving two runners stranded. Davey Johnson's team pushed across another run in the third on consecutive singles by Darryl Strawberry and Kevin McReynolds, and a two-out double by Kevin Elster. Two innings later, they added a brace of runs to their total, chasing Dodgers starter Tim Leary in the process. Leary walked Strawberry and paid for it immediately when Kevin McReynolds belted a home run, upping the score to 4–0. L.A. scored their only run of the game in the fifth when relief pitcher Brian Holton singled for his first hit of the season, Sax walked, and Hatcher drove in Holton with a single. Holton gave that run back in the top of the sixth on a double by Dykstra and a single by Hernandez. Kirk Gibson, who was 0 for 4 on the day, played with his usual aggressiveness in spite of his hamstring and knee injuries, and aggravated them when he slid into second base trying to break up a double play. Ironically, in the three games following Howell's suspension, Dodgers relief pitchers made eleven appearances for a total of fifteen innings, and allowed only one run for a brilliant 0.60 ERA.

Game seven matched Orel Hershiser, trying to put the finishing touches on a sensational season, and Ron Darling, trying to bring the New York Mets their second world championship in three years. Hershiser had trouble with his mechanics in the first inning and the Mets put two men on base with one out, but the gutty Dodgers ace retired both Darryl Strawberry and Kevin McReynolds, ending New York's only scoring opportunity of the game. In the bottom of the first, Steve Sax led off with a single and raced around to third on a hit-and-run double into the left field corner by Mickey Hatcher. Kirk Gibson then drove in the first run of the game with a long sacrifice fly to the warning track in center field. Mike Scioscia and Jeff Hamilton got the second inning underway with singles off Darling, bringing up Alfredo Griffin. As *The Sporting News* reported, "Everyone but Hernandez expected Griffin to bunt, even with Hershiser coming up next. Sure enough, Griffin bunted, a woeful pop-up that a charging Hernandez would have snagged easily. A flat-footed Hernandez watched the ball drop in front of him, untouched, and Griffin was safe at first to load the bases."[10] Pitcher Orel Hershiser hit a bouncer to third base that had double play written all over it, but once again the New York defense crumbled. Gregg Jeffries took his eye off the ball for a second to glance home and, in that instant, disaster struck. He dropped the ball, all hands were safe, and the Dodgers had a 2–0 lead. Steve Sax then put the final nail in Darling's coffin by lining a single up the middle for two runs. Dwight Gooden, making his first relief appearance in the major leagues, came on, with mixed results. Mickey Hatcher grounded out, and then Gooden walked Gibson intentionally to load the bases again. Mike Marshall bounced one to second base, but the Mets screwed up the double play again. This time it was Wally Backman, who slipped as he tossed the ball to shortstop Kevin Elster. The throw was high, everybody was safe, and Sax crossed the plate with the fourth run of the inning. The play would prove costly for the Dodgers, however, as noted by Gibson. "Trying to protect my bad leg, I made an ugly slide as I attempted to break up a double play. In doing so, I strained the medial collateral ligament in my other knee. Both legs were now shot."[11] John Shelby's sacrifice fly brought Gibson in, and the Dodgers were comfortably in front 6–0.

That ended the scoring for the day. All that remained was for Hershiser to keep Davey Johnson's powerful team under control for seven more innings. And Bulldog did just that. He actually got stronger as the game progressed, and the crowd gave him standing ovations several times, including in the sixth inning when he fanned both Keith Hernandez and Darry Strawberry. Gregg Jeffries' double in the seventh inning was the only hit Hershiser allowed after the fourth inning. In the ninth, he retired the first two batters, Gregg Jeffries and Gary Carter. Then before facing Howard Johnson, he stepped off the mound, as the crowd screamed with anticipation. Later Hershiser would say that he realized the electricity of the moment and he wanted to drink it all in so he would remember it for years to come. After surveying the crowd for a few seconds, he turned to face New York's last threat. He fanned Johnson on an inside sinker that the batter took for a called third strike as Dodger Stadium exploded. Hershiser knelt on the mound in a moment of silent prayer as his teammates rushed to congratulate him. His complete game shutout gave him a new NLCS record of 24⅔ innings pitched.

In the Dodgers clubhouse, after the last out was recorded, the bubbly flowed like water one more time. As the celebration got underway, "the players set about spraying each other with jets of eye-searing champagne. Only one Dodger had the foresight to wear a pair of swim goggles during the celebration. Guess Who?"[12] It was the team flake, Mickey Hatcher, of course.

Players from both teams who were interviewed after game seven were pretty much in agreement. The best team lost the series, but the team that played the best won the series. "Because we played like —," said New York first baseman Keith Hernandez, reflecting on the way the Mets lost the National League Championship Series to the Dodgers in seven games." The Dodgers players were in accord with Hernandez. "I've never seen a team play more as a 'team' than this one," said right fielder Mike Marshall. "The Mets have better talent, there is no question about that. But we got as much out of our talent as we could. We did all the little things to win." Good thing too, according to Mickey Hatcher, who played first base and left field. "If we don't do little things," he said, "we can play like a high school team."[13]

The statistics confirmed that the two teams played on an equal footing. The Mets had a .242 team batting average compared to .214 for the Dodgers, while the Dodgers had a 3.32 ERA compared to 3.94 for the Mets. But the Dodgers made the big hits when they counted. Kirk Gibson, for instance, hit only .154 for the series, but batted in six runs, hit the game-winning home run in game four, and blasted a three-run homer in game five, won by the Dodgers 7–4. Mike Marshall batted a weak .233, but knocked in five runs. When all was said and done, the team that couldn't did. They defeated a New York Mets squad that was vastly superior to them, a team that had beaten them ten times in eleven meetings during the regular season. The Dodgers won the series on courage — on heart — on determination — and on team chemistry.

Los Angeles Dodgers Batting

Name	Pos	AB	R	H	D	T	HR	RBI	BA
Dempsey	C	5	1	2	2	0	0	2	.400
Gibson	LF	26	2	4	0	0	2	6	.154
Griffin	SS	25	1	4	1	0	0	3	.160
Hamilton	3B	23	2	5	0	0	0	1	.217
Hatcher	IF-OF	21	4	5	2	0	0	3	.238
Marshall	RF	30	3	7	1	1	0	5	.233

Name	Pos	AB	R	H	D	T	HR	RBI	BA
Sax	2B	30	7	8	0	0	0	3	.267
Scioscia	C	22	3	8	1	0	1	2	.364
Shelby	CF	24	3	4	0	0	0	3	.167

Los Angeles Dodgers Pitching

Name	G	CG	IP	W	L	H	SO	BB	SV	ERA
Belcher	2	0	15.1	2	0	12	16	4	0	4.11
Hershiser	4	1	24.2	1	0	18	15	7	1	1.09
Holton	3	0	4	0	0	2	2	1	1	2.25
Howell	2	0	0.2	0	1	1	1	2	0	27.00
Leary	2	0	4.1	0	1	8	3	3	0	6.23
Orosco	4	0	2.1	0	0	4	0	3	0	7.71
Peña	3	0	4.1	1	1	1	1	5	1	4.15
Tudor	1	0	5	0	0	8	1	1	0	7.20

New York Mets Batting

Name	Pos	AB	R	H	D	T	HR	RBI	BA
Backman	2B	22	2	6	1	0	0	2	.273
Carter	C	27	0	6	1	1	0	4	.222
Dykstra	CF	14	6	6	3	0	1	3	.429
Elster	SS	8	1	2	1	0	0	1	.250
Hernandez	1B	26	2	7	0	0	1	5	.269
Jeffries	3B	27	2	9	2	0	0	1	.333
Johnson	SS-3B	18	3	1	0	0	0	0	.056
McReynolds	LF	28	4	7	2	0	2	4	.250
Strawberry	RF	30	5	9	2	0	1	6	.300

New York Mets Pitching

Name	G	CG	IP	W	L	H	SO	BB	SV	ERA
Aguilera	3	0	7	0	0	3	4	2	0	1.29
Cone	3	1	12	1	1	10	9	5	0	4.50
Darling	2	0	7	0	1	11	7	4	0	7.71
Fernandez	1	0	4	0	1	7	5	1	0	13.50
Gooden	3	0	18.1	0	0	10	20	8	0	2.95
Leach	3	0	5	0	0	4	4	1	0	0.00
McDowell	4	0	6	0	1	6	5	2	0	4.50
Myers	3	0	4.2	2	0	1	0	2	0	0.00

The Dodgers' World Series opponent was determined in the American League Championship Series (ALCS) that matched the Boston Red Sox against the powerful Oakland Athletics, winners of 104 games during the regular season. The first two games were played in Boston, with the next two games scheduled for Oakland, and the fifth game, if necessary, back in Boston. Managers Joe Morgan of the Red Sox and Tony LaRussa of the A's led with their best, with Dave Stewart (21–12) facing left-hander Bruce Hurst (18–6) in the opening game, played on October 5. Oakland was slightly favored in the series based on their superior pitching staff. The Sox held a slight advantage from an offensive standpoint, leading the league in runs scored with 813, but the A's were close behind with 800 runs scored. And the A's could score quickly as attested to by their 156 home runs, led by the "Bash Brothers," José Canseco and Mark McGwire, who hit 74 home runs between them. The A's also had more speed with 129 stolen bases to just 65 for the Sox. Boston had a better defense, but the A's had a deeper starting staff with four pitchers with more than ten victories compared to two for Boston. And the A's also had Dennis Eckersley, who had 45 saves to 29 saves for the Red Sox closer, Lee Smith.

To make matters worse for Joe Morgan's crew, the Oakland Athletics held an advantage in the head to head competition between the two clubs during the regular season, going 3–3 against the Sox in Boston and sweeping all six games in Oakland. In the ALCS opener, both Stewart and Hurst set the other side down without a run over the first three innings, but in the top of the fourth, José Canseco, the American League home run king, lofted a Hurst curveball over the Green Monster in left field to give his team a 1–0 lead. Boston tied the game in the seventh when Wade Boggs' sacrifice fly off Rick Honeycutt scored pinch runner Kevin Romine. The tie didn't last long however, just two pitches in fact. In the Oakland eighth, Carney Lansford ripped a double on the first pitch from Hurst, and Dave Henderson singled on Hurst's next pitch, sending Lansford home with the eventual winning run.

Oakland	0 0 0	1 0 0	0 1 0-2-6-0		
Boston	0 0 0	0 0 0	1 0 0-1-6-0		

WP-Honeycutt
LP-Hurst

In game two, it was more of the same. Storm Davis started for LaRussa, facing Roger "Rocket" Clemens, Boston's eighteen-game winner during the regular season. Once again, both pitchers kept the opposing hitters in check, this time for 5½ innings. Boston broke the ice in the bottom of the sixth inning, scoring two unearned runs on two-out walks to Dwight Evans and Mike Greenwell, an error by center fielder Dave Henderson on a ball hit by Jim Rice that allowed one run to score, and a single by Ellis Burks that brought in run number two. But, like the first game, the resilient A's came right back to grab the lead in the top of the seventh. Dave Henderson singled to center off a rapidly tiring Clemens to open the inning, and the next batter, all-world José Canseco, drove an 0–2 pitch over the Monster to tie the game, and they added another run on a Mark McGwire single, giving the A's a 3–2 lead. That lead didn't last long either as Rich Gedman slammed a home run off Greg Cadaret in the bottom of the inning. Lee Smith, Boston's closer, was called in to keep Oakland's batters under control, but he failed in his assignment. Ron Hassey singled with one out in the ninth and scampered around to third on Tony Philips' single. 'Walt Weiss, the no. 9 hitter, admitted,' (I) looked over my shoulder as I went to the plate. I've been pinch-hit for in that situation a few times." Oakland manager Tony LaRussa, however, stayed with Weiss, who drove an 0–2 fastball into center field for the go-ahead run."[14] Dennis Eckersley was called upon for the second straight night, and earned his second save of the ALCS, retiring the Sox in order.

Boston was in dire straits now, having dropped both games at home and having to travel to Oakland for games three and four, where they were 0–6 during the season. Mike Boddicker, who was 7–3 with Boston after being obtained in a mid-season trade with Baltimore, was Joe Morgan's choice to open festivities in the Oakland Coliseum. Tony LaRussa countered with 6', 3", 193-pound fireballer Bob Welch, who finished the season with a mark of 17–9. The 31-year-old right-hander didn't have it on this day however, and the Red Sox drove him to cover in less than two innings, scoring five runs on six hits. That's when the A's pulled out their big bats and went to work, putting four balls out of the park, en route to a convincing 10–6 win. Mark McGwire started the A's hit parade by slamming a solo home run in the bottom of the second inning. Later in the same inning, Walt Weiss drove in a run with a double, and then scored ahead of Carney Lansford's homer, cutting the Boston lead to 5–4. Ron Hassey followed a two-out single by McGwire with another A's homer and they suddenly had the lead by a 6–5 score. They added a run in the fifth, both teams scored in the seventh, and Dave Henderson hit a cloud-banger with a man on base in the eighth to close out the scoring for the day, the A's winning 10–6.

Boston	3 2 0	0 0 0	1 0 0-6-12-0
Oakland	0 4 2	0 1 0	1 2 0-10-15-1

WP-Nelson
LP-Boddicker

The fourth game played in the Coliseum was anti-climactic. The Red Sox were already beaten, at least mentally. Morgan came back with Bruce Hurst in an effort to revive the listless Sox, but he struggled through four innings, yielding two runs on four base hits. José Canseco was the culprit again, slamming a first inning home run to give his team a running start. They added a run in the third on singles by Weiss and Lansford and a double by Henderson. Boston had a golden opportunity to send Dave Stewart to an early shower when they loaded the bases in the first inning, but Stew fanned Dwight Evans to end the Red Sox threat and effectively end their season. "(Stewart) then retired 12 of the next 13 batters before issuing a walk to Marty Barrett in the sixth. A single (Wade Boggs), a fielder's choice (Mike Greenwell), and a groundout produced Boston's only run."[15] Tony LaRussa's warriors put a two-spot on the board in the bottom of the eighth, to close out the scoring. José Canseco singled and stole second. Mark McGwire drove him in with a single and, after another single by Stan Javier and a walk to Luis Polonia, McGwire scored on a sacrifice fly by Don Baylor. Dennis Eckersley picked up his fourth save of the series pitching an almost-flawless ninth. The A's, as a team, raised havoc with Boston's top pitchers, scoring twenty runs, with eight doubles, seven home runs, and a .299 batting average in four games. Their pitching staff was just as impressive, holding the high scoring Red Sox to eleven runs, good for a 2.00 ERA. Six of their eight pitchers had perfect 0.00 ERAs, including Storm Davis and Dennis Eckersley. Dave Stewart was not far behind with a 1.35 ERA for 13⅓ innings.

Boston	0 0 0	0 0 0	1 0 0-1-4-0
Oakland	1 0 1	0 0 0	0 2 0-4-10-1

WP-Stewart
LP-Hurst

José Canseco led the Oakland A's at the plate with three home runs, four RBIs, and a .313 batting average. Dave Henderson also had four RBIs and hit .375, and Mark McGwire hit one homer, drove in three runs, and batted .333. Gene Nelson went 2–0 on the mound, and Dennis Eckersley had four saves. With their combination of power, speed, and pitching, the Oakland Athletics were heavy favorites to defeat the Los Angeles Dodgers in the World Series. Wade Boggs hit .385 for Boston and Rich Gedman batted .357, but the rest of the position players, with the exception of Jody Reed who hit .273, were helpless with a bat in their hands. And the Sox pitching was almost as bad. Bruce Hurst had a 2.77 ERA, but finished with an 0–2 record thanks to his offense which scored only two runs in the two games he pitched. And Roger Clemens, who had an ERA of 3.86, was the only other Red Sox pitcher with an ERA under 5.79.

9

THE WORLD SERIES

Typewriters clicked away incessantly between the end of the NLCS on October 12 and the start of World Series festivities on October 15, as beat writers struggled to fill the void with analyses and introspective on the upcoming battle between the Oakland Athletics and the Los Angeles Dodgers. On the surface, the Series appeared to be a mismatch, another David and Goliath confrontation, with L.A.'s popgun attack no match for the fearsome power of the Bash Brothers, José Canseco, Mark McGwire, Dave Parker, and Dave Henderson whose 110 home runs combined were more than the Dodgers' entire team total of 99 homers. The experts predicted that the Bash Brothers would raise havoc with Dodgers pitchers, and that even Orel Hershiser would feel the fury of the Oakland bats. They also predicted that A's pitchers Dave Stewart (21–12), Bob Welch (17–9), Storm Davis (16–7), and Dennis Eckersley (4–2 with 45 saves and a 2.35 ERA) would throttle Dodgers hitters rather easily, particularly with L.A.'s biggest slugger possibly out for the entire series with leg injuries. After the NLCS, according to Gibson, The doctors "had done all they could, hoping for some miracle that I would wake up and be ready to play. But when I tried to jog, my legs were nearly ready to collapse from the pain. I was afraid I wouldn't be able to play in the type of game I lived for, where the World Championship was at stake."[1]

Oakland's José Canseco became the first man in baseball history to hit at least 40 home runs and steal at least 40 bases in the same year when he slammed a league-leading 42 home runs and stole 40 bases in 1988. The one-man team also led the league in runs batted in with 124, scored 120 runs, and batted .307. His Bash Brother, Mark McGwire, hit 32 home runs and drove in 99 teammates. Dave Henderson, another right-handed power hitter, sent 24 balls screaming into the evening sky, drove in 94 runs, and batted .304. Dave Parker, in an injury-plagued season, hit 12 home runs in 377 at-bats. As a team, the A's were the most dominating team in the American League. They hit 156 home runs in 162 games, second only to the Toronto Blue Jays who hit 158, and they scored 800 runs, trailing only the Boston Red Sox who scored 813. The A's pitching staff led the American League with a 3.44 ERA and 64 saves.

Oakland, who won 104 games in sweeping to the Western Division title by 13 games over the Minnesota Twins, crushed the Boston Red Sox in the American League Championship Series, four games to none. Tony LaRussa's team came into the World Series brimming with confidence after putting such a monstrous hurt on a team of Boston's caliber. On the other hand, Tommy Lasorda's warriors were also feeling good about their chances after disposing of their season-long nemesis, Davey Johnson's New York Mets. "As Vin Scully says, 'This is a team that shakes its head when it wins.' Orel Hershiser added, 'Not so much in disbelief, but maybe more like, "Can you believe it worked out?"'"[2]

In the days before the World Series got underway, there was already controversy brewing, something that Los Angeles Dodgers manager Tommy Lasorda welcomed. The motivational force behind the L.A. machine always used controversial comments by opposing players, managers, or media experts to incite his team, to bring out the best in them and, in many cases, to convert them into overachievers. The culprit in this case was Oakland's designated hitter, Don Baylor, who questioned the courage of Dodgers closer Jay Howell, when he was quoted as saying, "What's he ever done? He couldn't save games over here (with the A's), so they got rid of him. He was right where he wanted to be in games 4 and 5 in New York (he was serving a suspension). He didn't want to be pitching with all the people screaming at him. He can't handle that. He couldn't handle it when he was in New York with the Yankees. I know, I played with him." Mickey Hatcher, never one to shy away from a fight, said, "They (the A's) can say what they want. If they want to light our fire, let 'em go ahead. We feed off publicity like that."[3] Baylor went on to say that the A's would have preferred to face the New York Mets, who they considered to be the best team in the National League, rather than the Dodgers, who were not in the Mets' class.

Game one was played in Dodger Stadium on Saturday, October 15, with the A's Dave Stewart opposing the Dodgers' rookie fireballer, Tim Belcher, who had been tested by the pressure of the NLCS, and who showed his courage and poise in that environment by winning two games against New York's finest. Before the opening game of the World Series got underway, Kirk Gibson arrived at Dodger Stadium early to talk to his manager. "'Tommy, this is bad. I'm really hurt. I don't know if I can do it tonight.' Dr. Frank Jobe — one of the world's leaders in sports medicine — and his staff came into the office, sized up the situation, and we unanimously agreed that I was out."[4] After Nancy Reagan threw out the first ball, and the band played the national anthem, the 26-year-old Belcher strode to the mound and went to work. He struck out the first Oakland batter to face him, Carney Lansford, but then the A's threatened. Dave Henderson slapped a single up the middle, José Canseco was hit on the hand by an inside fastball, Dave Parker flied to John Shelby in short center field, and Mark McGwire walked to load the bases. But Belcher wriggled out of the predicament by inducing Terry Steinbach to send a harmless fly ball out to John Shelby in center field.

Dave Stewart was not as fortunate in the bottom of the inning. He retaliated for Belcher hitting Canseco by plunking Sax on the shoulder with his first pitch of the game, Sax jumped up unhurt and raced to first base. Plate umpire Harvey immediately warned both managers to stop the beanball war. Franklin Stubbs flied to Henderson in left field but, after Stewart balked the runner to second, Mickey Hatcher caught hold of an 0–1 pitch and drove it into the bleachers in left-center field, 380 feet from home plate, to give his team a quick 2–0 lead. With both arms raised skyward, the former University of Oklahoma football player, who had hit only one home run all season, was so excited that he raced around the bases at breakneck speed, almost catching Sax at home plate. Third base coach Joey Amalfitano refused to shake Hatcher's hand as he passed third, fearing an injury. But, in the blink of an eye, the A's fought back. Glenn Hubbard singled leading off the second and, after Walt Weiss fanned, Belcher lost the location of the plate and walked both the opposing pitcher, Dave Stewart, and Lansford to load the bases. Belcher took a deep breath and struck out Henderson for out number two. But before he could get out number three, he had to pitch to Canseco. His first pitch was a ball. The second pitch never reached home plate. Canseco, arms extended for maximum power, caught a hanging curveball on the fat part of the bat, and hit it on a line to dead center field. José watched the flight of the ball all the way, knowing full well it would leave the park. The ball was hit like a rocket, never getting more than twenty feet off the ground, and it cleared the center field fence with plenty to spare, bouncing off an NBC television camera, and putting a three-inch dent in it, before coming to rest some 420 feet from home plate. When the ball left the park, a slight smile played on the Cuban's lips. He carried the bat down the first base line for four or five steps, then gingerly tossed it away and broke into his home run trot. Canseco, and other Bash Brothers, celebrated with their now-famous, high-five, forearm salute (striking each other's forearm with their own, in a macho celebration of brute power). Lasorda sat quietly alone on the Dodgers bench, arms folded, contemplating the rapid change of fortune.

Belcher was allowed to bat for himself in the bottom of the inning, but his work on the mound was done for the day. Tim Leary came on to work the third and threw three shutout innings at Tony LaRussa's crew, aided by some smart defensive plays by his infielders. In the A's fourth, Dave Henderson hit a ground-rule double down the right field line, but fell victim to some razzle-dazzle by Griffin and Sax. José Canseco hit a hard ground ball between short and third that was run down by Griffin but, instead of throwing Canseco out at first, Griffin tossed the ball to Sax at second base. Henderson, who was returning to second with the ball hit ahead of him, now found himself trapped off base. Putting on the brakes, he turned back toward third but was run down by Sax for the first out.

The Dodgers pared the lead to 4–3 in the bottom of the sixth. With one out, Mike Marshall singled to right field on a low, outside fastball. John Shelby followed with a shot that struck the pitching rubber and bounded into center field, with Marshall going to second. Mike Scioscia also saw a low outside fastball, and he rode it to left field for another single, with Marshall coming across with L.A.'s third run. The rally ended almost as soon as it began when Jeff Hamilton hit a shot to third base that was taken on one bounce by Carney Lansford, who stepped on third and gunned down Hamilton at first.

Dave Stewart continued to hold L.A. at bay through eight innings, and Leary, Holton, and Peña threw goose eggs at Oakland after Canseco's blast. While the game was being played out, a frustrated and edgy Kirk Gibson sat watching the action on the clubhouse TV, nursing two bad knees and one bad hamstring. When he heard Vin Scully tell his audience that "Gibson will not be playing tonight. He's not even in the dugout," he fumed.[5] As the game neared its end, Scully said, "Looking to the ninth for the Dodgers, it will be Mike Scioscia, Jeff Hamilton, and Alfredo Griffin, followed by the pitcher. All the Dodgers have remaining on the bench are Dave Anderson, Mike Davis, and Kirk Gibson, but we know he's not going to be playing."[6] That was all the Dodger's MVP needed to hear. "Bull." He began to get himself game ready. "I began visualizing the crowd, thinking of their response when I walked out of the dugout. I thought, 'When I hear 55,000 loyal Dodger fans going nuts, I won't hurt anymore.' Now I had the image, as big as a movie screen, vividly developed in my mind. I was going to sting Eckersley and win the game."[7] Gibson tore the icebags from his legs, asked Mitch Poole, the clubhouse attendant to set up a batting tee in the net at the top of the runway leading to the dugout, and took a few practice swings. Then he told Mitch to go get Lasorda. When Tommy arrived, he was visibly upset that Gibson wanted to see him at the most critical juncture of the game. "What do you want," he scowled. "I've got a game to manage." Gibson said, "Let Davis pinch hit for Griffin and I'll hit for the pitcher." A wildly ecstatic Lasorda raced back to the dugout before Gibson could change his mind.

Meanwhile, the atmosphere in Dodger Stadium quieted as Dennis Eckersley raced in from the bullpen and tossed his jacket to the batboy. The A's closer, who had led the American League with 46 saves during the season, capped the Oakland pennant drive by saving all four victories in the American League Championship Series. Now he was anxious to close out the game for the A's first World Series win. Things looked bleak in Dodger town as Eckersley did a workman-like job of disposing of the first two Dodgers hitters. He retired Mike Scioscia on a pop-up to the catcher, and then set Jeff Hamilton down on three straight strikes, the last one a mean sidearm fastball that caught the Dodgers third baseman looking. Mike Davis, the Dodgers' last hope, stepped in to face the major league's top closer. Eckersley, working carefully to Davis, realizing that he was the last Dodger on the bench with home run power with Gibson incapacitated, walked the left-handed slugger on a 3–1 pitch. Suddenly, as if in a Hollywood B movie, a wounded Kirk Gibson limped out of the Dodgers' dugout and made his way slowly to the plate, as 55,983 Dodgers fans practically tore the park apart. Vin Scully broadcast the action to his television audience. "And look who's comin' up. All year long, they looked to him to light the fire, and all year long he answered the demands until he was physically unable to start tonight, with two bad legs. With two out, you talk about the roll of the dice, this is it."[8] Gibson remembered the moment clearly. "The place rocked, and the sounds were numbing. I shuffled to the on-deck circle, grabbed a rosin bag, threw it down, and walked straight to the plate. Just as I had anticipated, the pain became secondary to the deafening roar of the crowd."[9] Eckersley's first pitch, high and outside, was fouled away upstairs by the gimpy Gibson, who was in obvious distress. He had to hop away on his follow-through to keep from falling down. It was impossible for him to take his normal swing with his two injured legs. He could only lunge at the ball with his front foot, making sure to put no weight on his rear foot. His swing was all wrist and arms, with no body movement whatsoever. Gibson fouled the second pitch over the roof to the left. Eckersley was quickly in the driver's seat, 0 and 2. The Dodgers were down to their last strike. The miracle of the NLCS was a distant memory. This moment was reality. The noise was deafening as Gibson topped the next pitch down the first base line, and hobbled down the line. The ball rolled foul. Eckersley gave the Dodgers MVP another fastball, but it was outside for ball one. Sax, on deck, was watching the drama unfold, anxious to get his turn at bat. Gibson lined another fastball down the left field line, foul. The sixth pitch of the at-bat was taken for ball two. Eckersley threw to first to keep Davis close to the bag, but when he gave Gibson a breaking ball, Davis took off for second and stole the base without a throw. The count was now full at 3–2. Dodger Stadium was electric. While he was waiting for pitch number eight, Gibson remembered the words of L.A.'s top scout, Mel Didier. "'Parrrtner,' he drawled, speaking to me before the Series began, 'as sure as I'm standing here breathin',' if Eckersley goes 3 and 2 on you, you're goin' to see a backdoor slider. I've seen him freeze George Brett with it. I've seen him freeze Wade Boggs with it. If you get him to 3 and 2, get ready to step into it, because it will be that backdoor slider.'"[10] Gibson was ready, and Eckersley didn't disappoint. He threw the backdoor slider just as Didier had predicted, but the ball got too much of the plate. Gibson got all his weight up front and whipped his bat through with lightning speed, to generate as much power as he could, using only his arms and wrists. When he made contact with the ball, he hit it one-handed and with his back foot off the ground. The ball shot off his bat and disappeared into the evening sky, on its way to a rendezvous in right field, while the hushed audience waited to explode. Eckersley turned to watch the trajectory of the ball, his expression one of disbelief and dejection. José Canseco took three steps back, then stopped to watch. The ball sailed over his head and settled into the right field stands for a game-winning home run. Vin Scully reported the final scene. "High fly ball into right field. SHE — IS — GONE. In a year that has been so improbable, the impossible has happened."[11] The screams emanating from Dodger Stadium sent tremors up and down the West Coast. A visibly elated Gibson hobbled around the bases slowly, pumping the air with his fist in celebration of what would go down in Los Angeles Dodgers lore as the greatest moment in L.A. Dodgers history. Lasorda leaped out of the dugout, with both arms thrown skyward, and raced for home plate, followed by the entire Dodgers team. A grinning Gibson gave two more arm-pumps between second and third base and then made the turn for home. His teammates were all waiting there, yelling and smiling, forming a welcoming line between third base and home to congratulate him on his historic feat. Hugs, backslaps, and high-fives followed Gibson down the line, and the team surrounded him as he crossed home plate, but he warned them not to put any weight on his shattered body. He did get a bear hug from manager Tommy Lasorda, however.

Oakland					Los Angeles				
Name	*Pos*	*AB*	*R*	*H*	*Name*	*Pos*	*AB*	*R*	*H*
Lansford	3B	4	1	0	Sax	2B	3	1	1
Henderson	CF	5	0	2	Stubbs	1B	4	0	0
Canseco	RF	4	1	1	Hatcher	LF	3	1	1
Parker	LF	2	0	0	Marshall	RF	4	1	1
Javier	PR-LF	1	0	1	Shelby	CF	4	0	1
McGwire	1B	3	0	0	Scioscia	C	4	0	1
Steinbach	C	4	0	1	Hamilton	3B	4	0	0
Hassey	C	0	0	0	Griffin	SS	2	0	1
Hubbard	2B	4	1	2	M. Davis	PH	0	1	0
Weiss	SS	4	0	0	Belcher	P	0	0	0
Stewart	P	3	1	0	Heep	PH	1	0	0
Eckersley	P	0	0	0	Leary	P	0	0	0
					Woodson	PH	1	0	0
					Holton	P	0	0	0
					González	PH	1	0	0
					Peña	P	0	0	0
					Gibson	PH	1	1	1
Totals		34	4	7			32	5	7

Oakland	0 4 0	0 0 0	0 0 0-4-7-0
Los Angeles	2 0 0	0 0 1	0 0 2-5-7-0

Double-Henderson
Home Runs-Hatcher, Canseco,Gibson

Name	IP	W	L	H	R	ER	SO	BB
Oakland								
Stewart	8	0	0	6	3	3	5	2
Eckersley	⅔	0	1	1	2	2	1	1
Los Angeles								
Belcher	2	0	0	3	4	4	3	4

Dennis Eckersley, the game's greatest closer, tried to slip a backdoor slider past Kirk Gibson in Game 1, with disastrous results (Jay Sanford).

Name	IP	W	L	H	R	ER	SO	BB
Leary	3	0	0	3	0	0	3	1
Holton	2	0	0	0	0	0	0	1
Peña	2	1	0	1	0	0	3	0[12]

Tommy Lasorda's confidence grew by leaps and bounds after Gibson's Hail-Mary home run catapulted his team into the victory circle in game one. He now believed that his team had a chance to pull off the upset of the century, and defeat the Oakland Athletics for the World Series championship. After all, he had his ace, Orel Hershiser, going in game two and, perhaps, later in the Series if needed. And since Hershiser had been in a zone since his last loss on August 24, pitching 82⅔ innings with a perfect 6–0 record and a miniscule 0.32 ERA, there was every reason to believe that he could sustain the magic for two more games. Then Lasorda would need only one more victory in the remaining four games to claim the crown.

Game two paired Orel Hershiser against 6', 4", 200-pound right-hander George Earl "Storm" Davis, Jr., who had gone 16–7 with Oakland during the regular season. Hershiser, who was making his fourth appearance in a game, and his third start, in nine days, forgot to take the videotape of Game 1 home to study the A's players, but he did watch some of it in the clubhouse in the morning. Then he made a crib sheet and laminated it, a concise summary of how to pitch to the Oakland players. When he reached the field prior to the start of game two, he showed the card he carried in his back pocket to home plate umpire Doug Harvey, and received his permission to use it during the game. The Dodgers ace set the A's down in order in the top of the first, and the Dodgers got a two-out single from Hatcher in the bottom of the inning, but couldn't do anything with it. Inning two was uneventful, and Tony LaRussa's sluggers were put away in order in the top of the third. The Dodgers then proceeded to blow the game wide open in the bottom of the third inning when they tattooed Davis for five runs, three of them coming on a home run by Mike Marshall. Even Hershiser got into the act. With one out, the Dodgers pitcher faked a bunt, and then pulled the bat back and hit a single through the middle. Steve Sax hit a soft single to right field, and Hershiser took off, intent on going all the way to third. He rounded second at full speed, catching Canseco asleep at the switch, and slid into third base without a throw. Franklin Stubbs got around on a fastball, pulling a ground ball through the right side, scoring Hershiser and sending Sax to third. Dodger Stadium was bedlam now as the Dodgers faithful sensed history in the making. On a hit-and-run play, the irrepressible Mickey Hatcher hit a seeing-eye Baltimore chop through the middle that eluded Weiss and Hubbard on its way to center field. Sax scored, Stubbs went to third, and Hatcher bounced into second base on his stomach as the throw tried unsuccessfully to cut down Stubbs at third. The next batter, Mike Marshall, strode into an 0–2 pitch and hit a towering fly ball

Kirk Gibson connected for a historic home run off Dennis Eckersley in the bottom of the ninth inning of Game 1 to give the Dodgers a 5–4 victory (courtesy of Los Angeles Dodgers).

Gibson pumped his fist in celebration as he began his victorious journey around the bases after hitting his game-winning homer (courtesy of Los Angeles Dodgers).

The irrepressible Mickey Hatcher celebrated, helmet askew, after a head-first slide into second base. A's shortstop Walt Weiss looks on (courtesy of Los Angeles Dodgers).

to left field. Dave Parker chased it all the way to the wall, then watched helplessly as it dropped beyond his leaping reach for a three-run homer. Lasorda, on the top step of the dugout, threw his arms up as the ball disappeared.

With a big five run lead, and the unbeatable Bulldog on the mound, the game was essentially over. L.A. added a run in the bottom of the fourth when Alfredo Griffin got an infield single between first and second that Hubbard made a diving stop on, but couldn't make a throw. The next batter, Orel Hershiser, electrified the crowd with his bat handling. He fouled off two pitches trying to bunt, and then slapped at an outside pitch and hit a rope down the right field line. It dropped less than a foot fair for a double as Griffin came home with run number six. That ended the scoring for the day, but Hershiser was still not through. Facing southpaw Curt Young in the sixth inning, he lined a ground-rule double past third base, for his third hit of the game in three at-bats, becoming the first pitcher to have three hits in a game since Art Nehf accomplished the feat for the 1924 New York Giants. His three hits also matched the A's total for the game, and his five total bases were one more than the Bash Brothers could muster.

Hershiser was coasting much of the game, and when the A's looked like they might mount an attack, L.A.'s defense came to the rescue. Dave Parker led off the second inning with a single, but Mark McGwire hit a slow bouncer into the hole between short and third. Alfredo Griffin ran it down deep in the hole, and then in one fluid movement, threw the ball back across his chest to Steve Sax at second. Sax's pivot and throw to Franklin Stubbs, while eluding a sliding Parker, completed an electrifying double play as Hershiser walked around the mound talking to himself in wonderment and appreciation. After the Dodgers ace had retired nine men in a row, Parker once again led off with a single, this time in the fifth inning. And once again, McGwire hit the ball to short, and the Dodgers pulled off another double play, Griffin to Sax to Stubbs. Oakland put two men on base in the seventh inning on an error and a two-out single by Parker, his third hit of the game, but Hershiser once again retired McGwire, this time on a fly ball to left field. Glenn Hubbard walked with one out in the eighth, but Weiss hit into a force play and Parker went down on strikes, chasing a 55-foot curveball. As the ninth inning got underway, 56,051 wild Dodgers fans stood as one, chanting, "Orel, Orel, Orel." Carney Lansford quieted them temporarily by walking to open the inning, but the next three men went down in order, with Parker, once again chasing a 55-foot breaking ball in the dirt, and the Dodgers owned a two game to none lead in the Fall Classic. The 6–0 whitewashing of the vaunted A's was Hershiser's second straight shutout in the postseason.

Oakland	0 0 0	0 0 0	0 0	0-0-3-0
Los Angeles	0 0 5	1 0 0	0 0	x-6-10-1

WP-Hershiser
LP-S. Davis

After the crowd had dispersed, and silence had descended on the great stadium, a string of Gray Line buses silently positioned themselves along the first base line, waiting to take the shell-shocked Oakland Athletics team back home to the Oakland Coliseum. The next three World Series games, if they were all needed, would be played on the A's home turf, and Tony LaRussa's boys were still confident that they would come back and win the Series. They believed, to a man, that they had a much superior team to that of the Los Angeles Dodgers, and they were sure they could sweep Tommy Lasorda's upstarts in the Coliseum. And they had their 17-game winner, Bob Welch, rested and ready to face L.A.'s crafty southpaw, John Tudor. Both pitchers had World Series experience, with Welch pitching for the Dodgers in both the 1978 and 1981 Series, and Tudor with five starts under his belt for the St. Louis Cardinals in 1985 and 1987, while posting a 3–2 Series won-loss record. The Las Vegas betting line that originally had the Los Angeles Dodgers as long shots to win the World Series now had the Dodgers pegged as 2–1 favorites to win it all.

Fans turned out in force, confident that the Bash Brothers could come back and beat up on the no-name team from Southern California. There was some concern in baseball circles, however, that Bob Welch might have a psychological problem as far as post-season play was concerned, similar to that experienced by Don Newcombe in the 1950s. Newcombe, it may be recalled, was a great pitcher for the Brooklyn Dodgers who once won 27 games in one season, and who batted .357 with seven home runs in another season. Newk pitched a great game against the New York Yankees in the 1949 World Series opener, only to lose the game 1–0 on a ninth inning home run by Tommy Henrich. He could never forget that loss, and he became less and less effective with each World Series start after that. The head games caused the great pitcher to suffer through an 0–4 World Series record with an 8.59 ERA. Now, baseball people were afraid that Bob Welch might suffer the same fate. Welch was an outstanding pitcher in Los Angeles, but the pressure seemed to get to him in the World Series, when every mistake is magnified a hundredfold. He pitched in two World Series for the Dodgers and, after a sensational start where he struck out Reggie Jackson with two men on base and two out in the bottom of the ninth inning to preserve L.A.'s 4–3 victory in game two of the 1978 World Series, his fortunes went south. He subsequently lost game four, and yielded a home run to Jackson in the Series finale, won by the Yankees 7–2. Now the pressure was on him again to prove his first two Series meltdowns were flukes.

Steve Sax grounded a single through the right side of the infield to get Game 3 underway, but just when A's fans began squirming in their seats, the 6', 3", 193-pound fireballer settled down and struck out Franklin Stubbs, Mickey Hatcher, and Mike Marshall in order. John Tudor, who was bothered by a tender elbow, mowed down the A's in the first inning, as Lasorda watched intently. Welch fanned two more Dodgers in the second inning, and seemed to be in a zone now. In the Oakland second, with Mark McGwire at bat, Tudor uncorked a high curve ball on an 0–2 count. As McGwire swung and missed for strike three, John Tudor headed for the dugout, kicking dirt in disgust. TV announcer Joe Garagiola stammered in disbelief, "He's walkin' off the mound," to which Vin Scully replied, "Yeah. He's had it." Vin was right. Tudor's elbow was completely gone. Tim Leary was rushed to the mound to relieve the Dodgers' courageous veteran, and he set the A's down in order. L.A. went quietly in the third, with Stubbs becoming Welch's sixth strikeout victim. In the bottom of the inning, the Oakland bats came to life. Glenn Hubbard hit a ball off the left field wall. Mickey Hatcher played the ball perfectly, grabbing it on one bounce and making a perfect throw to second to hold Hubbard to a long single. With Ron Hassey at bat, Hubbard stole second and continued to third when Scioscia's errant throw bounced into center field. Hassey went with an outside pitch and grounded a single between third and short, scoring the A's first run in eighteen innings. The wounded Dodgers suffered more woes in the fourth when their last power hitter, Mike Marshall, was forced out of the game with a bad back. Mickey Hatcher, Mr. Everyman, moved to right with Danny Heep going to left. Hatcher made his presence felt almost immediately. José Canseco lifted a fly ball into no-man's land in short right-center. Shelby and Hatcher converged on the ball and, at the last instant, Hatcher threw himself at the ball. With his body fully extended, the amazing Stuntman made a spectacular diving backhand catch. He rolled over several times, then bounced back up on his feet, glove held high to show the umpires the ball.

In the Dodgers' fifth, Jeff Hamilton lined a Welch fastball back through the middle for a single. Griffin moved the tying run up ninety feet with a well-executed sacrifice. After Sax was retired, Franklin Stubbs, another of the Dodgers players who rose to the heights in the Series, drove the ball to deep right-center field, hitting the 375 foot sign on one bounce. Hamilton trotted in from second base with the tying run as Stubbs glided into second with a double. He died there as Hatcher lined back to Welch. In the next inning, Welch hit the wall, and the Dodgers prepared to break the game wide open. Danny Heep duplicated Stubbs' feat, only this time to left field. John Shelby grounded a single to left. Heep stopped at third and Shelby slid into second when Luis Polonia's throw missed the cutoff man and went through to the plate. When Mike Davis walked to load the bases with no outs, Welch was yanked in favor of left-hander Greg Cadaret. With Scioscia, Hamilton, and Griffin, due up to face the young lefty, the Dodgers were only a couple of hits away from taking a three-game to none advantage. But Tony LaRussa's A's were not about to cave in. They took a hitch in their belts and went to work. Cadaret's pitch to Scioscia was in tight and the Dodgers catcher popped it up down the third base line where Carney Lansford gathered it in for out number one. Having done his job, Cadaret handed the ball over to Gene Nelson, whose job it was to nail the right-hander. Hamilton obliged with a high bouncer to third. Lansford's throw home forced Heep for the second out. Now it was up to Griffin, but Alfredo couldn't do it this time. He hit a bouncing ball to first base that was grabbed by McGwire, who stepped on the bag for out number three. The A's had momentarily escaped from the jaws of death. The game remained tied at 1–1.

The seventh and eighth passed without incident, and the Dodgers were retired in order in the top of the ninth. The A's had the heart of their batting order coming up to face Dodgers closer Jay Howell in the bottom of the ninth. Canseco, McGwire, and Parker, stood ready to end the game. Canseco went after a high fastball. He missed the sweet spot by a fraction of an inch and lofted a harmless fly ball to second baseman Steve Sax. The determined Mark McGwire stepped in, looking for a good fastball he could drive. With the count 2–2, McGwire found a pitch to his liking. He jumped on a heater down the middle and sent it screaming to left field. It dropped over the fence at the 370-foot mark as Danny Heep and John Shelby could only watch. The Oakland dugout came alive for the first time since Canseco's grand-slam homer in the second inning of game one. There were smiles and high-fives all around, and a team meeting at home plate to greet Big Mac after he completed his triumphant trip around the bases. Forearms cracked at home plate as the mighty McGwire accepted congratulations from his excited teammates. The big guy's game-winning home run had gotten the A's back into the Series. Down only 2–1 now, and with two more games at home, the Oakland team stood poised to sweep the remaining contests and realize their destiny.

Los Angeles	0 0 0	0 1 0	0 0 0-1-8-1
Oakland	0 0 1	0 0 0	0 0 1-2-5-0

WP-Honeycutt
LP-J. Howell

In the visitor's clubhouse, however, the Dodgers were not about ready to lie down and play dead for their Northern California rivals. Despite the fact that their lineup had been decimated by injuries, their confidence remained steadfast. Tommy Lasorda's battlers didn't know how they were going to pull out the Series, but they believed they would find a way to win it somehow. And NBC announcer Bob Costas played right into their hands when he reviewed their lineup for game four in a pre-game broadcast on Wednesday, October 19. Pointing out the fact that the entire Dodgers lineup had accounted for only thirty-six home runs all year, six less than José Canseco had hit by himself, Costas declared that this was the weakest hitting team to ever play in the World Series. Dodger manager Tommy Lasorda, never one to lose an opportunity to incite his troops, jumped on Costas' statement to fire up his team. He taped the comments to the clubhouse door for all to see, then played on his team's emotions to get their adrenaline flowing for another charge up Mt. Everest, walking around the clubhouse screaming, "Kill Costas, Kill Costas."

The pitching matchup for game four was a repeat of game one, with Oakland ace Dave Stewart going against Dodgers rookie Tim Belcher. No sooner had the game begun than the hyped-up Dodgers had Stewart in deep trouble. Steve Sax, leading off, took advantage of Stewart's wildness and cajoled a base-on-balls from the big right-hander. After Stubbs had been retired, the wheels began to turn as manager Lasorda, determined to take advantage of every opportunity to manufacture runs, sent super-sub Mickey Hatcher to the plate to execute a hit-and-run. Hatcher did his job perfectly, hitting a ground ball between first and second, with Sax scooting around to third. The weakest lineup in World Series history was already threatening, with runners on the corners and only one out in the top of the first. Stewart, somewhat rattled by the turn of events, uncorked a wild pitch with Mike Davis at the plate and Sax scampered home with the first run of the game. Davis then hit a routine ground ball toward second base, but the gremlins were still at work and Hubbard couldn't find the handle on the ball. The Dodgers were in business again, with runners at first and third and still only one out. Moments later, Hatcher crossed the plate as Shelby grounded out, and suddenly the lowly Dodgers were in front by a 2–0 score before the A's ever came to bat.

Stunned but not beaten, the A's fought back. Luis Polonia, protecting the plate on an 0–2 pitch, looped a single to left field. He went to second on a passed ball, advanced to third on a groundout by Mark McGwire, and scored on a ground ball by Canseco. Danny Heep opened the Dodgers' second with a base hit but was caught stealing, Steinbach to Weiss. Hamilton and Griffin went without a whimper. The A's went down in order in their half. The Dodgers rattled their chains again in the third. Franklin Stubbs drove a Stewart blazer up the gap in right-center field for a two-base hit. After Hatcher popped to Polonia, Mike Davis smashed a line drive that went off shortstop Weiss' glove for an error, and Stubbs brought home L.A.'s third run. Weiss was disconsolate. The usually reliable shortstop had mistimed his leap and the ball just passed over his outstretched fingers, leading to another unearned Dodgers run, their second of the game. Tim Belcher breezed through the third inning, retiring the side in order for the second straight inning.

Mike Scioscia opened the Dodgers' fourth with a single to right field. Then, with a count of 3–1 on Danny Heep, Scioscia made an ill-advised attempt to steal second, but was gunned down, Steinbach to Weiss. And more importantly for the Dodgers, Scioscia twisted his right knee sliding into second base and had to be helped off the field. He would be lost to the Dodgers for the remainder of the Series. But L.A. had a more-than-average backup catcher. Rick Dempsey filled the breach and kept the Dodgers' spirit alive with a steady performance. He put on the tools of ignorance in the bottom of the fourth inning, and would handle the catching chores the rest of the way. In an emergency, Mickey Hatcher was ready to go behind the plate.

Tim Belcher got into a minor jam in the fourth inning. Dave Henderson led off with a single, breaking a string of nine consecutive batters Belcher had retired. When José Canseco walked on four pitches, suddenly the A's had the tying and go-ahead runs on base with no one out. But the 26-year-old rookie remained cool under pressure and set down the next three A's in order, Parker striking out, McGwire sending a fly ball to Shelby in right-center, and Lansford, on a checked swing, tapping to Stubbs at first base. Belcher labored a little more in the sixth when, for the fourth time in the game, the A's put the leadoff man on base, Henderson grounding a single through the hole in the left side. Franklin Stubbs made a great play on a foul ball by Canseco, catching it as he fell into the Dodgers' dugout. After Parker flied out, McGwire walked and Lansford hit a flare to right field, scoring Henderson and making the score 3–2. The Dodgers got that run back in the top of the seventh. Alfredo Griffin walked on four pitches with one out. Steve Sax followed with a single up the middle that just got by a diving Hubbard, and Griffin legged it to third. Pinch-hitter Tracy Woodson, facing southpaw Greg Cadaret, hit a tailor-made double play ball to short, but a heads-up play by Sax broke up the potential inning-ending play. Sax, who took off with the pitch, got a great jump, and beat Weiss' throw to Hubbard as Griffin came across with the Dodgers' fourth run. The Dodgers bench was on their feet cheering as Griffin headed for the dugout.

Tim Belcher, who had been laboring for three innings, finally ran out of gas in the seventh. With one out, Walt Weiss beat out an infield hit behind first base that bounced off Tracy Woodson's glove. Polonia hit a skimmer to Sax, whose throw to Griffin was too late to get Weiss, but Griffin's quick relay to first retired Polonia for out number two. Dave Henderson, a thorn in L.A.'s side the entire Series, then lined a double into the left field corner, and Weiss brought in run number three. That was it for Belcher. He had pitched 6⅔ innings, fanning seven and walking two, with three runs being scored against him, two earned. Jay Howell came in for his second appearance of the Series. Howell, hearing it from the crowd about the home run McGwire had hit against him in his last appearance, walked Canseco, putting runners on first and second. The next batter, Dave Parker, reached safely when his line drive bounced off the heel of Griffin's glove for an error. That brought up Mark McGwire and, as he strode to the plate, 49,317 A's fans erupted in wild hysteria, as they anticipated a repeat of the previous night's McGwire–Howell duel. But this was a new day and a new duel, and this time Jay Howell came away victorious. He gave McGwire a moving fastball up and away and the Oakland slugger just missed it, hitting a popup to Tracy Woodson at first base. Howell later admitted that he was hoping to meet his tormenter in a non-critical situation, in a relaxed atmosphere, but it wasn't to be. He met him with the bases loaded, and he sucked it up and met the challenge. The Dodgers' closer also survived a two-out single in the eighth, and went to the mound in the ninth, protecting a slim 4–3 lead. The first batter, Luis Polonia, sent a fly ball to José González for out number one. Dave Henderson, that man again, lined a single to left field for his fourth hit of the game and his sixth hit of the Series. Howell, who had been throwing Canseco high fastballs, got him swinging on a 3–2 curveball. Dave Parker, representing the winning run, hit a foul popup to Jeff Hamilton at third base and the Dodgers were home free. Franklin Stubbs was the first Dodger to reach Howell on the mound after the last out was recorded, and he gave his closer a well-deserved high-five. Pitching coach Ron Perranoski, approaching from the other direction, hugged his pitcher from behind as the entire team converged on the scene.

Los Angeles	2 0 1		0 0 0		1 0 0-4-8-1		
Oakland	1 0 0		0 0 1		1 0 0-3-9-2		

WP-Belcher
SV-J. Howell
LP-Stewart

As Ostler reported, "After that game, a 4–3 Dodger victory, Lasorda and most of the Dodgers were stomping around the clubhouse in self-righteous indignation over Costas' pre-game remark, which they had taken as an insult. Hatcher, who had contributed a key single to a two-run first-inning rally, was more realistic. 'I think we believe too, that this was one of the worst lineups ever,' he said. 'You go down our lineup — who *are* those guys?'"[13]

Now it was on to game five with the Dodgers sitting atop a convincing 3 to 1 lead in games. And with Orel Hershiser, sitting in the wings, ready to start two of the last three games if necessary, things looked mighty bleak for Tony LaRussa's mighty A's. They had their backs to the wall now, and they had to win three games in a row if they were to realize their dream of a world championship. It was not an impossible task, but facing the Dodgers' Bulldog, who had not lost a game in fifty-five days, certainly didn't make it any easier. And Oakland starter Storm Davis felt the fury of the Dodgers' bats immediately. Franklin Stubbs pulled a one-out curveball to right field for a single in the opening stanza. Then, Mickey Hatcher climaxed his great Series by crushing a Davis fastball, sending a screamer to left field. Left fielder Stan Javier had the ball in his sights, but as he scaled the wall in hopes of catching it, he ran out of real estate, and the ball sailed six rows deep into the left field stands for a home run, giving Hershiser a 2–0 lead before the game was ten minutes old. Hatcher raced around the bases in record time, as was his habit, and as he entered the dugout, he flailed away in his exuberance, waving his arms in all directions, knocking Ron Perranoski's hat off, and causing his amused teammates to run for cover. Ostler reported that he even "mimicked the Oakland sluggers by trying a forearm bash with a teammate in the dugout. He didn't get it quite right though, because he instantly recoiled in pain. 'I thought I broke my arm,' he said."[14]

Hershiser, who was having trouble finding his rhythm, stifled the A's through two innings, but the green and gold threatened to get back into the game in the third. The Dodgers ace paced around the mound nervously, unable to get comfortable, and he didn't have good control of his fastball, which was sailing high and wide. He was forced to live with his curve and his change, and the A's took advantage of that situation. Carney Lansford grounded a single up the middle, leading off the third inning. Tony Philips then hit a shot into the hole between third and short that Griffin dove for and kept in the infield, holding runners at first and second. Once again, buzzing began in the grandstand as the Oakland fans tried to revive their apparently indifferent team. Walt Weiss dropped a bunt in front of the plate and was thrown out, Dempsey to Sax, as the runners each moved up a base. Stan Javier then ended Hershiser's string of twenty-one consecutive scoreless innings in post-season play with a sacrifice fly to Mickey Hatcher in left field. The A's had demonstrated that the Dodgers' ace was not invincible. Now they had to prove that they could beat him.

The A's scored no more in the third, and the Dodgers came up, leading 2–1. Again, it was Mickey Hatcher who ignited the team. He hit a high chopper to third and beat Lansford's bare hand grab and throw to first. "To avoid a possible swipe tag by first baseman Mark McGwire, Hatcher dove into the dirt and sort of burrowed his way to the bag. He was safe. It was ungraceful, almost comical, but it worked."[15] Hatcher held his base while the A's 16-game winner struck out both Mike Marshall and John Shelby. Then, just when it seemed as if Oakland would get out of the inning, Storm Davis quickly fell behind the next batter, Mike Davis, 3 and 0, and the final piece of managerial strategy on the part of Tommy Lasorda pushed the Dodgers to the brink of the championship. He gave Mike Davis the green light on the 3–0 pitch and, when the A's starter laid his fastball down the middle, the Dodgers right fielder jumped all over it, hitting a high drive that carried deep into the right field seats for a two-run homer and a 4–1 Dodgers lead. After the Oakland fourth inning ended, Hershiser, still out of synch, walked disgustedly to the dugout and threw his glove against the wall. Then he sat down and closed his eyes. When the TV cameras scanned the Dodgers dugout, they caught him appearing to be napping. But he said that wasn't true. "I just didn't want this to be the one bad outing that would have everyone saying that this guy couldn't handle the pressure when it counted. So when you saw me relaxing in the dugout (with his eyes closed) I was just trying to think 'just one pitch at a time,' because I couldn't cope with any more." Another time he seemed to be singing, "admitting that he was singing some favorite hymns to himself. 'You don't want to hear my singing,' he said afterward when asked. 'They were just some hymns I learned in church. I was just singing to relieve the pressure.'"[16] When Hershiser went back out to the mound in the bottom of the fifth inning, he was a different pitcher. He had suddenly found his rhythm, and he set down nine men in a row from the fifth inning to the seventh inning.

The Dodgers meanwhile, added to their lead. With Mike Davis on first following a walk by Gene Nelson, Rick Dempsey took a high slider to the right field wall for a double and a 5–1 L.A. lead. The TV cameras, scanning the stands at the end of the seventh inning, caught Hershiser's father gesturing to a friend by holding up six fingers, meaning six outs to go. By this time, the Oakland batters were trying anything they could to disrupt Hershiser's timing. One Oakland tactic of stepping out of the batters' box did work to some extent. After talking to Rick Dempsey in a stage whisper so the batter and umpire could hear him, about stopping the delaying tactics, he walked the batter, Tony Philips. "He started to throw a lot of changeups in the seventh," said Dempsey, "and he lost his control a little."[17] Hershiser retired Walt Weiss on a grounder to first base, with Philips advancing to second, from where he scored on a single by Stan Javier. The next batter, Dave Henderson walked, with the Oakland fans now screaming "Orel, Orel," in an effort to further distract the Dodgers pitcher. But Bulldog, after throwing a wild pitch that advanced both runners, settled down. He clenched his teeth together in a spirited demonstration of determination. He backed off the mound, vigorously rubbing up the baseball and gathering his thoughts. The Dodgers bullpen squirmed around, and in the dugout the coaches surrounded Lasorda for direction. Was Hershiser losing it? Was the pressure and excessive workload of the past three weeks catching up with the Dodgers' ace? Fresh arms were ready in the bullpen, but Lasorda said, "Let him go." He stuck with his man. It was Hershiser's game to win or lose. The noise was deafening as Canseco stepped in, representing the tying run. The fans exhorted Canseco to put Hershiser's fastball into orbit, but it didn't happen. Bulldog jammed the A's slugger and induced him to hit a soft pop fly to Stubbs at first base. A dejected Canseco walked slowly back to the dugout shaking his head. Meanwhile, on the mound, Dempsey and Hershiser put their heads together to discuss the strategy of pitching to the ever-dangerous Dave Parker. The "Cobra" stood at the plate as Hershiser uncorked a wild pitch, moving the runners to second and third. Remembering that Parker had chased a fifty-five foot curveball in game two, Hershiser decided to test the waters again. Parker was fooled again, and he swung and missed the sinker in the dirt, as the Oakland dugout became deadly silent and their fans hung their heads in disbelief.

In the Oakland ninth, Mark McGwire hit a towering drive to left-center field, but John Shelby ran it down at the wall. Ron Hassey took a called third strike for out number two. The next batter, Carney Lansford, hit a chopper in the hole between third and short that Griffin gloved, but Lansford beat it out for a hit. Tony Philips, the A's last hope, went down swinging at a high outside fastball. Orel Hershiser dropped to one knee in silent prayer just before catcher Rick Dempsey reached the mound, caught him in a low bear hug, and lifted him off the ground. Soon the entire Dodgers team converged on the mound and the wild celebration began. Vin Scully screamed into his microphone, "Got him. Like the 1969 Mets, it's the impossible dream revisited."

Los Angeles					Oakland				
Name	*Pos*	*AB*	*R*	*H*	*Name*	*Pos*	*AB*	*R*	*H*
Sax	2B	4	0	2	Javier	LF	3	0	1
Stubbs	1B	4	1	2	Henderson	CF	2	0	0
Hatcher	LF	4	2	2	Canseco	RF	4	0	0
González	LF	0	0	0	Parker	DH	4	0	0
Marshall	RF	4	0	0	McGwire	1B	4	0	0
Shelby	CF	3	0	0	Hassey	C	3	0	0
M. Davis	DH	2	1	1	Lansford	3B	4	1	2
Dempsey	C	4	0	1	Philips	2B	3	1	1
Hamilton	3B	4	0	0	Weiss	SS	2	0	0
Griffin	SS	4	0	0	S. Davis	P	0	0	0
Hershiser	P	0	0	0	Cadaret	P	0	0	0
					Nelson	P	0	0	0

THE CELEBRATION !! (courtesy of Los Angeles Dodgers)

Name	Pos	AB	R	H	Name	Pos	AB	R	H
					Honeycutt	P	0	0	0
					Plunk	P	0	0	0
					Burns	P	0	0	0
Totals		**33**	**5**	**8**			**29**	**2**	**4**

Los Angeles	2 0 0	2 0 1	0 0 0-5-8-0
Oakland	0 0 1	0 0 0	0 1 0-2-4-0

Double-Dempsey
Home Runs-Hatcher, M. Davis

Name	IP	W	L	R	ER	H	SO	BB
Los Angeles								
Hershiser	9	1	0	2	2	4	9	4
Oakland								
S. Davis	4⅔	0	1	4	4	6	5	1
Cadaret	0	0	0	0	0	1	0	0
Nelson	3	0	0	1	1	1	1	2
Honeycutt	⅓	0	0	0	0	0	0	0
Plunk	⅔	0	0	0	0	0	0	0
Burns	⅓	0	0	0	0	0	0	0[18]

Many of the Dodgers players remained on the field for several minutes after the last out, hugging their wives and families, waving to fans in the stands, and just absorbing the moment. The Los Angeles clubhouse was sheer bedlam as players made the rounds of the room spraying anyone within shooting distance with a stream of the bubbly. They were especially on the lookout for Lasorda and anyone wearing a suit, Dodgers' executives, owners, reporters, and broadcasters. And, of course, they found time to inhale a little of the beverage themselves. At one point in the festivities, Tommy Lasorda climbed on a stool and yelled for quiet with both arms raised. "Nobody thought we could win the division," he screamed. "Nobody thought we could beat the mighty Mets. Nobody thought we could beat the team that won 104 games. But we believed it." The Dodgers' loquacious manager was just getting started, but before he could add to his soliloquy, he was inundated by a torrent of champagne, directed at him by Kirk Gibson and other fun-loving participants.

During the madness, one of the beat reporters cornered Mickey Hatcher, and mentioned that it looked like the two home runs he hit, in games one and five, were hit off identical pitches. Hatcher just shrugged his shoulders and said, "I'm glad someone saw those pitches. I didn't. I was just swinging."[19] When Lasorda was interviewed, he was asked about his surprise slugging star, Mickey Hatcher, who had powdered the ball to the tune of .368 during the five-game series with two home runs and five RBIs. The Dodgers manager looked surprised. "Mickey Hatcher? I thought his name was Jimmie Foxx!

What a job he's done. We wanted him to give us a spark and he did. He's one of the great, unsung heroes of the season. Every team needs a Mickey Hatcher. You can't win without foot soldiers, and Mickey Hatcher is one of the most valuable of my foot soldiers. No matter where I put him, he does the job."[20]

It was a shocking Series, an improbable end to a script that could only have been written in Hollywood. Los Angeles' domination over what many people considered to be one of the strongest teams ever to play in the World Series could not be explained in terms of personnel, or individual statistics. There was absolutely no way these teams could be compared that would lead to a Dodgers victory. The Dodgers' triumph was, in the final analysis, a miracle — the miracle of Chavez Ravine.

Orel Hershiser, deservedly, was voted the World Series Most Valuable Player. Now he had two bookends, this trophy and the one he received for being voted the MVP of the NLCS. Hershiser pitched a total of 18 innings against the powerful Oakland Athletics, holding them to a total of two runs on seven base hits, all singles, while sending 17 of them back to the bench in frustration. Kirk Gibson put it all in perspective when he said, "As long as we all live, none of us will ever see any pitcher accomplish what Orel has done. He'll go down in history."[21]

Hershiser, in return, credited Gibson with making the Dodgers a team, and a winning team, at that. "He has really been the heart and soul of this ballclub. His hard work gave him the right to talk to people and air them out and make them proud to be Dodgers."[22] "He made it cool to care about winning. He made it cool to be aggressive and to hustle and work hard."[23]

With all the accolades that were being handed out, to Hatcher, Hershiser, and Gibson, it is only right that the other twenty-two members of the team be recognized for their efforts. Every man on the team contributed to the final result, from the starters like Sax and Shelby and Scioscia, to the Stuntmen like Dempsey and Mike Davis and Woodson. And a special notice should be taken of Jeff Hamilton, who was, without a doubt, the hard luck hitter in the Series. His statistics looked pretty pathetic, with just two hits in nineteen at-bats for a .105 batting average. But he actually hit eight to ten balls hard, but they were right at somebody. With a little luck, the Dodgers' fine third baseman could have posted a batting average of .526 or higher.

The key to the Series was the Dodgers' scouting. Steve Boros, Mel Didier, and Jerry Stephenson did a fantastic job scouting the American League all year, including the teams in the American League Championship Series, and they felt the A's could be pitched to with fastballs above the belt and up. In addition to their comments on Eckersley's back-door slider, they told the Dodgers pitchers to keep the ball low to Dave Parker, which they did with exceptional success, and to pitch José Canseco high and tight, and not to let him extend his arms. The Dodgers didn't make more than five mistakes the entire Series in terms of execution of what the scouting reports read. One was the pitch down the middle to Canseco in game two, another was Howell's pitch over the plate to McGwire in game three. And two were Howell's pitches to Dave Parker in game four, but he got away with them when Parker popped up to Jeff Hamilton.

When the statistics for the two teams are reviewed, it is obvious that, once again, the team that played the best won the Series. The Dodgers scored twenty-one runs in the Series while their pitchers held the powerful A's to just eleven runs. L.A's team batting average of .246 eclipsed the embarrassing .177 batting average put together by Tony LaRussa's contingent. L.A.'s 41 base hits included fourteen for extra bases—eight doubles, one triple, and five home runs, while the powerful A's could produce only five extra base hits—three doubles and two home runs. The Bash Brothers, José Canseco and Mark McGwire, batted a combined .056 on two base hits in thirty-six at-bats. Canseco was 1 for 19, with five RBIs. His grand slam in game one accounted for his only homer and four of his five RBIs in the Series. McGwire's home run in game three accounted for his only hit and his only RBI of the Series. Terry Steinbach, who batted .364, and Dave Henderson, who hit .300, were the only Oakland batters to solve the deliveries of the Dodgers pitchers. The three Oakland starters had a combined ERA of 5.27, and Eckersley, who pitched only 1⅔ innings in two appearances in the Series, posted a 10.80 ERA.

On the other side of the ledger, Dodgers hitters were led by Mickey Hatcher, who pounded out seven base hits in nineteen at-bats, with one double, two homers, five runs batted in, and a .368 batting average. Hatcher was inserted into the number three spot in the Dodgers lineup throughout the entire World Series by manager Tommy Lasorda in hopes that he could light a fire under the team in Gibson's absence. And did he ever. He hit a two-run homer in the first inning of game one to get the Dodgers' attack underway. He contributed a run-scoring single in the big five-run inning in game two that cemented a Dodgers victory. He went one for four in game three. He grounded a hit-and-run single into right field in the first inning of game four, igniting a two run Dodgers rally that gave his team a lead it never relinquished. And he slugged another two-run homer in the first inning of game five to pace L.A. to a 5–2 win and a world championship. In other words, Mickey Hatcher could just as easily have been the Series MVP. He was that good. Steve Sax batted an even .300, and Franklin Stubbs checked in with a .294 average, with two doubles, and two RBIs. The L.A. mound corps was led by Hershiser, who tossed two complete game victories, striking out seventeen batters and holding the mighty A's to just seven base hits in eighteen innings. Tim Leary, selflessly pitching out of the bullpen the entire Series, posted a 1.35 ERA in two games, Alejandro Peña was perfect, with a 0.00 ERA in two games, while Brian Holton and John Tudor had 0.00 ERAs in one game. Jay Howell had one save and a 3.38 ERA, and Tim Belcher who had a 6.23 ERA, mostly as a result of Canseco's grand-slam homer in game one, came back to win game four, holding the A's to two earned runs on seven base hits in 6⅔ innings while fanning seven batters and walking only two.

In retrospect, the 1988 World Series reminded one of a statement made by legendary boxing manager Cus D'Amato when referring to a boxing match. "Every match is a test of will versus skill, with the will always prevailing unless the skill is so superior that the will is never tested." Oakland had the skill. Los Angeles had the will. And the will triumphed.

10

AFTERWARD

The Dodgers, on their return to Los Angeles following their World Series miracle, spent the weekend partying. Then, on Monday morning, October 24, as the sun burned off the early morning fog, the team gathered at the corner of Ninth Street and Broadway to begin a parade that would carry them to City Hall where they would be honored for their magnificent World Series achievement. A crowd, estimated to be between 50,000 and 100,000 began staking out their territory along the parade route at daybreak, and they spent the better part of the morning partying, talking, laughing, singing, and cheering, while vendors circulated through the crowd selling food and beverages. At precisely 11:00A.M., the Wilson High School band stepped out to begin the parade, while the players and staff, seated on five floats, waved to their delirious fans who lined the streets of the city, straining to catch a glimpse of their heroes as they passed. Orel Hershiser, standing behind the World Series trophy, waved to the crowd from one float, while Kirk Gibson, dressed in a white T-shirt with a white baseball hat, smiled and waved from another float. The parade wound its way through downtown Los Angeles, north on Broadway, and then east of First Street to the Plaza of Champions and City Hall. The ubiquitous street vendors worked their way along the parade route peddling their wares, particularly world championship memorabilia, like Dodgers hats, T-shirts, and pennants. And the food vendors continued to supply the hungry fans.

Several thousand more Angelinos filled the Plaza as Tommy Lasorda, Orel Hershiser, Kirk Gibson, and the rest of the Dodgers contingent assembled on the stage erected in front of City Hall. The stage was decorated with blue and white banners. A large blue banner, announcing the World Champion Dodgers, hung over the stage. Young boys watched the celebration from trees in the Plaza, and City Hall workers, taking a break from their duties, viewed the proceedings from the windows overlooking the stage. After the UCLA marching band played the national anthem, "the crowd greeted Mayor Tom Bradley with cheers and blasts from air horns, as he asked, 'Does L.A. love the Dodgers? You believed it and now the rest of the world believes it. The L.A. Dodgers are the Cinderella team of 1988. They are the team that displayed guts, grit, and bulldog determination.'"[1] Vin Scully, the master of ceremonies, introduced all the Dodgers players, the manager, the coaches and trainers, and the front office personnel. As each Dodgers speaker approached the podium, the fans cheered and waved signs. Hershiser thanked his fans for their support, and he thanked God for his ability, as chants of "Orel, Orel," filled the plaza. Tommy Lasorda gave another of his rambunctious pep talks, telling the crowd, "Pete Rose said, 'I'm not worried about the Dodgers, I'm worried about San Francisco and Houston.' He was right — When we went eight games above them, they were tied with San Francisco and Houston. Roger Craig said, 'I promise the Giant fans that we will be in the World Series.' He was right — He was there watching us play. Hal Lanier said, 'If we don't beat the Dodgers, I shouldn't be working here.' He was right — He's no longer working there. Then we played the Mets and the whole world said, 'You don't belong on the same field with the Mets — They were right, we didn't belong on the same field.' Then Lasorda said, "I promised you that if you stuck with this team, we would be dancing in the streets of Los Angeles," and with that he broke into an impromptu dance that resembled the twist, much to the delight of the big crowd who chanted, "Dance, Tommy, dance."[2] Kirk Gibson brought the crowd to a fever pitch when, called upon by Lasorda to come to the podium and give his famous clubhouse cry that followed each Dodgers victory, Gibby shouted to the enthusiastic crowd, "How sweet it is, to taste the fruits of victory." Gibson went on to say, joining the Dodgers "was the most important decision of my life and I want to thank you, the fans, for making it the best decision of my life. We made this impossible dream come true."[3]

As fall turned to winter, the honors came fast and furious to Los Angeles Dodgers players and executives.

• Fred Claire was named *The Sporting News* Executive of the Year, the UPI Co-Executive of the Year, and the *Baseball America* National League Executive of the Year. He was the first Dodger to win the *TSN* award since Buzzie Bavasi in 1959. It was Claire's personnel moves that were the secret ingredients to the Dodgers' amazing season. From the free agent signings of Mickey Hatcher, Mike Davis, Rick Dempsey, and Kirk Gibson, to the blockbuster trade that brought Jay Howell and Alfredo Griffin to Los Angeles from the Oakland Athletics and Jesse Orosco from the New York Mets, and the trade that brought Tim Belcher to L.A. from Oakland, Claire seemed to have the magic touch. Every deal turned to gold.

• Tommy Lasorda was named the National League Manager of the Year by the Baseball Writers Association, the UPI National League Manager of the Year, the *Baseball America* Manager of the Year, and *The Sporting News* National League Co-Manager of the Year. Lasorda, in his twelve years at the helm of the Dodgers, had won five division titles, three National League pennants, and one world championship prior to

1988, but he never got the recognition he deserved. However, after his phenomenal success in 1988, his immense talents were finally recognized. He utilized his entire 25-man roster to keep the pennant ship afloat through a multitude of injuries, and he kept the morale of the team at a high level through all the ups and downs. And as Jay Howell noted, Lasorda handled the bullpen pitching staff magnificently, utilizing every man but not overworking them, so when the post-season series arrived the relievers were fresh, strong, and ready to go.

- Tim Belcher was named *Baseball America* Rookie of the Year, and *The Sporting News* National League Rookie Pitcher of the Year. The 26-year-old power pitcher, who began his professional baseball career in 1984 with Madison in the Midwest League, made his Dodgers debut three years later when he went 4–2 in six games. In 1988, his first full season in the Big Time, he won 12 games against 6 losses with an outstanding 2.91 ERA. He also went 3–0 in post-season play, winning two games against the New York Mets and one game against the Oakland Athletics. He had the same post-season won-loss record as Orel Hershiser, and Hershiser was voted the MVP in both series.

- Kirk Gibson was named the National League Most Valuable Player by the Baseball Writers Association of America. He received 272 votes to 236 for Darryl Strawberry, 162 for Kevin McReynolds, and 160 for Andy Van Slyke of Pittsburgh. Gibson was the 12th Dodger to win the coveted award and the first Dodger outfielder to do so. He also earned *The Sporting News* National League Silver Slugger Award as the foremost offensive player at his position, and he was selected to the National League All-Star Team by *Baseball America*. Kirk Gibson was, as noted previously, the heart and soul of the Los Angeles Dodgers in 1988. He batted a hard .290 with 28 doubles, 25 home runs, 106 runs scored, 31 stolen bases, and 76 runs batted in. But his value was more than statistics. It was his never-say-die attitude, and his unselfish play, that sparked the Dodgers to the championship. Whether it was scoring from second base on a wild pitch, racing from first to third on a short single, or sliding hard into second base to break up a double play, Gibson showed the other Dodgers players how to win. And in the process, he destroyed his body, limiting his World Series appearances to just one at-bat. But what an at-bat it was!

- Orel Hershiser was the winner of the National League's Cy Young award as the league's best pitcher, as determined by the Baseball Writers Association of America. He was named on 120 ballots compared to 54 for Danny Jackson and 42 for David Cone. Hershiser was selected as *Sports Illustrated* Sportsman of the Year, *Sport Magazine*'s Player of the Year, the NLCS MVP, *Sport Magazine*'s World Series MVP, *The Sporting News* Player of the Year, the AP Male Athlete of the Year, and *Baseball*

America Pitcher of the Year. He was named to *Baseball America*'s National League All-Star team, *The Sporting News* National League All-Star Team, and he won the National League Gold Glove as the league's top fielding pitcher. Hershiser was another deserving role model. He, too, did whatever it took to win, as demonstrated by his aggressive base running in game two of the World Series. His season accomplishments included a 23–8 won-loss record, and a 2.26 ERA. He led the league with 23 victories, eight shutouts, fifteen complete games, and 267 innings pitched. Along the way, he set a major league record for consecutive scoreless innings pitched with 59, breaking Don Drysdale's old record of 58 scoreless innings, and he added eight more scoreless innings in the NLCS. He was 1–0 with a 1.10 ERA and a record 24⅔ innings pitched in the NLCS, and 2–0 with a 1.00 ERA in the World Series.

- Tim Leary was named the UPI National League Comeback Player of the Year, and *The Sporting News* National League Comeback Player of the Year. He also won *The Sporting News* National League Silver Slugger Award as the league's best hitting pitcher. He batted .268 on 18 base hits in 67 at-bats, with 9 runs batted in. Leary, who went 3–11 with the Dodgers in 1987, compiled a record of 17–11 in 1988, with a 2.91 ERA and six shutouts in 229 innings pitched.
- Steve Sax was named to the National League All-Star Team. The Dodgers' speedy second baseman batted .277 with 42 stolen bases while fielding .981.

Other notable performances by members of the Los Angeles Dodgers included:

- John Shelby's 24-game hitting streak, from May 14 through June 9, during which time he pounded out 32 hits in 89 at-bats for a .360 average.
- Mickey Hatcher's .308 pinch-hitting average, based on eight hits in twenty-six at-bats, with one home run and seven RBIs.
- Brian Holton's pitching. Holton was one of the unsung heroes during the Dodgers' world championship season. He pitched in 45 games for Tommy Lasorda, with a 7–3 record and an outstanding 1.70 ERA. He also pitched in 4 games in the postseason with one save and a 1.50 ERA.
- Mike Marshall and John Shelby's tie for the team lead in game-winning RBIs with 12 each. They were followed by Pedro Guerrero with 10, Kirk Gibson with 9, Mickey Hatcher and Steve Sax with 6, and Franklin Stubbs with 5.

In reviewing the Dodgers' postseason magic, Jay Howell felt that the home run hit by Mike Scioscia in the ninth inning of game four of the NLCS was their most important home run. According to him, it changed the entire momentum of the series, and good things began to happen from that moment on. Gibson's homer in the twelfth, Gibson's three-run homer the next day, Orel Hershiser's two consecutive shutouts, one in the NLCS and one in the World Series, Mickey Hatcher's two home runs, in games one and five of the Series, Gibson's dramatic home run in game one of the World Series, and the overall play of every member of the team, from Stubbs, to Hamilton, to Woodson, to Davis, and so on down the line, all followed Scioscia's mighty blast, and all contributed to the Dodgers' fantastic world championship triumph.

The Los Angeles Dodgers' unlikely World Series triumph brought some interesting, and often tongue-in-cheek, observations from baseball experts over the winter. "A funny thing happened to the Los Angeles Dodgers on their way to the 1988 World Series. They won the damn thing. They won it with a lineup that looked as though it might have had trouble winning the World Series at Williamsport. It was a lineup that would not have intimidated Taiwan. It was a lineup only a mother could love. Heck, it was a lineup only a mother could *stand*. Night after night, though, the Dodgers bravely went out there with their bowling-average batting averages and their understudy-replaces-the-star cast and those sickly little bodies of theirs, and somehow they licked the healthiest-looking bunch of ballplayers you have ever seen, the Oakland A's."[4]

"How in the world did it happen? How did a team with a lineup resembling that of the Albuquerque Dukes trounce a team reminiscent of the 1927 Yankees? How did the Los Angeles Dodgers beat the Oakland Athletics like a drum, four games to one, in the 1988 World Series? How come manager Tommy Lasorda and the rest of his Dodger Glue team get to go to the White House and shake hands and schmooze with the Prez while Tony LaRussa and his Abashed Brothers have gone home shaking their heads?"[5]

"Quite a World Series it turned out to be, this one between the Oakland Athletics and the Los Angeles Arthritics. It was nearly the first World Series ever forfeited because the commissioner refused to permit one side's players to be carried to and from the batter's box on stretchers. It was a World Series in which, instead of players dropping flies, they kept dropping *like* flies. It was a World Series in which the disabled list almost certainly outnumbered the able list. It was a World Series in which the Dodgers reportedly decided to celebrate by pouring bottles of iodine over one another's heads. By the time it ended Los Angeles manager Tommy Lasorda no longer filled out a lineup card with his best nine players. He just started asking for nine volunteers. Somehow the Dodgers kept scratching, clawing, and creeping along. This might have been the only ballclub in World Series history to use pine-tar rags for tourniquets. But give the Dodgers credit. They played a great World Series. And some of them even lived to tell about it."[6]

"Don't discredit the A's. Credit the Dodgers. They kept pulling rabbits out of hats and punching ground balls into the hole. They were more aggressive, maybe because they had to be. The A's kept waiting for an explosion. Silence was all they heard."[7]

Some people were unable to explain the World Series outcome in logical terms, but they insisted it wasn't the result of a miracle. One such skeptic was Oakland Athletics slugger José Canseco, who said, "Emotion is overrated. You put your talent on the field and let the straws fall where they may. Maybe it wasn't our year. Maybe no matter what we did we would have lost."[8]

Maybe that's the definition of a miracle.

Appendix: Los Angeles Dodgers Selected Players Statistics 1981–1988

Batters

Name	Pos	AB	H	D	T	HR	RBI	SB	BA
Anderson, D.	SS	2026	490	73	12	19	143	49	.242
Baker, D.	OF	7117	1981	320	23	242	1013	137	.278
Brock, G.	1B	3202	794	141	6	110	462	41	.248
Cey, R.	3B	7162	1866	328	21	316	1139	24	.261
Dempsey, R.	C	4692	1093	223	12	96	471	20	.233
Duncan, M.	SS	4677	1247	233	37	87	491	174	.267
Garvey, S.	1B	8835	2599	40	43	272	1308	83	.294
Gibson, K.	OF	5798	1553	260	54	255	870	284	.268
Griffin, A.	SS	6780	1688	245	78	24	527	192	.249
Guerrero, P.	OF	5392	1618	267	29	215	898	97	.300
Hamilton, J.	3B	1205	282	61	3	24	211	0	.234
Hatcher, M.	OF	3377	946	172	20	38	375	11	.280
Landreaux, K.	OF	4101	1099	180	45	91	479	145	.268
Lopes, D.	2B	6354	1671	232	50	155	614	557	.263
Marshall, M.	OF	3593	971	173	8	148	530	26	.270
Monday, R.	OF	6136	1619	248	64	241	775	98	.264
Russell, B.	SS	7318	1926	293	57	46	627	167	.263
Sax, S.	2B	6940	1949	278	47	54	550	444	.281
Scioscia, M.	C	4373	1131	198	12	68	446	29	.259
Shelby, J.	OF	3090	739	128	24	70	313	98	.239
Stubbs, F.	1B	2591	602	109	12	104	348	74	.232
Yeager, S.	C	3584	816	118	16	102	410	14	.228

Pitchers

Name	G	IP	W	L	Pct.	SO	BB	H	ERA	SVS
Belcher, T.	394	2443	146	140	.510	1519	860	2423	4.16	5
Crews, T.	281	423	11	13	.458	293	110	444	3.44	15
Hershiser, O.L.	510	3130	204	150	.576	2014	1007	2939	3.48	5
Holton, B.	185	370	20	19	.513	210	125	401	3.62	38
Honeycutt, R.	797	2160	109	143	.433	1038	657	2183	3.72	38
Hooton, B.C.	480	2652	151	136	.526	1491	799	2497	3.38	7
Howe, S.R.	497	606	47	41	.534	328	139	586	3.03	91
Howell, J.	568	844	58	53	.523	666	291	782	3.34	155
Howell, K.	245	613	38	48	.442	549	275	534	3.95	31
Leary, T.	292	1491	78	105	.426	888	535	1570	4.36	1
Niedenfuer, T.	484	653	36	46	.439	474	226	601	3.29	97
Pena, A.	503	1057	56	52	.519	839	331	959	3.11	74
Reuss, J.	628	3670	220	191	.535	1907	1127	3734	3.64	11
Stewart, D.	523	2629	168	129	.566	1741	1034	2499	3.95	19
Valenzuela, F.	453	2930	173	153	.531	2074	1151	2718	3.54	2
Welch, R.L.	506	3092	211	146	.591	1969	1034	2894	3.47	8

Player career statistics used with authorization of Pete Palmer, *Baseball Encyclopedia*.

CHAPTER NOTES

Chapter 1

1. William F. McNeil, *Dodger Chronicles*, p. 641.
2. *The Berkshire Eagle*, May 16, 1981, p. 24.
3. *The Transcript*, September 18, 1981, p. 10.
4. Rich Coberly, *The No-Hit Hall of Fame: No-Hitters of the 20th Century*, p. 187.
5. Jay Johnstone and Rick Talley, *Over the Edge*, p. 113.
6. Johnstone, *Temporary Insanity*, p. 2.
7. *The Berkshire Eagle*, October 20, 1981, pp. 24 to 25.
8. McNeil, *Dodger Chronicles*, pp. 192 to 202.
9. Ibid, pp. 192 to 202.
10. *The Series*, p. 215.

Chapter 2

1. McNeil, *Dodger Chronicles*, p. 265.
2. *Times-Union*, August 9, 1982, p. D1.
3. *Daily News*, October 4, 1982, p. C27.
4. McNeil, *Dodger Chronicles*, p. 272.
5. *Dodger Blue* 7, no. 12 (August 1987): 8.
6. *Dodger Blue* 3, no. 17 (October 15, 1983): 29.
7. McNeil, *Dodger Chronicles*, p. 276.
8. Jack Canfield, et al., *Chicken Soup for the Baseball Fan's Soul*, p. 37.
9. Orel Hershiser, *Out of the Blue*, pp. 9–10.
10. William McNeil, *Dodger Diary*, p. 82.
11. *Dodger Blue* 4, no. 14 (August 31, 1984): 27.
12. McNeil, *Dodger Diary*, pp. 81–82.
13. Ibid.
14. Jay Johnstone, *Over the Edge*, pp. 3–4.

15. *USA Today*, July 12, 1985, p. 6C.
16. Johnstone and Talley, p. 6.
17. *The Series*, pp. 320–321.

Chapter 3

1. Randy Youngman, *Dodger Blue* 6, no. 3 (March 15, 1986): 7.
2. Terry Johnson, *Dodger Blue* 6, no. 10 (June 30, 1986): 7.
3. *The Berkshire Eagle*, September 23, 1986, p. D8.
4. Joe Resnick, *Dodger Blue* 6, no. 18 (October 30, 1986): 13.
5. Dan Beck, *Dodger Blue* 6, no. 18 (October 30, 1986): 14.
6. *Dodger Blue* 7, no. 2 (February 15, 1987): 13.
7. *The Berkshire Eagle*, April 8, 1987, p. D3.
8. Morrow, ESPN.com.
9. Joe Gergen, "L.A. 'Stuntman' Thrives in Rare Leading Role," *The Sporting News*, October 31, 1988, p. 7.
10. Mickey Hatcher, *Dodger Blue* 7, no. 18 (December 1987): 14.
11. Joe McDonnell, *Dodger Blue* 7, no. 6 (May 15, 1987): 19.
12. *The Berkshire Eagle*, July 6, 1987, p. D1.
13. Brian Golden, *Dodger Blue* 7, no. 11 (August 1987): 6.
14. *Dodger Blue* 7, no. 12 (mid–August 1987): 14.
15. *The Berkshire Eagle*, August 26, 1987, pp. D1, D2.
16. *Dodger Blue* 7, no. 16 (mid–October 1987): 9.
17. Joe McDonnell, *Dodger Blue* 8, no. 1 (mid–January 1988): 8–9.

Chapter 4

1. Kirk Gibson with Lynn Henning, *Bottom of the Ninth*, p. 113.
2. Joe McDonnell, *Dodger Blue* 8, no. 2 (February 1988): 5.
3. Ibid., pp 6–7.
4. Ibid., p. 7.
5. *Dodgers Dugout*, January 1988, pp. 5–6.
6. *Baseball America's 1989 Almanac*, p. 233.
7. *The Sporting News*, February 29, 1988, p. 41.
8. *Dodgers Dugout*, September 1988, p. 10.
9. Gibson, p. 116.
10. *Dodgers Dugout*, March 1988, p. 10.
11. Ibid.
12. *Dodgers Dugout*, January 1988, p. 13.
13. Ibid., March 1988, p. 12.
14. Ibid., p. 13.
15. Ibid., p. 13.
16. Gordon Verrell, *The Sporting News*, March 7, 1988, pp. 13–14.
17. Scott Ostler, *The Sporting News 1989 Baseball Yearbook*, pp. 61–64.
18. *Dodgers Dugout* 3, no. 3 (April 15, 1988): 7.
19. *Dodgers Dugout* 3, January 1988, p. 11.
20. Ibid.

Chapter 5

1. *Sports Illustrated*, April 4, 1988, p.96.
2. Ibid., pp. 93–94.
3. *The Sporting News*, March 7, 1988, p. 31.
4. *Dodgers Dugout* 3, no. 3 (April 15, 1988): 11.
5. *Dodgers Dugout* 3 (May 15, 1988): 2.
6. *The Dodgers Reader*, p. 212.
7. *The Sporting News*, May 23, 1988, pg. 31.
8. *The Sporting News*, June 6, 1988, pg. 32.
9. *Dodgers: The First 100 Years*, pp. 219–220.
10. *Dodger Blue* 8, no. 12 (August 1988): 6.
11. Ibid., p. 11.
12. Ibid., p. 12.
13. *Dodgers Dugout*, June 15, 1988, p. 4.
14. Ibid.
15. Ibid., p. 9.

16. Ibid., July 15, 1988, p. 10.
17. Ibid., July 30, 1988, p.7.
18. Ibid., July 15, 1988, p. 10.
19. Ibid.

Chapter 6

1. Gordon Verrell, *The Sporting News*, August 1, 1988, p. 23.
2. Ibid., August 8, 1988, p.16.
3. *Dodgers Dugout*, July 30, 1988, p. 15.
4. *The Sporting News*, August 8, 1988, p. 17.
5. *Dodgers Dugout*, July 30, 1988, p. 3.
6. Ibid., August 15, 1988, pp. 4, 10.
7. *The Sporting News 1988 Box Score Book, National League*, p. 88.
8. *The Sporting News*, September 5, 1988, p. 18.
9. *Dodgers Dugout*, August 15, 1988, p. 5.
10. Ibid., p. 2.
11. Ibid., August 30, 1988, p. 5.

Chapter 7

1. Orel Hershiser, *Out of the Blue*, p. 109.
2. Ibid., pp. 109–110.
3. Ibid., pp. 111–112.
4. Hal McCoy, *The Sporting News*, September 26, 1988, p. 24.
5. Ibid.
6. Hershiser, pp. 119–120.
7. William F. McNeil, *The Dodgers Encyclopedia*, 2001, pp. 394–395.
8. Hershiser, pp. 125–126.
9. *The Sporting News*, October 10, 1988, p. 32.
10. Hershiser, p. 130.
11. *Dodgers Dugout*, September 30, 1988, p. 5.
12. *The Sporting News 1988 Box Score Book, National League*, p. 121.

Chapter 8

1. *The Ballplayers*, p. 531.
2. *The Sporting News*, October 17, 1988, p. 16.
3. Ibid.
4. *Street & Smith's Baseball 1989*, p. 115.
5. *The Sporting News*, October 17, 1988, p. 16.
6. Ibid.

7. Ron Fimrite, *Sports Illustrated*, October 17, 1988, pp. 31–32.
8. *Dodgers Dugout*, October 30, 1988, p. 20.
9. *The Sporting News 1988 Box Score Book National League*, p. 125.
10. Paul Attner, *The Sporting News*, October 24, 1988, p. 17.
11. Gibson, p. 128.
12. Scott Ostler, *The Sporting News 1989 Baseball Yearbook*, p. 61.
13. Paul Attner, p. 17.
14. *Street & Smith's Baseball 1989*, p. 119.
15. Ibid., p. 121.

Chapter 9

1. Gibson, p. 128.
2. *Dodgers Dugout*, October 30, 1988, p. 3.
3. *The Sporting News*, October 24, 1988, p. 36.
4. Gibson, pp. 128–129.
5. Ibid., p. 130.
6. Ibid., p. 131.
7. Ibid.
8. Orel Hershiser with Jerry B. Jenkins, *Out of the Blue*, p. 186.
9. Gibson, p. 132.
10. Ibid., p. 133.
11. Hershiser, p. 188
12. *The Sporting News*, October 24, 1988, p. 43.
13. Scott Ostler, "Hats Off to Hatcher," *The Sporting News 1989 Baseball Yearbook*, pp. 61–64.

14. Ibid.
15. Ibid.
16. C. W. Nevius, "Who Killed the A's? The Choir Boy Did It," *Baseball Digest*, February 1989, pp. 20–21.
17. Ibid., p. 22.
18. *Street & Smith's Baseball 1989*, p. 126.
19. Ostler, p. 61–64.
20. John Kuenster, "Mickey Hatcher a 'Foot Soldier' Who Helped Dodgers Win It All," *Baseball Digest*, February 1989, pp. 17–18.
21. Nevius, p. 20.
22. Gibson, p. 123.
23. Steve Wulf, *Sports Illustrated*, October 31, 1988, p. 34.

Chapter 10

1. Josh Meyer and Rick Orlov, *Daily News of Los Angeles*, October 25, 1988, p. N1.
2. Tot Holmes, "Celebrate," *Dodgers Dugout*, October 30, 1988, p. 11.
3. Meyer and Orlov, p. N1.
4. Mike Downey, "Dodgers in La La Land," *Street & Smith's Baseball 1989*, p. 38.
5. Steve Wulf, "Destiny's Boys," *Sports Illustrated*, October 31, 1988, p. 32.
6. Mike Downey, *The Sporting News*, October 31, 1988, p. 4.
7. Art Spander, "Dodgers Produced Like a Team of Destiny," *The Sporting News*, October 31, 1988, p. 5
8. Ibid.

BIBLIOGRAPHY

Books

Canfield, Jack, Mark Victor Hansen, Mark Donnelly, Chrissy Donnelly, and Tommy Lasorda. *Chicken Soup for the Baseball Fan's Soul*. Deerfield Beach, FL: Health Communications, 2001.

Carter, Craig, and Larry Wigge, eds. *1988 Box Score Book, American League*. St. Louis: The Sporting News, 1988.

_____. *1988 Box Score Book, National League*. St. Louis: The Sporting News, 1988.

Caruso, Gary. *The Braves Encyclopedia*. Philadelphia: Temple University Press, 1995.

Coberly, Rich. *The No-Hit Hall of Fame: No-Hitters of the 20th Century*. Newport Beach, CA: Triple Play, 1985.

Cohen, Richard M., and David S. Neft. *The World Series*. New York: Collier Books, 1986.

Cohen, Stanley. *Dodgers! The First 100 Years*. New York: Birch Lane Press, 1990.

Gallagher, Mark, and Walter LeConte. *The Yankee Encyclopedia*. Champaign, IL: Sports Publishing, 2000.

Gewecke, Cliff. *Day by Day in Dodgers History*. New York: Leisure Press, 1984.

Gibson, Kirk, with Lynn Henning. *Bottom of the Ninth*. Chelsea, MI: Sleeping Bear Press, 1997.

Hershiser, Orel, with Jerry B. Jenkins. *Out of the Blue*. Brentwood, TN: Wolgemuth & Hyatt, 1989.

Holmes, Tot. *Dodgers Blue Book*. Gothenburg, NE: Holmes, 1988, 1989.

_____. *Dodger's Dugout*. Gothenburg, NE: Holmes, 1988, 1989.

Hoppel, Joe, and Craig Carter. *The Series: An Illustrated History of Baseball's Postseason Showcase*. St. Louis: Sporting News Publishing, 1989.

Johnstone, Jay, and Rick Talley. *Over the Edge*. New York: Bantam Books, 1988.

_____. *Temporary Insanity*. Chicago: Contemporary Books, 1985.

Los Angeles Dodgers Blue Book. Edited by Tot Holmes, Gothenberg, NE: Tot Holmes, 1982 to 1989.

Los Angeles Dodgers Media Guide. Los Angeles: Los Angeles Dodgers, 1989.

Los Angeles Dodgers Yearbooks. Los Angeles: Los Angeles Dodgers, 1981 to 1989.

MacLean, Norman, ed. *Who's Who in Baseball*. New York: Who's Who In Baseball Magazine, 1982 to 1990.

McNeil, William F. *Dodger Chronicles*. Pittsfield, MA: William F. McNeil, 1993.

_____. *Dodger Diary*. Pittsfield, MA: Celtic, 1986.

_____. *The Dodgers Encyclopedia*, 2nd ed. Champaign, IL: Sports Publishing, 2003.

Metsky, Karen, ed. *1988 World Series*. New York: Sports Minded, 1988.

Murray, Jim. "They Won't Call Him Dr. Zero for Nothing," in *The Dodgers Reader*. Edited by Dan Riley. New York: Houghton Mifflin, 1992.

Nemec, David. *Great Baseball Feats, Facts, & Firsts*. New York: New American Library, 1987.

Palmer, Pete, and Gary Gillette, eds. *Baseball Encyclopedia*. New York: Barnes & Noble Books, 2004.

Sahadi, Lou. *The L.A. Dodgers: The World Champions of Baseball.* New York: Quill, 1982.
Schott, Tom, and Nick Peters. *The Giants Encyclopedia.* Champaign, IL: Sports Publishing, 1999.
Shatzkin, Mike, ed. *The Ballplayers.* New York: Arbor House, 1990.
Simpson, Allan, ed. *Baseball America's 1989 Almanac.* Durham, NC: American Sports Publishing, 1989.
Sporting News 1989 Baseball Yearbook. St. Louis: The Sporting News, 1989.
Street & Smith's Baseball Annual. New York: Conde Nast, 1988 to 1990.
Thorn, John, Michael Gershman, and David Pietrusza, eds. *Total Baseball.* New York: Penguin Books, 1997.
Whittingham, Richard. *The Los Angeles Dodgers.* New York: Harper & Row, 1982.

Periodicals

Baseball Digest, 1988 to 1989.
Berkshire Eagle, Pittsfield, MA, 1984 to 1988.
Boston Herald, 1984 to 1988.
Cleveland Press, 1981.
Democrat and Chronicle, Rochester, NY, 1981 to 1984.
Dodger Blue, Long Beach, CA, July 15, 1983, to mid–September 1988.
Meyer, Josh, and Rick Orlov. "Dodgers: How Sweet It Is." *Daily News of Los Angeles*, October 25, 1988, p. N1.
New York Daily News, 1982 to 1988.
New York Post, 1984 to 1988.
Rochester Democrat and Chronicle, Rochester, NY, June 12, 1981.
Sporting News, May 23, 1981; January 4, 1988, to October 11, 1988.
Sports Illustrated, 1988.
Sunday Republican, Springfield, MA, 1984 to 1988.
The Transcript, North Adams, MA, May 15, 1981, p. 16.
USA Today, 1984 to 1988.

INDEX